IMAGES
of America

ENFIELD

A SWEDISH-AMERICAN FARM COMMUNITY 1850–2002

To the memory of my great-grandparents
Erick & Kestin Trogen
who were among the homesteaders

And to the memory of my grandparents
Frank Abrahamson
Amanda Felien Abrahamson
Edward Joseph Trogen
Anna Westling Trogen
who came to Enfield in the 1890s

And to the memory of my parents
Edwin Theodore Abrahamson
Evelyn Anna Trogen Abrahamson
who lived their span of years in the Enfield community

And to my brother and sister
Bruce Edward Abrahamson
Mavis Abrahamson Ward
for their help in this and
many other endeavors

And to my children
Eric Edwin Abrahamson
Lisa Kristine Abrahamson Betz

And to my grandsons
Ryan Michael Abrahamson
Micki Eric Abrahamson
James Charles Betz
Daniel Abraham Betz
as a reminder to tend Lake Side Cemetery
and to not forget those who came before you

IMAGES of America

ENFIELD

A SWEDISH-AMERICAN FARM COMMUNITY 1850–2002

Dean E. Abrahamson

ARCADIA PUBLISHING

ISBN 978-0-7385-2309-5

Published by Arcadia Publishing
Charleston, South Carolina

Printed in the United States of America

Library of Congress Catalog Card Number: Applied For.

For all general information contact Arcadia Publishing at:
Telephone 843-853-2070
Fax 843-853-0044
E-mail sales@arcadiapublishing.com
For customer service and orders:
Toll-Free 1-888-313-2665

Visit us on the Internet at www.arcadiapublishing.com

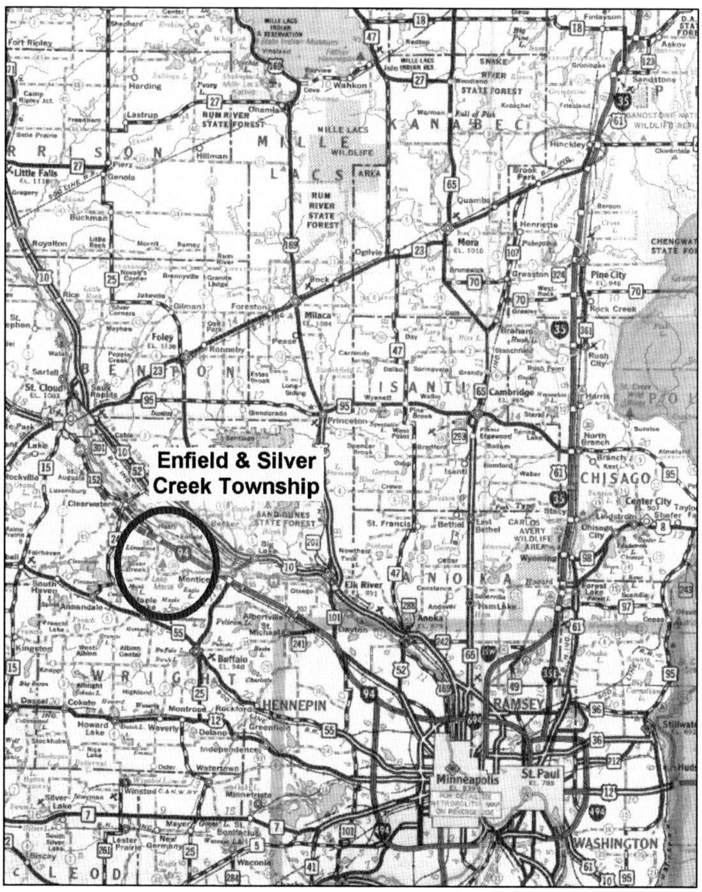

CENTRAL MINNESOTA: 2002.

Contents

Acknowledgments

This work could not have been completed without much help. The records and photographs collected by my mother, Evelyn Trogen Abrahamson, provided much of the basic information. I have drawn heavily on the memoirs written by my father, Edwin T. Abrahamson, and his brothers, Verner F. and Glenn E. Abrahamson. My sister, Mavis Abrahamson Ward, has read many drafts and has also put up with many calls and inquiries.

Members of my family spent many hours going through the photo collections of: my grandmothers Anna Westling Trogen and Amanda Felien Abrahamson, my mother, Evelyn Trogen Abrahamson, Bruce E. Abrahamson, Rebecca Abrahamson Barnett, Amelia Erickson Westman, Joyce Erickson DeVries, Frieda Westling Cullen and Marlys Cullen Lilja, and Ruth Westling Berg and Wesley "Bill" Berg. My aunt, Helen P. Abrahamson, and my uncles, Kenneth R. and Glenn E. Abrahamson, identified many of the individuals in old photographs, as did Gladyce Anderson and Rebecca Abrahamson Barnett. Other photographs were obtained from the Wright County Historical Society, the Minnesota Historical Society, the *Monticello Times*, Delores Frehner Ramerth, Lenore Platten Johnson, and the photo archives of the University of Minnesota Extension Division and the University of Louisville Ekström Library Photo Archives.

Betty Dircks, Wright County Historical Society Archivist, helped in many ways. Donald Smith, Editor and Publisher of the *Monticello Times*, gave me complete access to the *Times* archives of photographs from their 1968 to 1975 "Monticello Yesteryears" series. Peter Kissinger, Jim Tetlie, and Heidi Vinkemeier guided me through the records of the Faith Lutheran Church. Jerry Stockham and Lenore Johnson helped me with the original records of the Lake Side Cemetery Association. Lenore also gave me the history of the Enfield phone company. Diana Magnuson, Minnesota Swedish Baptist Conference archivist, tracked down the few remaining written records of the Enfield Baptist Church. David L. Hansen, photo archivist at the University of Minnesota Extension Division, gave me access to their collection. Chuck Thomas and Jennifer Claybourne-Torkelson, University of Minnesota Libraries Digital Collections Unit, made high-resolution scans of aerial photographs and of the negatives from the *Monticello Times* archives.

Richard Anderson identified for me the fate of the Enfield Baptist Church. Gahart Decker and Allan and Terri Nystrom did the same for the fate of the Enfield Town Hall, a.k.a. the Enfield IOGT Hall. Wesley "Bill" Berg confirmed the exact location and ultimate fate of the Enfield-Becker Ferry.

Finally, I thank my Arcadia Publishing editor, Jeff Ruetsche, and publisher, John Pearson.

I am indebted to them all, but any remaining errors or oversights are my own.

Introduction

Swedish emigrant farmers settled the Enfield community. They came with grub hoes, axes, and saws to Silver Creek Township, a small part of the massive, dense, mixed hardwood forest known as the Big Woods that covered central Minnesota.

They were young people and many of them came with small children. They left the Swedish villages where their ancestors had lived for centuries, knowing that they probably would never again see their parents. They came to a forest wilderness, cleared the land, built their farmsteads, and raised their families. In their spare time they created the community's schools, churches, cemetery, social and commercial institutions, and built their roads and bridges. They were a remarkable generation.

Like in other rural communities of the period, everyone knew each other, families became connected by marriage, they formed a cooperative corporation to build and operate commercial activities, they shared and traded work and tools, and they assumed responsibilities for township and local governance.

My ancestors and several of their siblings are among those who left their farms in Sweden and came to Silver Creek Township between 1868 and 1896. They carved farms out of forest and built the community. The Trogen family homesteaded in 1871 and the Abrahamson family settled in Enfield in 1900.

This book is an account of the origin and the subsequent fate of the Enfield, Minnesota farm community—from the first homesteaders through to the present time, when there are few farmers but a plethora of homes for commuters. It is also a capsule rendering of the evolution of farming techniques from the mid-1800s until the advent of large-scale commercial farming following the Second World War.

The family farms are gone and with them the community. Women welcomed the coming of electricity and a freezer that meant that they did not have to spend endless hours canning during hot summer days. Men did not mourn the passage from horses to tractors and did not seem to miss getting up to milk the cows 365 days per year. But we do mourn the passing of the era of tightly-knit families who worked together on everything from governance of the school district and township roads to farm tasks that needed many hands.

A limited edition of this book, in a somewhat different format, was originally published by DEA Press as *Enfield Minnesota A Swedish-American Farm Community—1850 to 2000*. The original edition is no longer available. It was intended primarily for descendants of the Enfield family farmers of the 1800s and 1900s. This edition is also for them, as well as for all descendants of Swedish immigrants who came to America.

The privately-printed edition contained about 50 pages of appendices that are not included in this book:

An explanation of Swedish person names during the emigration period.

Autobiographies of the Enfield community residents that were included in the 1915 History of Wright County, Minnesota.

Land-ownership plan maps for the Enfield community published from 1879 through 2001.

Detailed lists of burials in Enfield's Lake Side Cemetery from 1889 through 2001.

Copies of these appendixes are available from the author
for the cost of making copies and for mailing.

Dean Abrahamson
82 Orlin Avenue S.E.
Minneapolis, Minnesota 55414

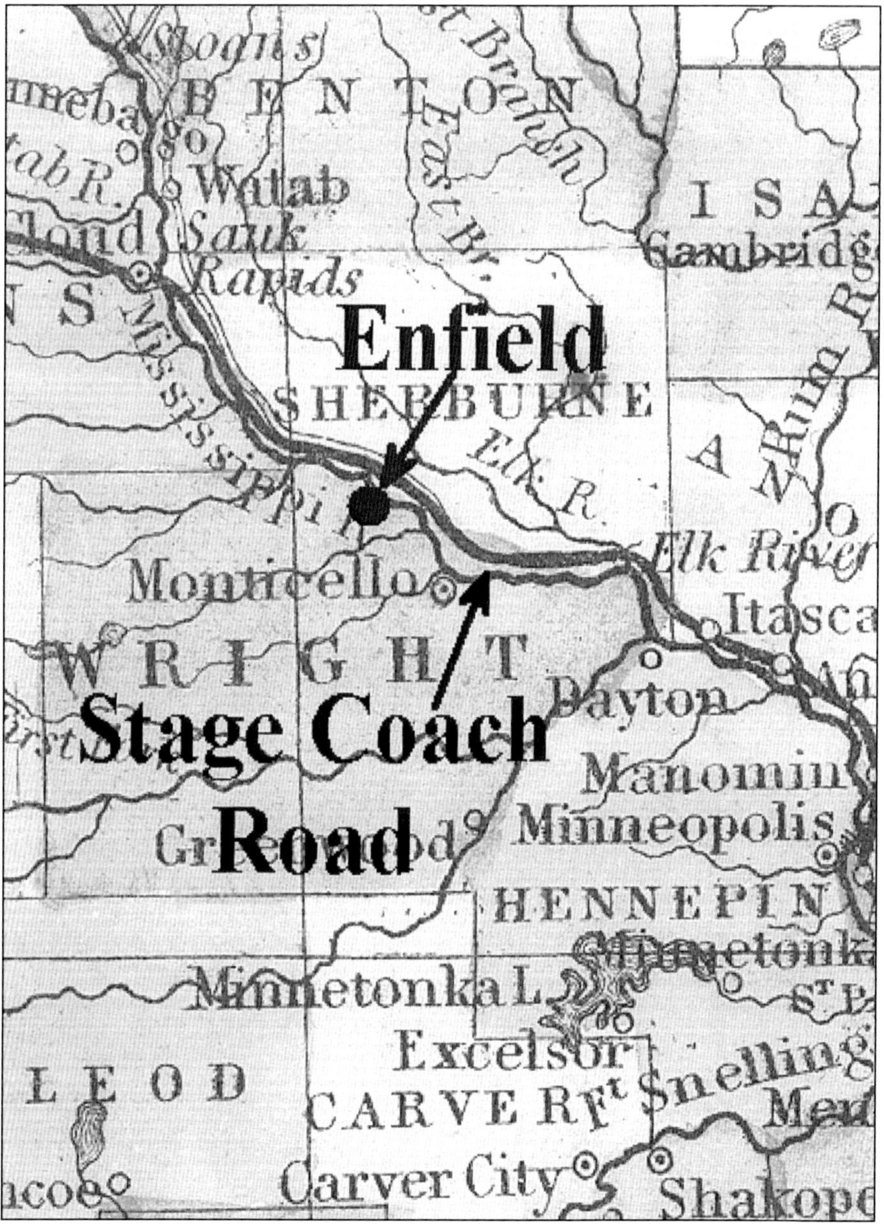

CENTRAL MINNESOTA: 1860S.

One

The Setting

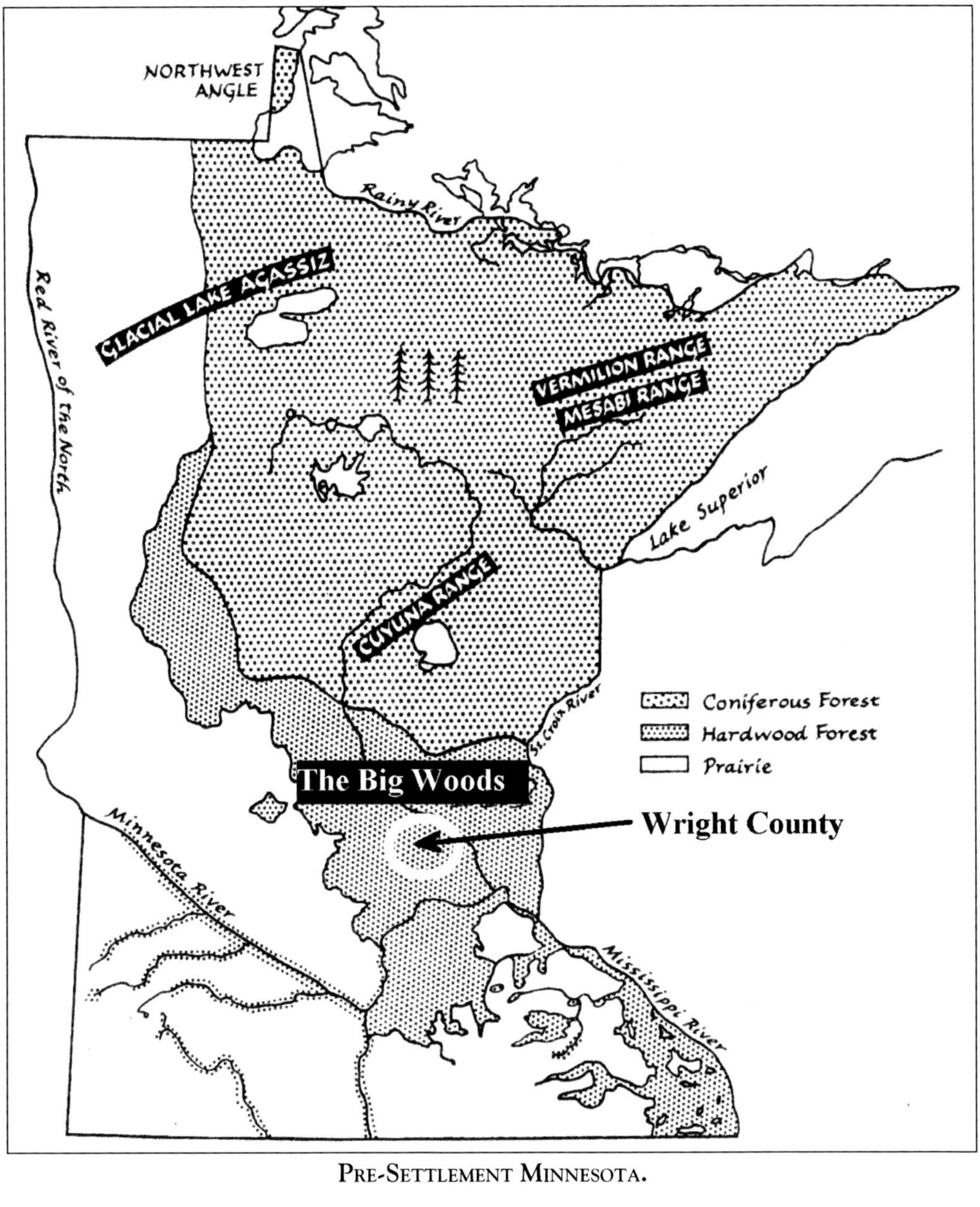

PRE-SETTLEMENT MINNESOTA.

European explorers began to come to Minnesota in the 1600s. Finally, only about 150 years ago, the settlers came to what would become the Enfield community, cleared the land, built their farmsteads, and created their local institutions—schools, churches, a cemetery, a town hall, general stores, a depot, potato warehouses, a cheese factory, as well as a baseball team, a town park, a band, and a community meeting hall. The rural community with its dairy farms grew and thrived for a century. The family dairy farms are now gone, some of the land is yet farmed, and the region is now evolving into a bedroom community in the outermost suburbs of Minneapolis and St. Cloud. The village that would become Enfield grew around the siding built in 1882 by the Minneapolis & St. Cloud Railroad Company in Wright County, Minnesota, Silver Creek Township. Wright County was organized in 1855. It has an area of 457,000 acres (714 square miles)—32,600 acres of which were under water in 1915. Many of the wetlands have since been drained. Wright County is located in the middle of what was known as The Big Woods, an extensive mixed hardwood forest bordered on the north by pine forests extending well into Canada and bordered on the southwest by prairie. Silver Creek Township, named for its creek, was first settled by Europeans in 1854. It was surveyed by A.H. Runyon in 1856 and was organized in 1858. The township includes Lake Maria State Park, created in 1963 to preserve a fragment of The Big Woods.

EARLY MAP OF THE ENFIELD COMMUNITY. Some of the land near the Mississippi River in the north part of the township had been acquired by non-Scandinavians prior to the passage of the Homestead Act, but Swedes had bought most of those tracts by the early 1900s. The Enfield community was then composed primarily of Scandinavian farm families, who were a diverse lot, including Baptists and Lutherans, and ranging from conservative Republicans to liberal Democrats. Supplies and outgoing commodities flowed through Enfield after the building of the railroad in 1882. Potatoes, grown on recently broken land, were a major cash crop from the 1880s and until about 1930. Cattle and hogs were sent to the St. Paul stockyards. Milk and cream were shipped to Minneapolis until the early 1920s, and after that to the cheese factory in Hasty, another small village about two miles to the northwest. The Enfield Farmers' Co-op cheese factory, built in 1927, operated until 1950.

THE APPROXIMATE EXTENT OF THE ENFIELD COMMUNITY

Northern Part of Silver Creek Township
Township 122N, Range 26W

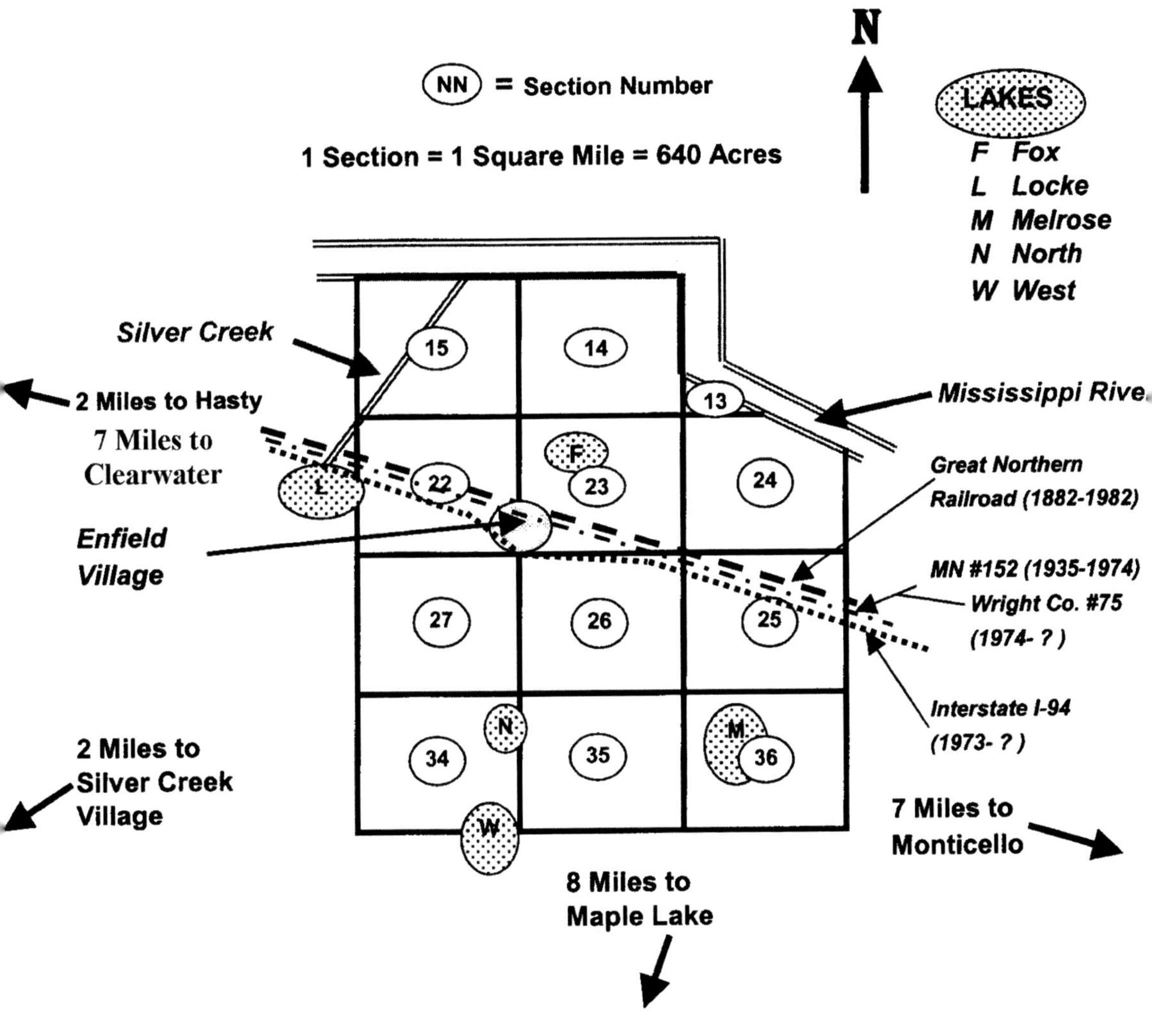

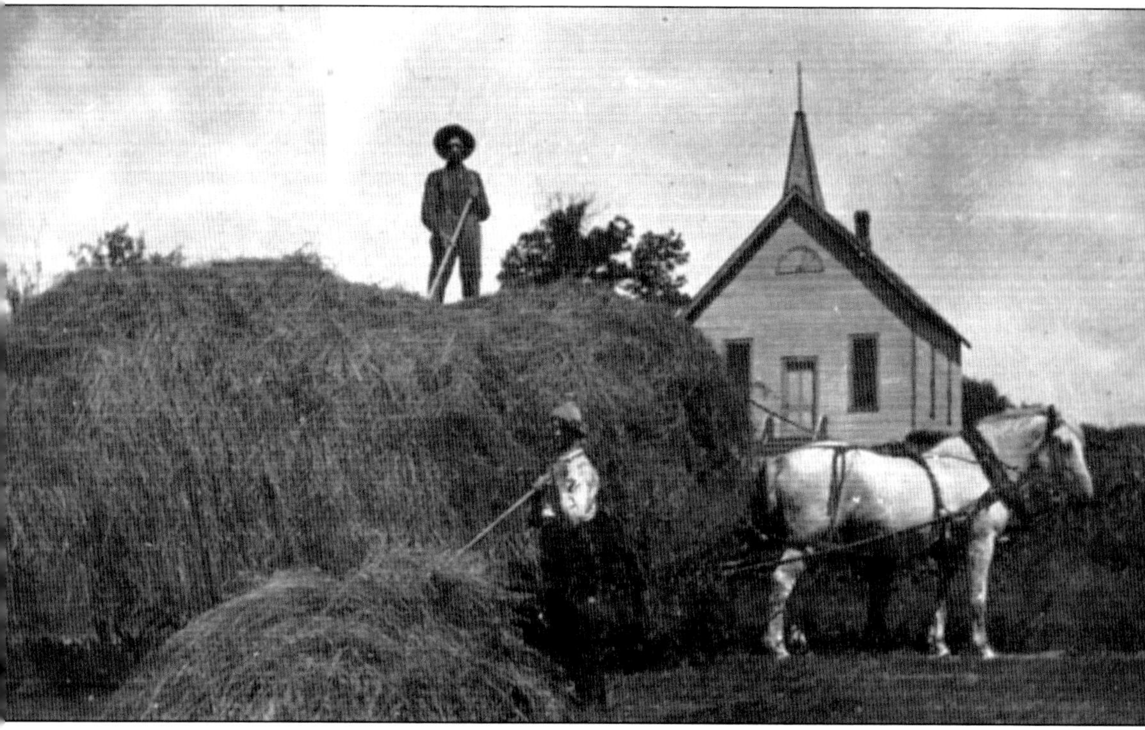

HAYING BY THE BAPTIST CHURCH, C. 1900. The Swedish immigrants formed a Baptist congregation in the late 1860s and constructed a church building in 1877. A Lutheran congregation began meeting a decade later; its church building was erected in 1891. The non-denominational cemetery was organized in 1889. Enfield had a baseball team, a band, and a town park. The Enfield Town Hall, which doubled as meeting hall for the International Order of Good Templars (IOGT, a temperance society), was built in 1910. The building was moved to Monticello in 1941.

10,000 B.C.	Ice Age retreats from Minnesota
1600s	First European explorers travel through Minnesota
1805-1806	Zebulon Pike explores Minnesota
1812	Red River Colony [Winnipeg] founded
1819	Fort Snelling established
1832	First mail-carrying steamboat to Fort Snelling
1849	Minnesota becomes a Territory with population of less that 5,000 people
1850s	First Silver Creek Township settlers -- along the Old River Road
1854	Congress grants purchase rights to claimants on unsurveyed land
1855	Ojibwa cede their lands in central Minnesota to the U.S.
1855	First Minnesota census: 598 non-Indian persons in Wright County
1855	Wright County organized
1856	Silver Creek Township surveyed
1858	Minnesota becomes the 32nd state
1858	Silver Creek Township organized
1862	Homestead Act opens surveyed land to settlement by homestead
1862	Last major Indian war in central Minnesota
1871	Erick & Kestin Trogen homestead in Section 26
1882	Railroad through Silver Creek Township
1896	My grandfather, Frank Abrahamson, bought 40 acres in Section 23
1935	First highway, Minnesota #152, through Silver Creek Township
1973	Interstate Highway I-94 through the township
2001	Enfield Village is becoming a memory

CHRONOLOGY OF SILVER CREEK TOWNSHIP. The farmers banded together in a cooperative to build a potato warehouse, a small stockyard, a town hall, a general store, a cheese factory, and other facilities. The village grew and peaked in the 1920s and 1930s. Minnesota Trunk Highway #152 was built through the village in 1935. This marked the start of the decline of the village. The cheese factory was forced to close in 1950 and, when farmers no longer had to come to the village daily, the general stores and post office were soon closed. The school was closed in 1951 and children began to be bussed to school in Monticello. Interstate I-94 was built just south of the village in the mid-1970s. It will not be long before Enfield can be found only by digging for old foundations and artifacts or with a global positioning system. There is no longer even a sign along Wright County #75.

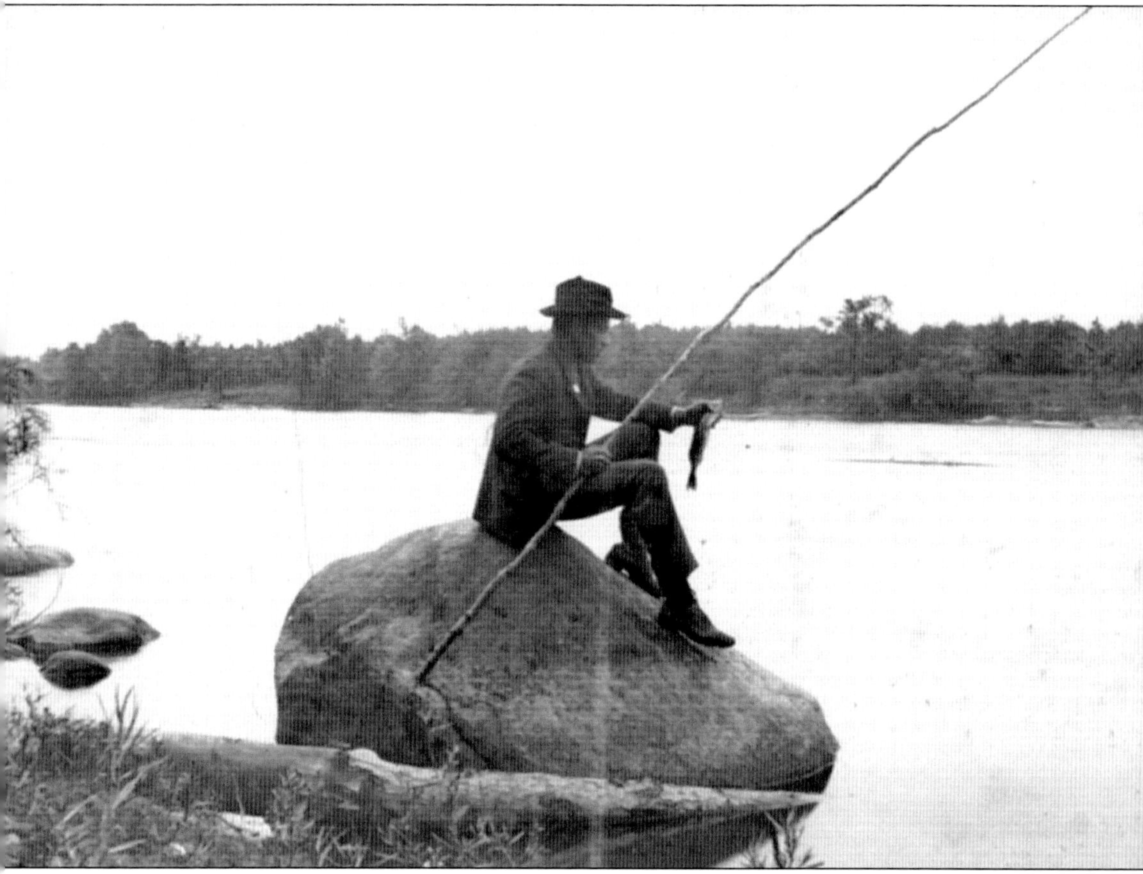

A Summer Afternoon near the Mississippi River. Willy Oswald was the Enfield community photographer from *c.* 1900–1915.

Two

The First Settlers 10,000 B.C. to the 1860s

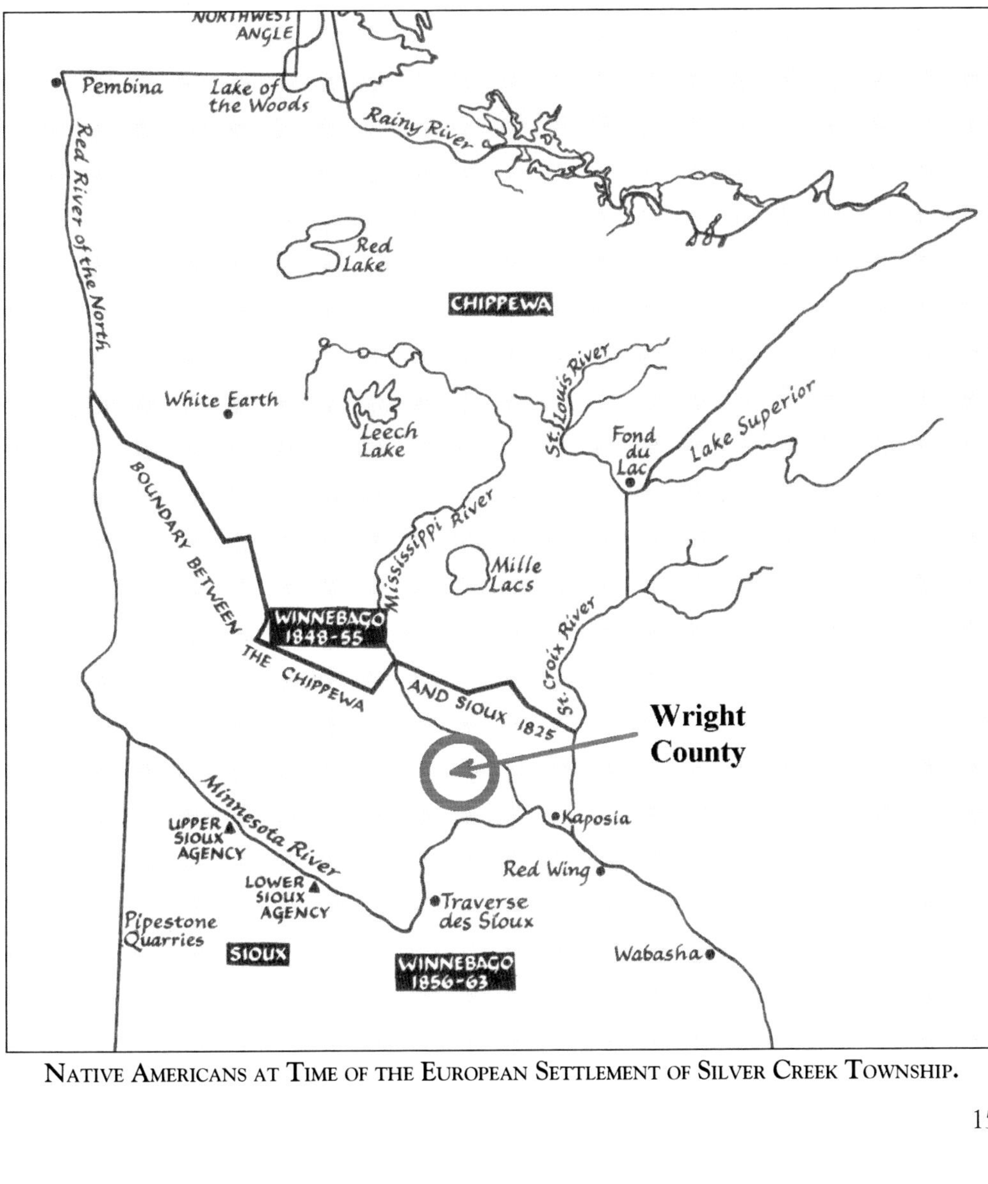

Native Americans at Time of the European Settlement of Silver Creek Township.

Minnesota's first settlers were the Native Americans who followed the retreat of the Wisconsin glaciation about 12,000 years ago. At the time of European settlement, in the early 1850s, Wright County was near the border of the territories of the Sioux or Dakotas, the plains Indians, and the Ojibwa or Chippewa, the forest Indians. It was a disputed border.

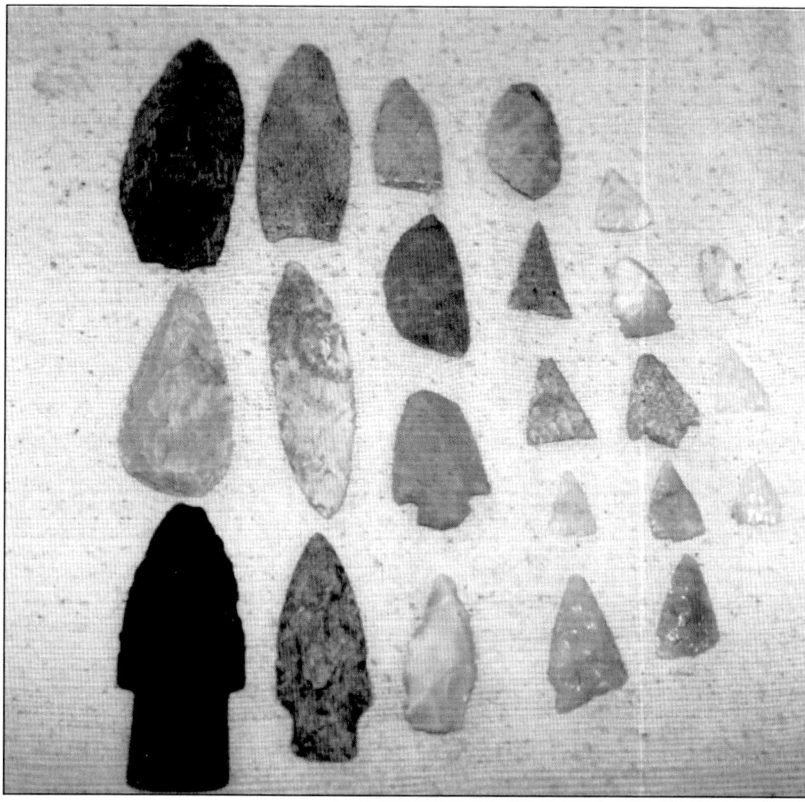

Spear Points Collected in the Enfield Area. The oldest spear points collected by my great-grandparents, Erick and Kestin Trogen, when breaking their land in Section 26 in the 1870s and 1880s, were dated as being from the Late Paleo-Indian period, 9,000 to 5,000 B.C., the period when Mammoth, Giant Bison, and other mega fauna were dominant. The larger spear points in the left-hand row are the oldest. Many of the original explorers and fur traders traveled along the Mississippi River beginning in the late 17th century and extending through the early days of the European settlement. They passed through the northern border of Silver Creek Township, but they did not tarry. The first settler recorded as having come to Wright County was a Canadian, Edmund Brissett, who established a trading post on Lake Pulaski north of present day Buffalo in 1849 or 1850. The first Minnesota census, in 1855, records 598 persons of European origin in Wright County, with 42 males and 20 females in Big Bend Precinct, which included Silver Creek, Clearwater, and other townships.

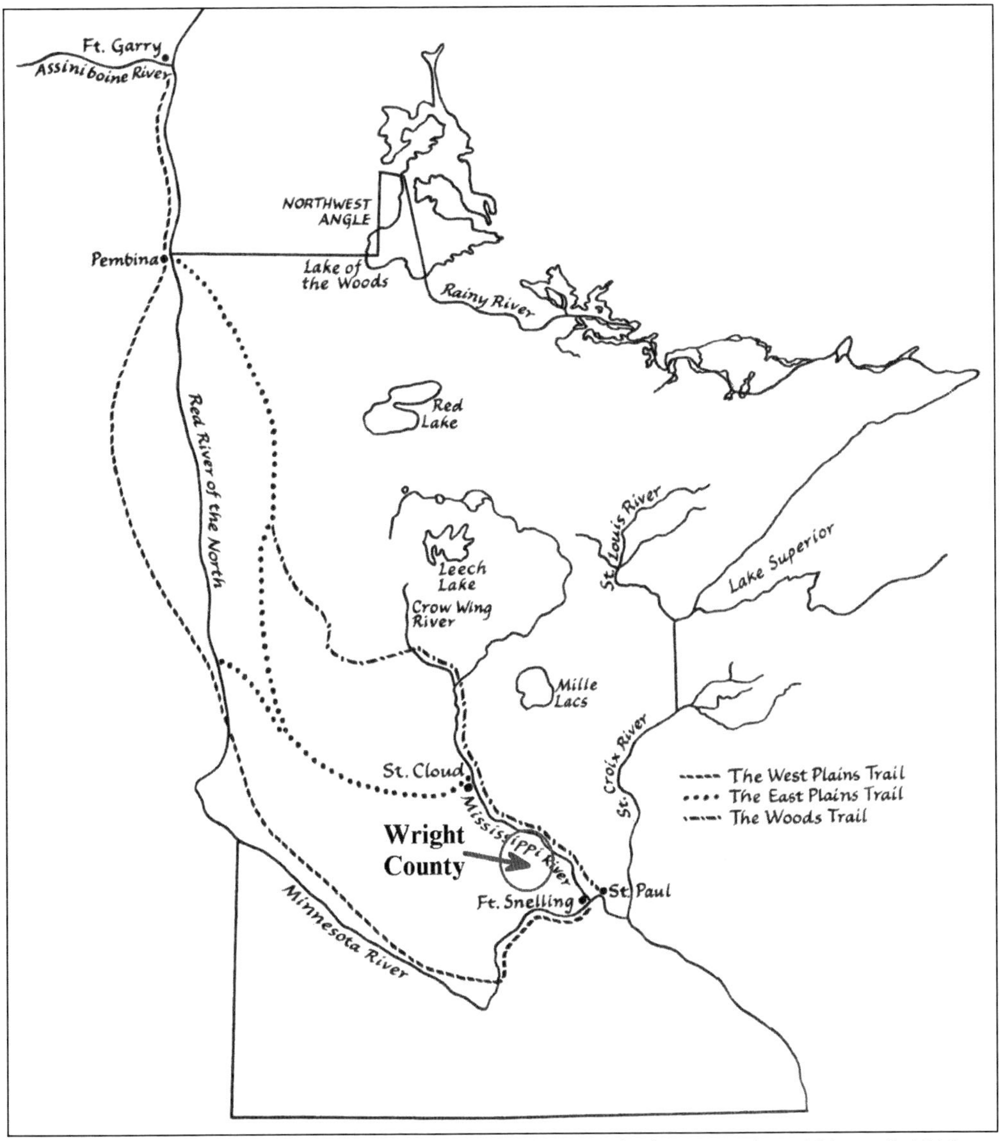

Pre-Settlement Military Trails. Military trails were laid out in the 1830s and 1840s to connect Fort Snelling, the head of steamboat navigation on the Mississippi River, with Fort Ridgley, on the Minnesota River upstream of New Ulm, and with Camp Ripley, north of present-day Little Falls, with the Euro-American settlements on the Red River in southern Canada. The Mississippi River Trail, surveyed by Corps of Engineers Captain John Pope in 1849, passed just north of what was to become Silver Creek Township. The trail split at the Sauk River near present-day St. Cloud into the East Plains Trail, which went west, and the Woods Trail that continued to follow the river to Camp Ripley and then angled northwest to Pembina and present day Winnipeg. A wagon road was cut along the southwest side of the Mississippi River to Monticello in 1854 and extended to Clearwater shortly thereafter. This trail, the Old River Road, was first used by Red River carts in summer and dog sleds in winter and then by a regular stagecoach system. A stagecoach station and hotel were located where the Old River Road crossed Silver Creek in Section 15. This was probably the overnight stop for the stagecoach, which at that time would have been one full day out of Minneapolis.

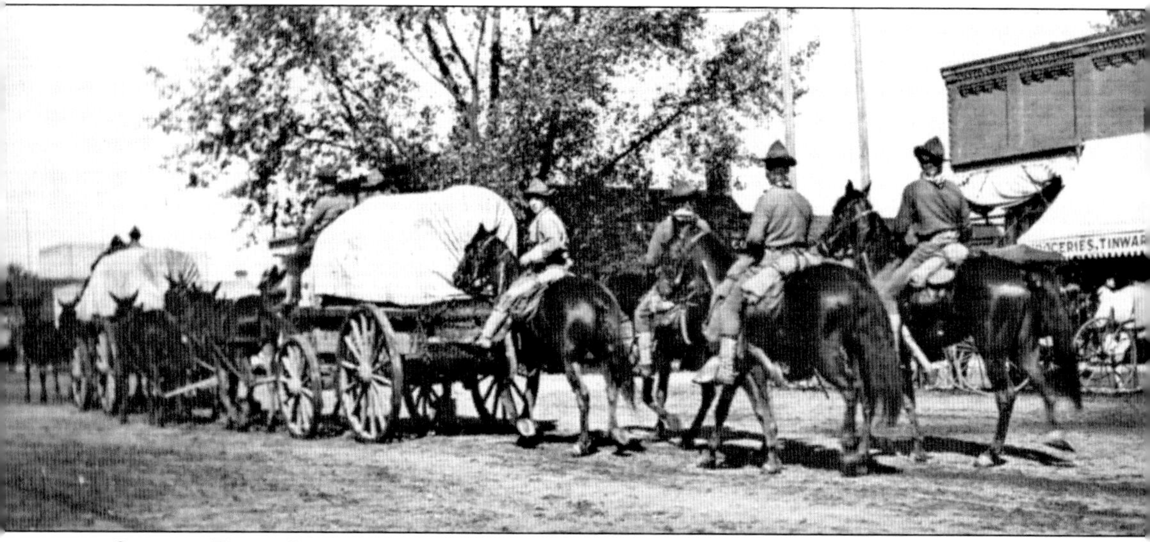

Cavalry Troop Passing Through Monticello, 1898. These gentlemen were probably going from Fort Snelling to Camp Ripley on the Old River Road through Silver Creek Township. Ruts left in the road by the stages and wagons were still visible c. 1950. The highways now designated as part of the National Great River Road roughly follow the old Minnesota portion of the post-settlement River Road from Minneapolis to St. Cloud and then north to Lake Itasca, the source of the Mississippi River. The first European settlers to the township were located along the stage road and along streams used for water-powered mills. Both Clearwater and Monticello had streams large enough for mills. In the late 1800s and early 1900s, Silver Creek village had sorghum, feed, and a sawmill. There were water-powered pulp and sawmills in Clearwater, and a flourmill at Monticello. Facilities not dependent upon waterpower included brick kilns at Hasty and Monticello and a sawmill and a canning factory in Monticello.

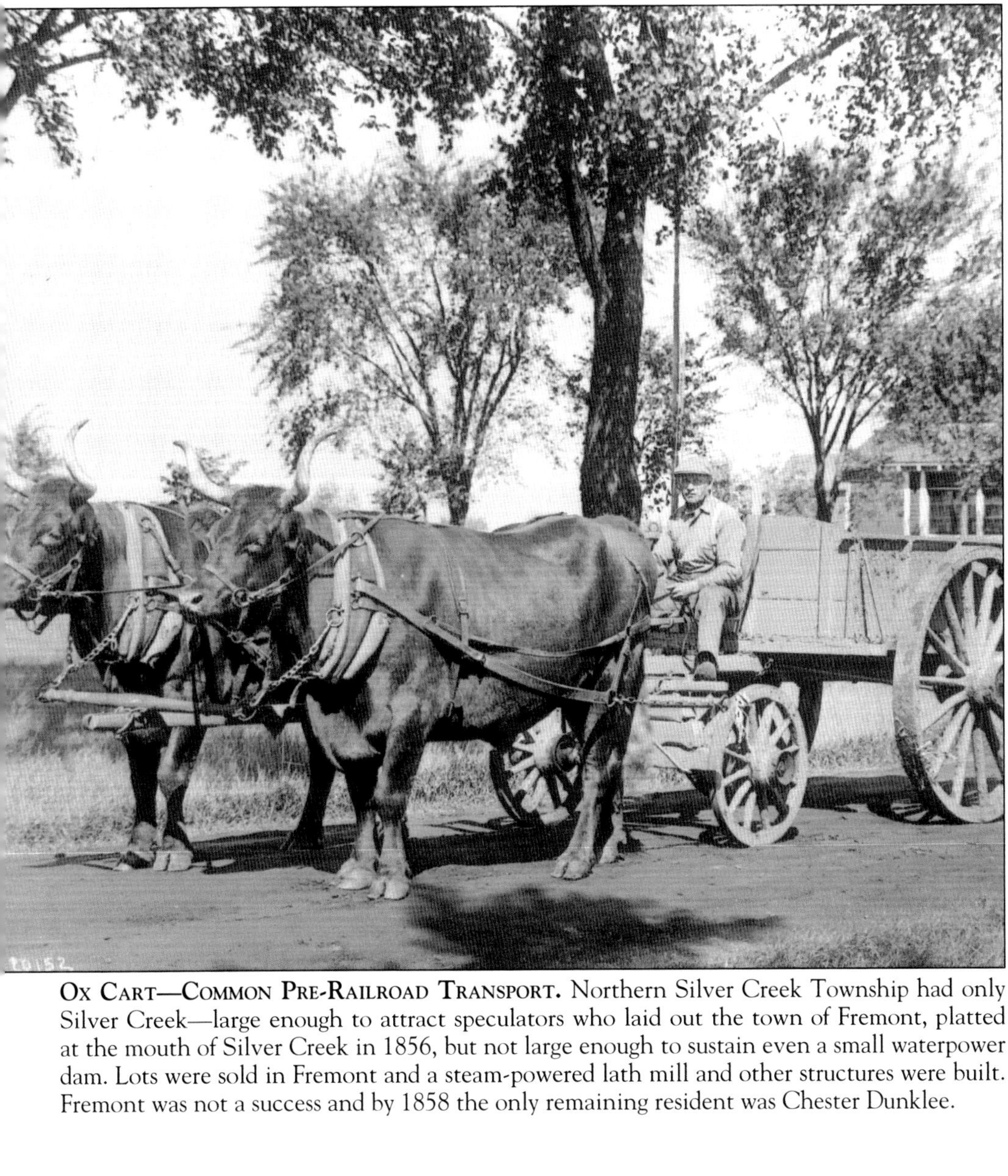

OX CART—COMMON PRE-RAILROAD TRANSPORT. Northern Silver Creek Township had only Silver Creek—large enough to attract speculators who laid out the town of Fremont, platted at the mouth of Silver Creek in 1856, but not large enough to sustain even a small waterpower dam. Lots were sold in Fremont and a steam-powered lath mill and other structures were built. Fremont was not a success and by 1858 the only remaining resident was Chester Dunklee.

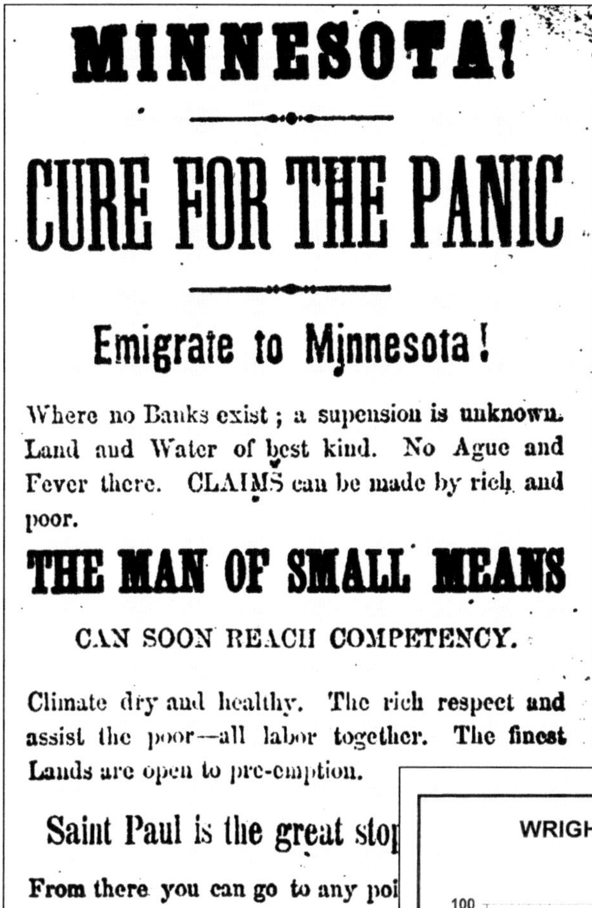
MINNESOTA!

CURE FOR THE PANIC

Emigrate to Minnesota!

Where no Banks exist; a supension is unknown. Land and Water of best kind. No Ague and Fever there. CLAIMS can be made by rich and poor.

THE MAN OF SMALL MEANS

CAN SOON REACH COMPETENCY.

Climate dry and healthy. The rich respect and assist the poor—all labor together. The finest Lands are open to pre-emption.

Saint Paul is the great sto

From there you can go to any poi

Come to Minnesota. Land speculators and developers again appeared 130 years later, creating the Fremont Heights Subdivision in the 1980s, and then the Forest Bend Subdivision, and the ongoing division of the farms into small tracts.

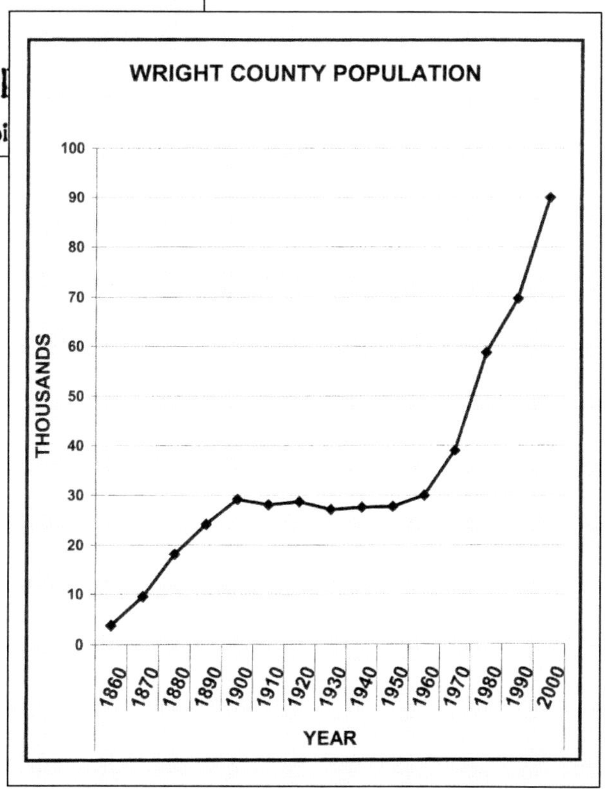

Rapid Population Rise. The population grew steadily from 1855 to 1900, a period of homesteaders with 40- and 80-acre farms. Farms began to be consolidated into larger units around 1900 but the population remained stable until the early 1960s. The transition from a farm community to a bedroom community at the outer ring of suburbs is yet under way. The population of Wright County increased from about five in 1850 to about 30,000 between 1900 and 1960, and then expanded to nearly 100,000 persons by 2000.

Three

SWEDISH FARMERS ARRIVE 1860S TO EARLY 1900S

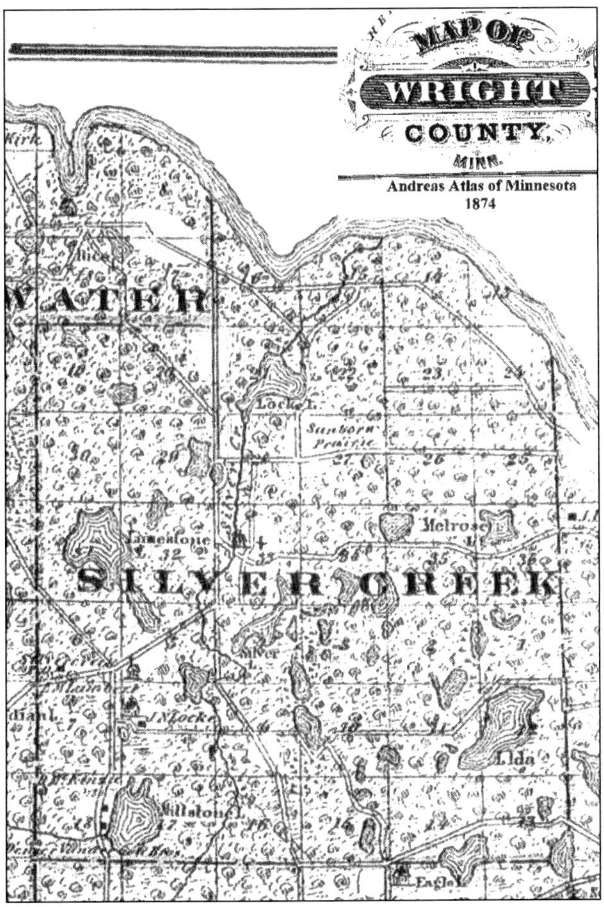

FROM THE FIRST MINNESOTA ATLAS, 1874—DENSE HARDWOOD FOREST COVERED THE TOWNSHIP. Wright County began to be settled following the land cessions by the treaties of Traverse des Sioux and Mendota in 1851. The land was surveyed in 1856, and the Homestead Act was passed in 1862.

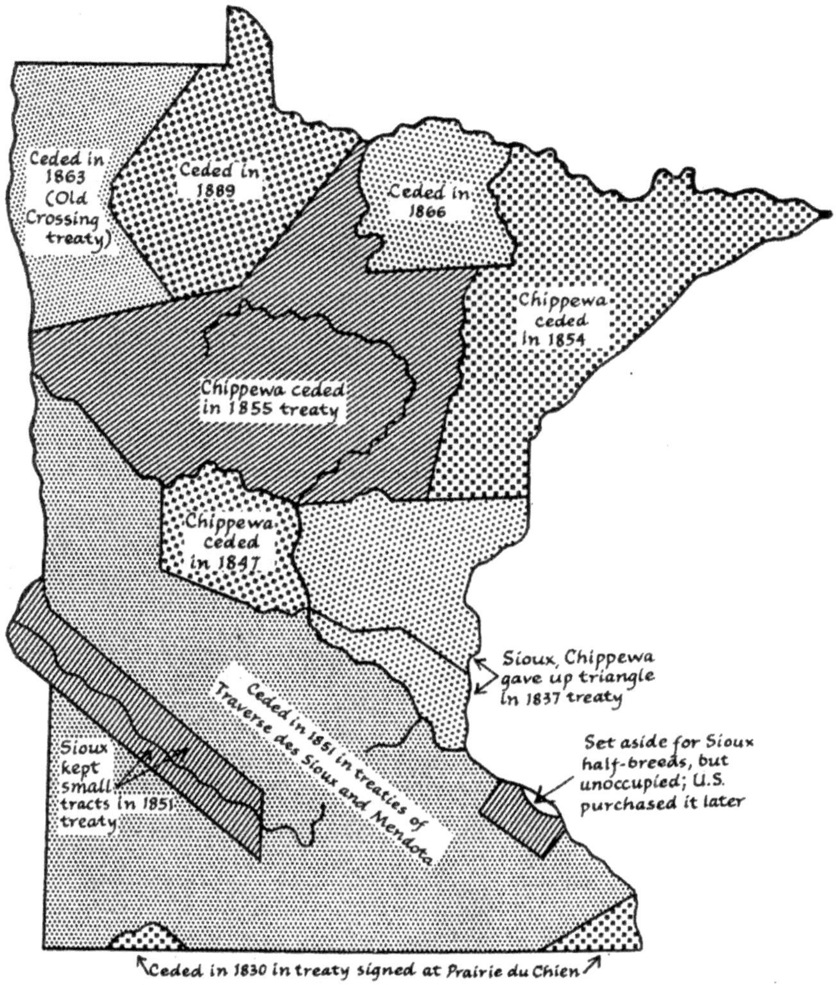

The land cessions by the Indians in Minnesota (adapted from Poatgieter and Dunn's *Gopher Reader*)

Land Cessions in Minnesota. Silver Creek Township was settled later than other parts of Wright County, perhaps because only the Swedes recognized its beauty and value. The part of Wright County with the most hills, ponds, and wetlands extends from the Mississippi River at the mouth of Silver Creek southeast to Lake Ida in Section 12. Nordic blood first flowed in North America when Bjarni Herjólfsson, Thorsteinn Eiríksson, Leif Eríksson, and other Vikings came to North America in about 1000 A.D. But these first Viking explorers did not stay nor did they get to central Minnesota. Swedes established their lower Delaware River colony in 1638. These early colonizers were seeking commercial interests to compete with the English or Dutch, or were simply adventurers. Large numbers of emigrants did not leave Sweden until the 1800s when sizable Swedish communities were established in Illinois and elsewhere.

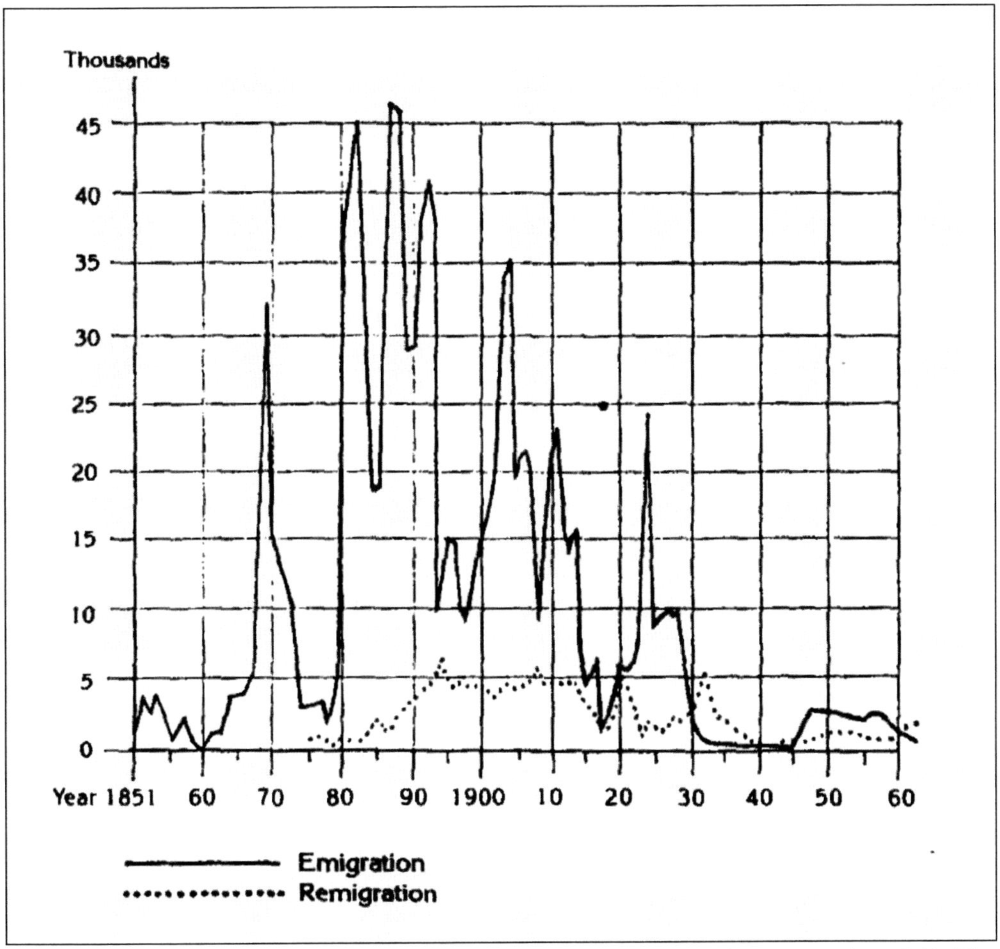

EMIGRATION AND REMIGRATION BETWEEN SWEDEN AND THE UNITED STATES: **1851–1963.** The first substantial Swedish presence in Minnesota was the community, immortalized by Vilhelm Moberg with his historical novels, established around Isanti County's Lindstrom and Center City in the mid-1850s. Many early Silver Creek Township homesteaders were Baptists who were fleeing the intolerance and oppression inflicted by the Swedish Kings and the priests of the Swedish Lutheran Church. Lutheranism formally became the State Church in 1593. Lutheran clergymen, appointed for life, became Government employees, and the Roman Catholic Church was banned in Sweden. In 1726, a law was passed prohibiting all religious assembles not conducted by a priest ordained by the State Lutheran Church. The worst parts of these laws were repealed by 1858, but Swedish citizens did not achieve full religious freedom until 1951. The first peak of Swedish emigration to the United States occurred from 1868 to 1874. A significant fraction of these emigrants left Sweden to escape what they regarded as religious intolerance—including the extended Trogen family that played a major part in the settlement of Silver Creek Township. The majority of the immigrants who came later, from the 1880s through the early 1900s, left Sweden for economic reasons.

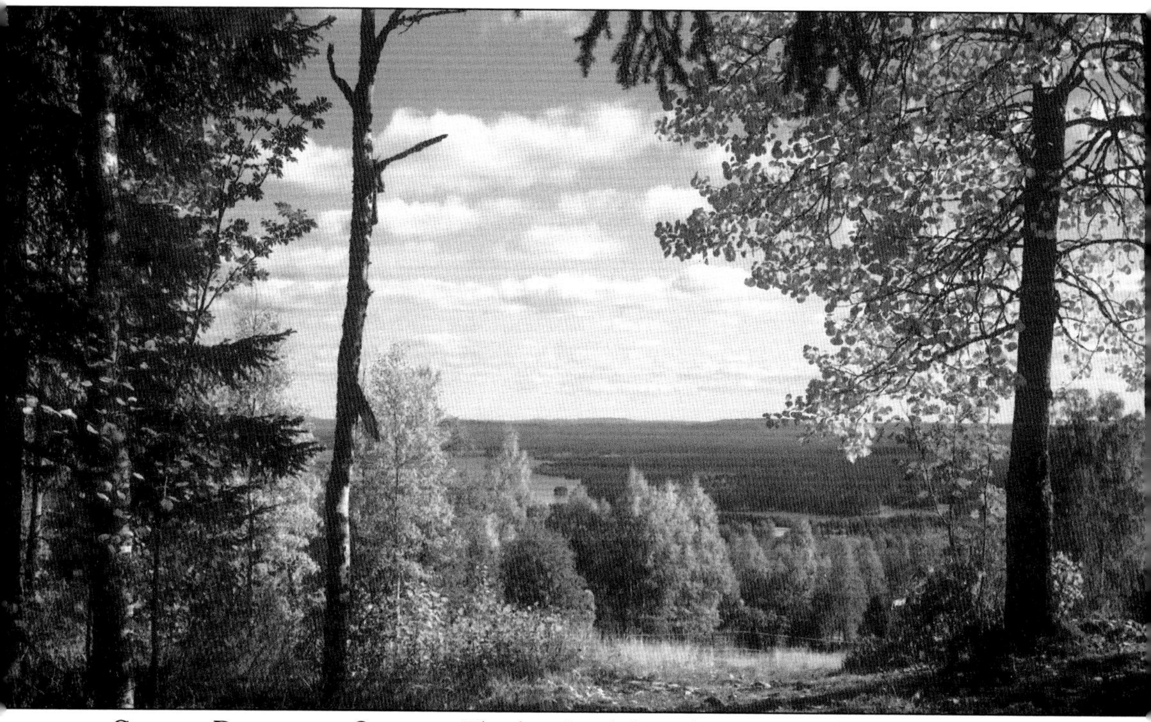

Central Dalarna in October. The first Swedish settlers came to the Township because the land was then open for homesteading and because the terrain and the vegetation are very much like that of their homes in central Sweden and particularly Dalarna—the home of Gustaf Vasa, of Swedish democracy, and of the artists Anders Zorn, Carl Larson, and Ottilia Adelborg. The northern part of Silver Creek Township was remarkably similar to that of their Swedish homes, with fertile soil, hills, streams, lakes, and an abundance of oak and other hardwoods. And a few emigrants from Gagnef and their other home communities had earlier settled in the southern part of Wright County. But they first had to travel from Sweden to Silver Creek Township. The trip took at least three months for those who came in the 1860s and 1870s.

Opposite: **Land Ownership at the Time of Silver Creek Township Settlement.** The emigrants sold nearly everything of what they owned, in part to pay for their passage, and in part because they could bring only limited baggage. A ticket from Sweden to Minnesota cost twice the annual cash wage of a farmhand or a housemaid in the 1860s. By 1900 competition between shipping companies had brought fares down, but passage for a family of four was still nearly half of the average worker's yearly salary. About half of the emigrants from 1870 to 1914 had pre-paid tickets sent from relatives or friends in America who had earlier emigrated. Most emigrants kept only the things that they would most need during the trip and in their new homes. They also kept their most cherished personal possessions. My great-grandmother, Kestin Trogen, kept her *högtidsdräkt*, homespun linen fabrics, and lace that she had made. Her husband, Erick Jonsson Trogen, kept the family bible and the photographs taken of Kestin and of himself when they were married in 1863.

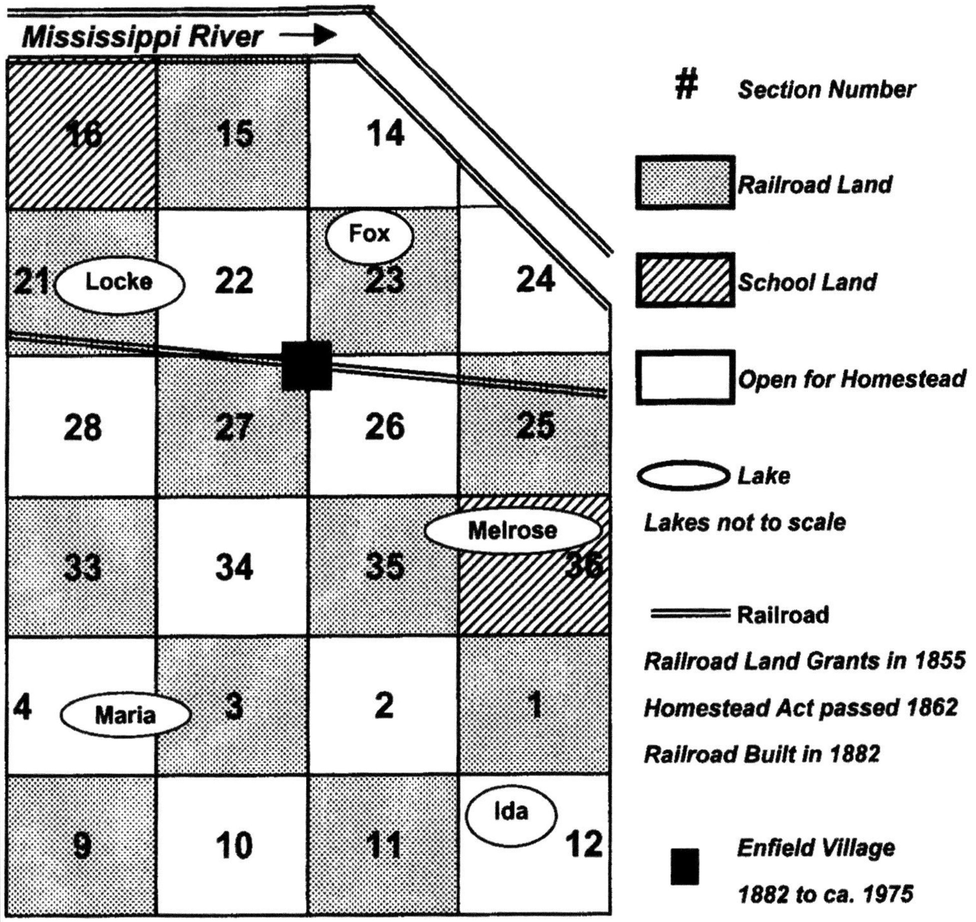

LAND OWNERSHIP PATTERN AT THE TIME OF SILVER CREEK TOWNSHIP SETTLEMENT

The odd-numbered sections in Silver Creek Township had been given to the proposed Minneapolis-St. Cloud Railroad Company in 1855. The Homestead Act became law in 1862. Even-numbered sections were open for homestead, except sections 16 and 36, which were school lands, revenues from the sale of which were to be used to establish rural schools. An 1854 Act of Congress gave squatters, who had come prior to the Homestead Act, land patents. Civil War veterans could also get land patents. Half of Silver Creek Township was given to the railroad barons, leaving emigrant farmers the choice of homesteading the scarce government land, or of buying land from the railroads or from earlier settlers.

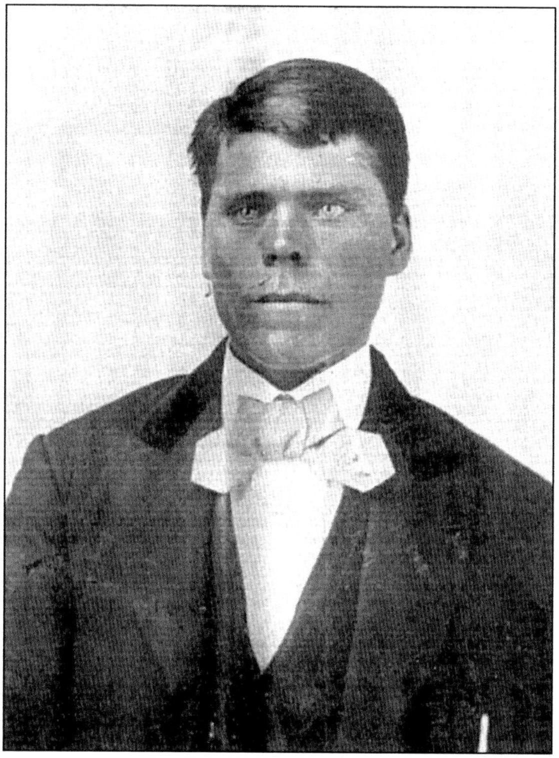

ERICK TROGEN IN 1863. A homesteader couple, Erick and Kestin Trogen, came to Silver Creek Township with three young children in 1871. The Trogen family, like most of the early emigrants, traveled by horse-drawn wagons from their home of Gagnef, Dalarna to Göteborg, a trip that took ten days over rough roads. They knew that they were leaving their families and their ancestral homes behind, probably forever. Neither Erick nor Kestin Trogen ever returned to Sweden, nor did any of their three young children who were born in Sweden.

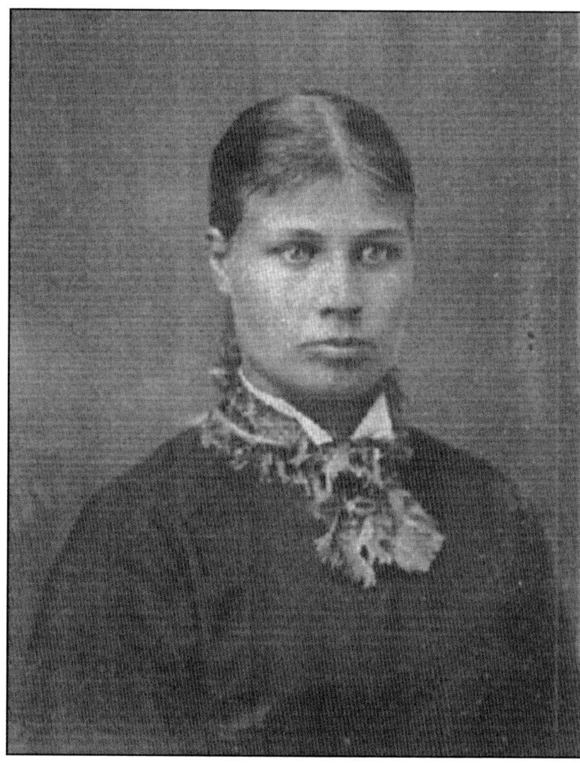

KESTIN TROGEN IN 1863. The Trogen family departed from Göteborg harbor on May 12, 1871 on the ship *Rollo*, bound for Hull, England. They then traveled over land from Hull to Liverpool and embarked on a larger emigrant ship for the Atlantic Ocean crossing. There were several hundred other emigrant passengers. About 30 of them were from the Gagnef community, each bound for Minneapolis or St. Paul, Minnesota.

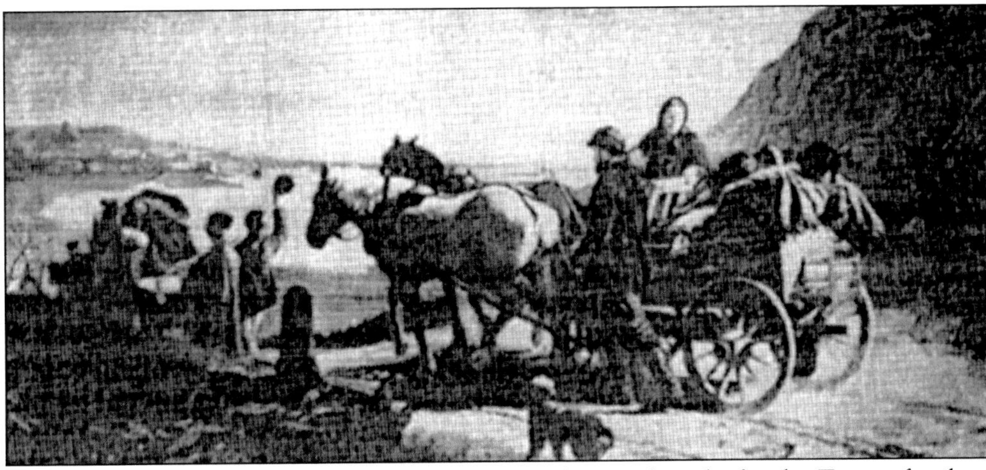

EMIGRANTS EN ROUTE TO GÖTEBORG, 1872. It took several weeks for the Trogen family to travel from Gagnef to Göteborg to Hull to Liverpool and then to New York. They disembarked at Castle Garden, the emigration center located on the east shore of lower Manhattan that was the main portal until the emigrant center on Ellis Island opened in 1892.

The Trogens took the railroad from New York to Chicago, and then took the recently-opened railroad from Chicago to La Crosse, Wisconsin, and continued on a riverboat to St. Paul. They arrived in St. Paul in August.

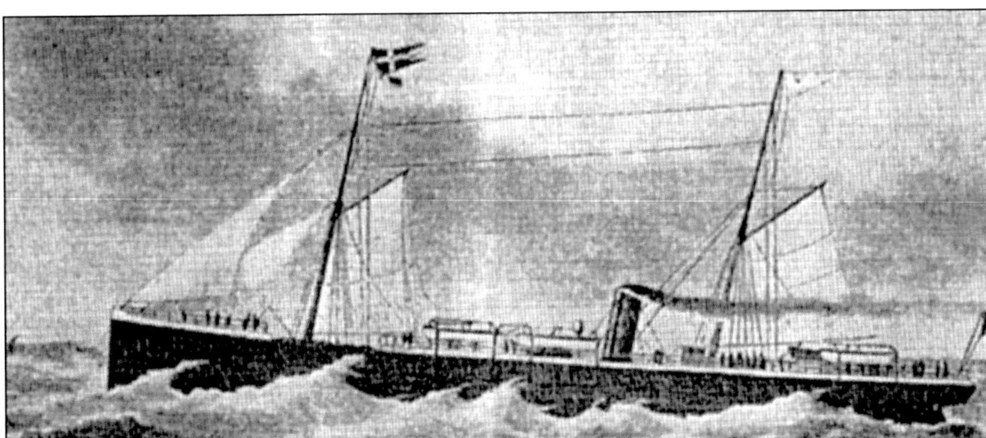

AN EMIGRANT SHIP OF THE ENGLISH WILSON LINE, 1860S. The emigrants went by stagecoach on the Old River Road through Dayton and Monticello to their new home. Another family from their home village in Sweden had come three years earlier to scout out the land. Olof Anderson, his wife Anna, and Jacob Peterson met them at the stage station located where the Old River Road crossed Silver Creek in northern Silver Creek Township. Olof and Anna took them into their home for the few weeks it took Erick and Kestin to build a log house on their own homestead.

They came to Minnesota's Big Woods, the dense hardwood forest extending from the prairies of the southwest to the Pine forests of northern Minnesota. Trees were so tightly spaced that several had to be removed just to make room for a cabin. Fragments of the Big Woods are preserved in Lake Maria State Park, about two miles southwest of the Trogen homestead, and in the Harry Larson Forest Wright County Park. The Larson Park includes the Bengt Larson homestead (Bengt was Harry's grandfather), immediately south of Erick and Kestin's farm, and the south part of Andrew Tatting's homestead.

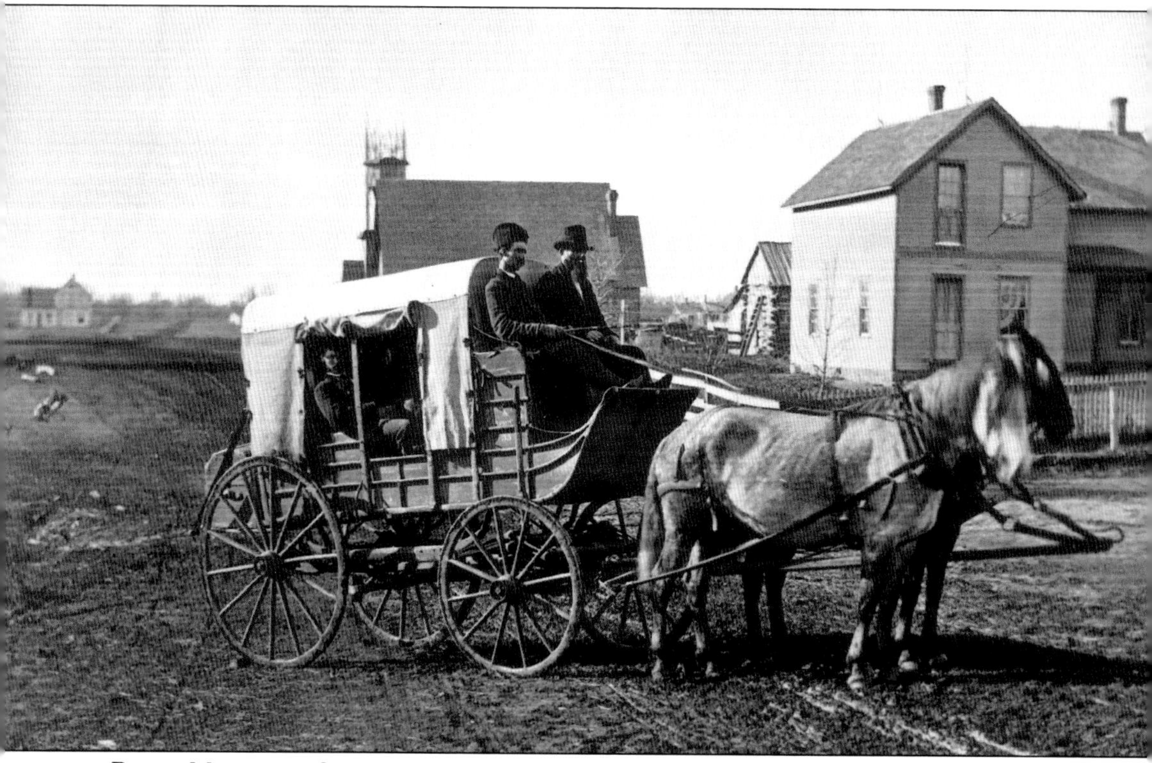

Rural Minnesota Stagecoach, 1876. It was too late in the year to clear land and plant their first crops, but not too late to raise a log house that would shelter them through the Minnesota winter. Erick and Kestin built the log house that would be home to their growing family for ten years. They also built a log barn for their team of oxen and two milk cows. The log house was replaced by a substantial, two-storied frame house in 1881.

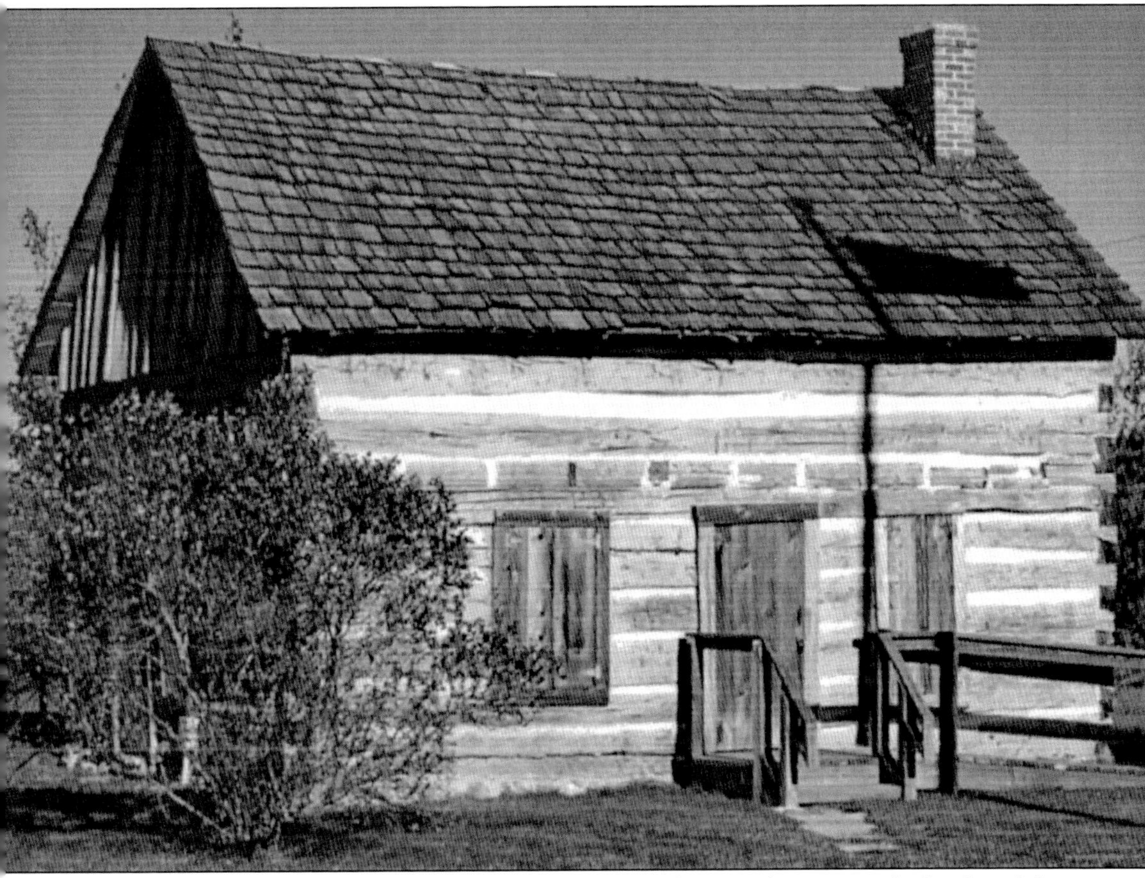

Wright County Homestead Cabin, 1870. Silver Creek Township was at the border of the lands of the prairie Indians, the Dakota or Sioux, and of the forest Indians, the Ojibwa or Chippewa. The U.S. Army, from its base at Fort Snelling, had suppressed local Indian tribes soon after Minnesota's last Indian war in 1862. Kestin Trogen related how groups of Indians occasionally came through their farm. The community was composed of a dozen or so newly claimed homesteads separated by dense forest. The settlers first lived on basic staples that they carried on their backs or by ox cart the seven miles from Monticello, and from the fruits, berries, nuts, and game gathered from the forest. There was no source in the community for even flour, sugar, salt, or coffee until Aleck Swanson, another Swedish emigrant, began to barter groceries for eggs from his farmhouse in the 1880s.

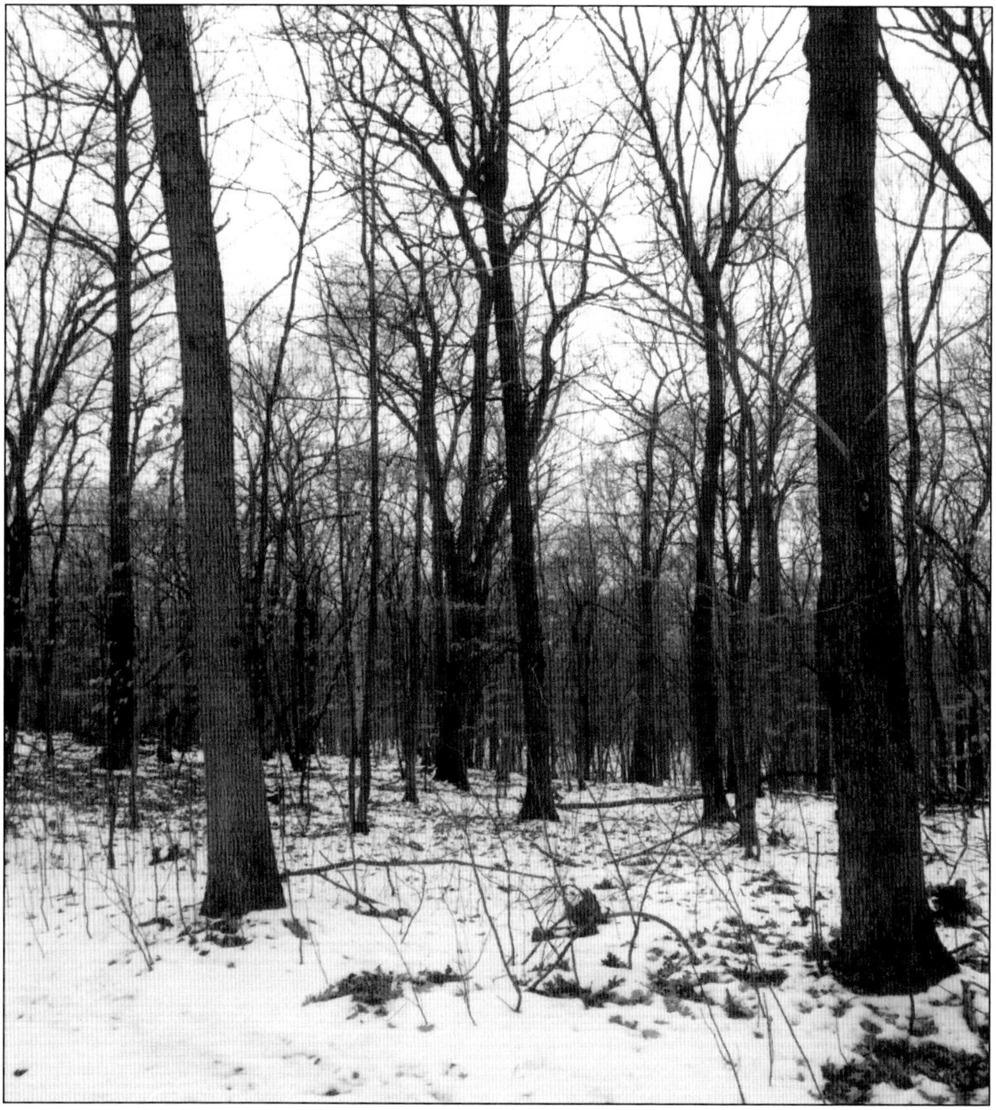

The Big Woods. Counties, townships, and school districts had been created when Minnesota gained statehood in 1858, but they were little more than paper. The emigrants cleared their land, built their farms, and raised their children. In their spare time they organized and built their churches, schools, roads, bridges, and cemeteries. As with many emigrants coming to the United States, one or two individuals were soon followed by their extended families. The first members of my extended Trogen family to come to Minnesota, Erick Peterson and Olof Anderson, homesteaded in Section 26 in 1868. Erick's half-sister, Kestin Trogen, and her husband, Erick Johnson Trogen, followed in 1871 with their three oldest children, Andrew Ezra, Anne, and Kerstin. The author's Westling ancestors, who were also from Dalarna, and his father's family, the Abrahamsons from Uppland and the Feliens from Småland, came to the Enfield community a generation later, in the 1890s. The homestead days were then past, but land was available for purchase from land granted to railroads, from speculators, and from earlier settlers. Swedish immigrants had bought out nearly all of the original squatters and non-Scandinavian settlers by *c.* 1900. The Enfield community became a homogenous collection of Scandinavian-American dairy farmers.

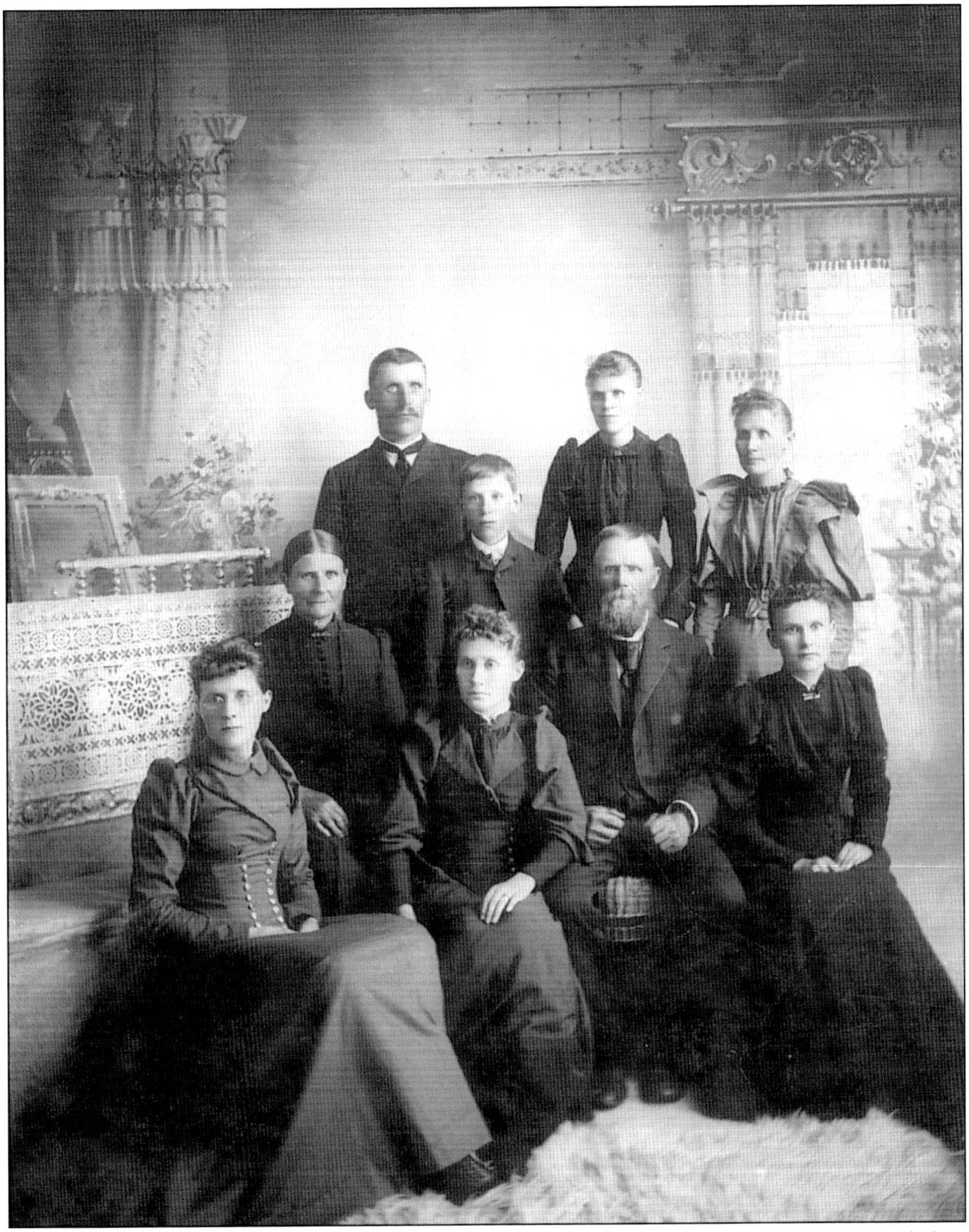

THE ERICK AND KESTIN TROGEN FAMILY IN 1893. They had emigrated and homesteaded in 1871. Pictured are: (front row) Carrie and Julia Anderson; (middle row) Kestin (Christine), Edward, Erick, and Ellen; (back row) Andrew Ezra, Anna Norling, and Kerstin Day.

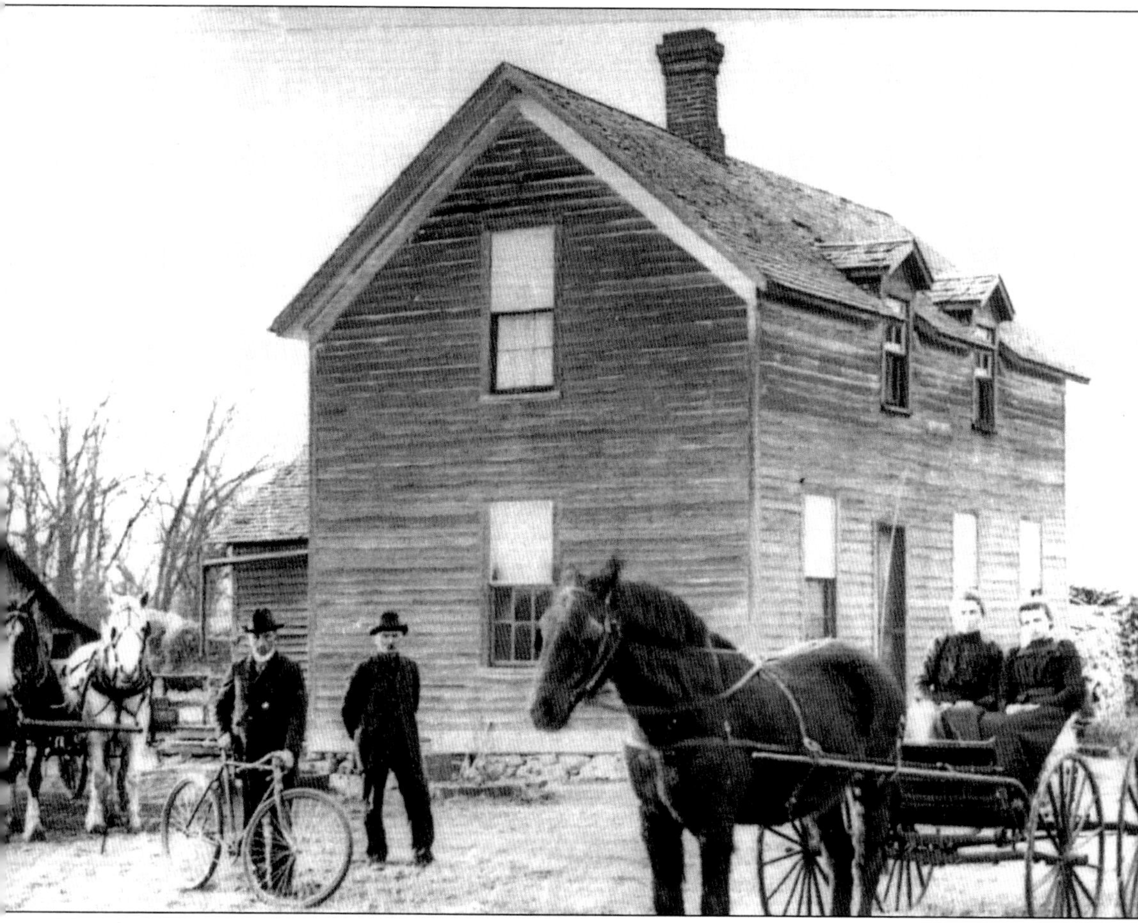

An Early Enfield Family. The picture was probably taken to send back to Sweden to demonstrate the family's prosperity in Minnesota.

Four

Schools 1856 to 1951

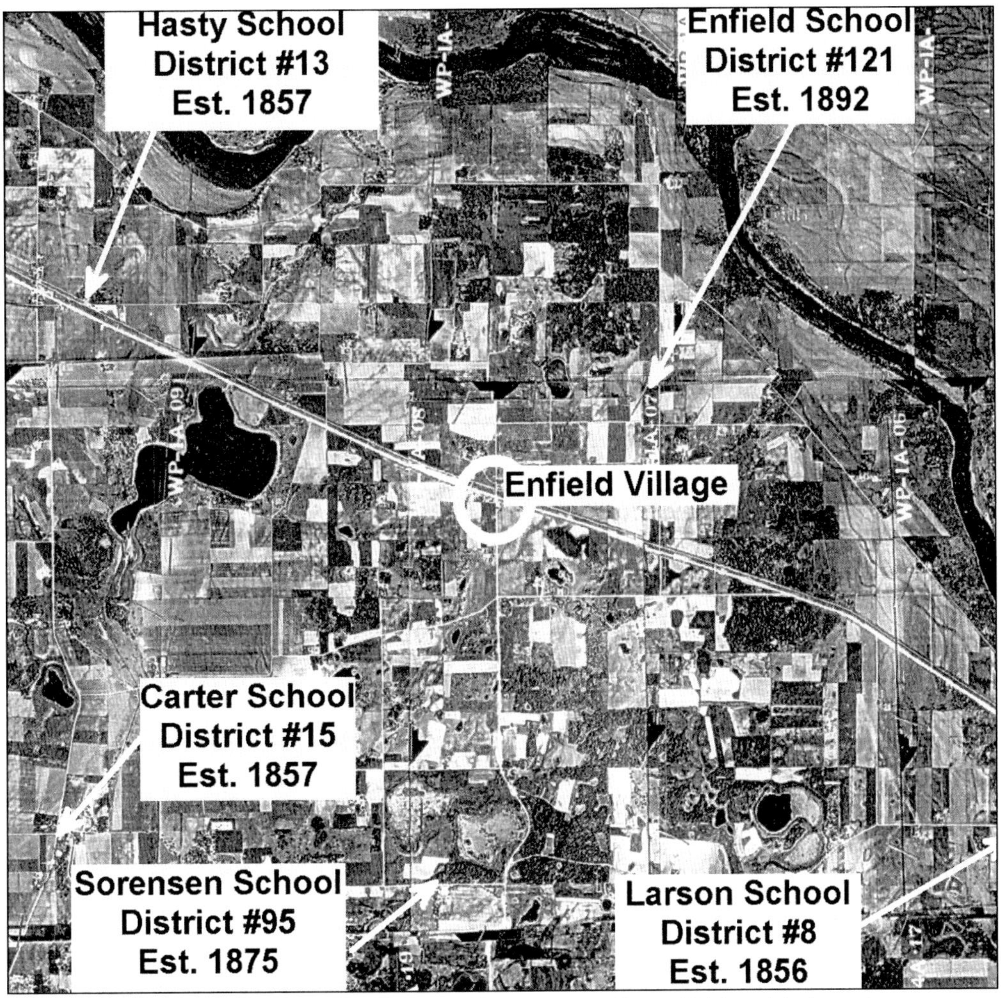

Schools Serving the Enfield Community. (June 1940 aerial photo.)

Schools districts were among the first institutions established in pioneer Minnesota. The average area served by a school was about five square miles (five sections). Most farmsteads were less than two miles from a school. The Monticello district, Wright County School District #2, was the second established in Wright County in 1855; the district, which included what was to become Enfield, reported 22 students in all classes in 1857. Eventually there would be 141 school districts in Wright County—schools within walking distance of every farmstead. The vast majority were one or two-room country schools, 11 of which served parts of Silver Creek Township. By 1859–1860, 712 children between the ages of four and 21 were recorded as living in Wright County, 536 of whom were reported to be enrolled in school.

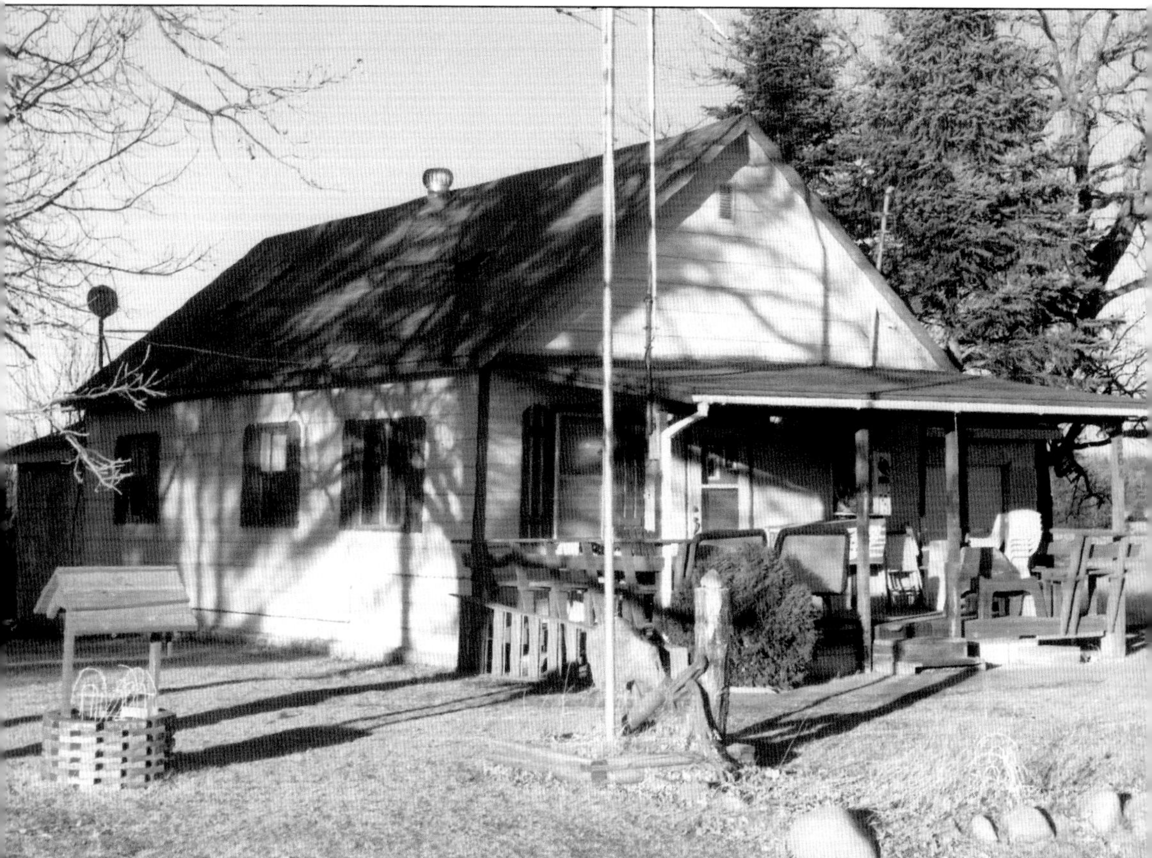

LARSON SCHOOL BUILDING, DISTRICT #8, 2002. The Silver Creek Township rural schools were closed in 1951 and 1952 when the districts were consolidated into town-centered school systems. The Enfield, Larson, Sorensen, and Hasty School districts were put into the Monticello school system, and the Carter district into that of Annandale. Five schools would serve the Enfield community. District #8, the Larson School, with the school building in Monticello Township Section 33, was chartered in April 1856. District #13, the Hasty School, in Silver Creek Township 16, and District #15, the Carter School, in Silver Creek Township Section 33, were chartered in January 1857. The northern portion of the future Enfield community was then in the Hasty school district, the southeastern portion in the Larson school district, and the southwestern portion in the Carter school district. Each served grades one through eight in one-room schools with one teacher, except for the Hasty school, which had two rooms and two teachers.

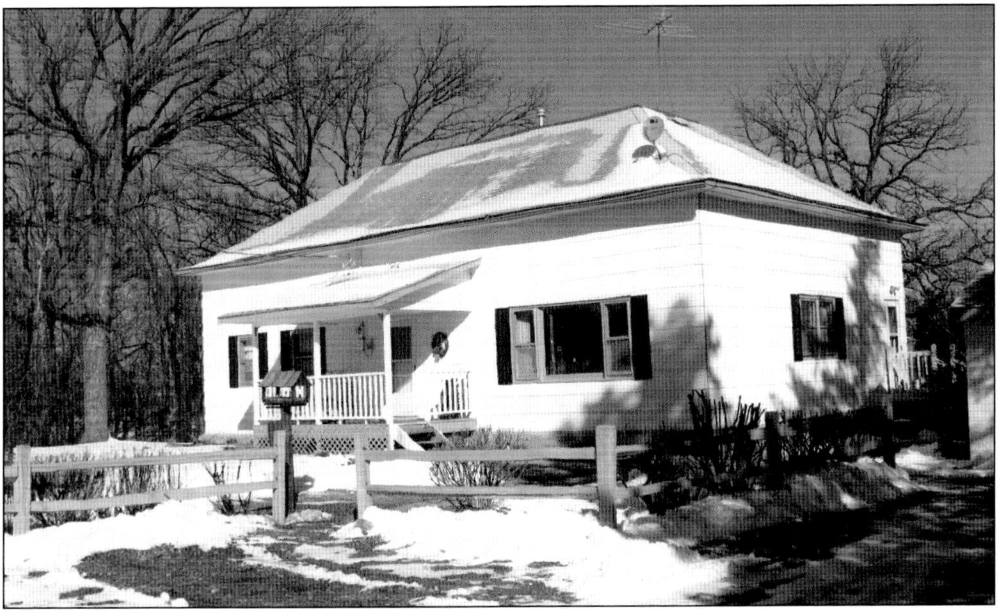

HASTY SCHOOL BUILDING, DISTRICT #13, 2002. The 1859–1860 student census for the northern part of Silver Creek Township was: District #8 (Larson), 32 students; District #13 (Hasty), 36 students; and District #15 (Carter), 21 students. The school year was about twelve weeks long in 1860. The average annual school attendance was 79 days per pupil in 1904, and had increased to 104 days by 1914. Nearly another twenty years passed before District 95, the Sorensen School, was established in March 1875 and incorporated a portion of the farms previously in Districts #8 and #15. After the school was closed in 1951, the building was sold and moved to the Maynard and Elsie Anderson farm, located just west of the original school location.

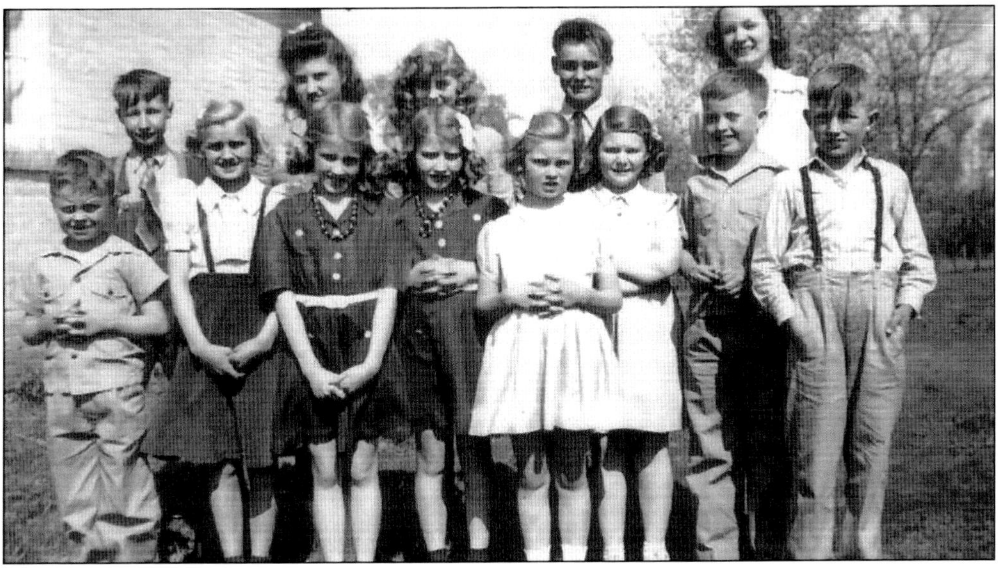

CARTER SCHOOL STUDENTS, 1942–1943. Pictured from left to right are: (front row) Bruce Abrahamson, Marilyn Betzler, Delores and Donna Rotsolk, Irene Olson, Gloria Peterson, Dean Abrahamson, and Richard Kramer; (back row) Kenneth Plaggerman, Margaret Borchert, Ralph Betzler, Olive Johnson, and the teacher.

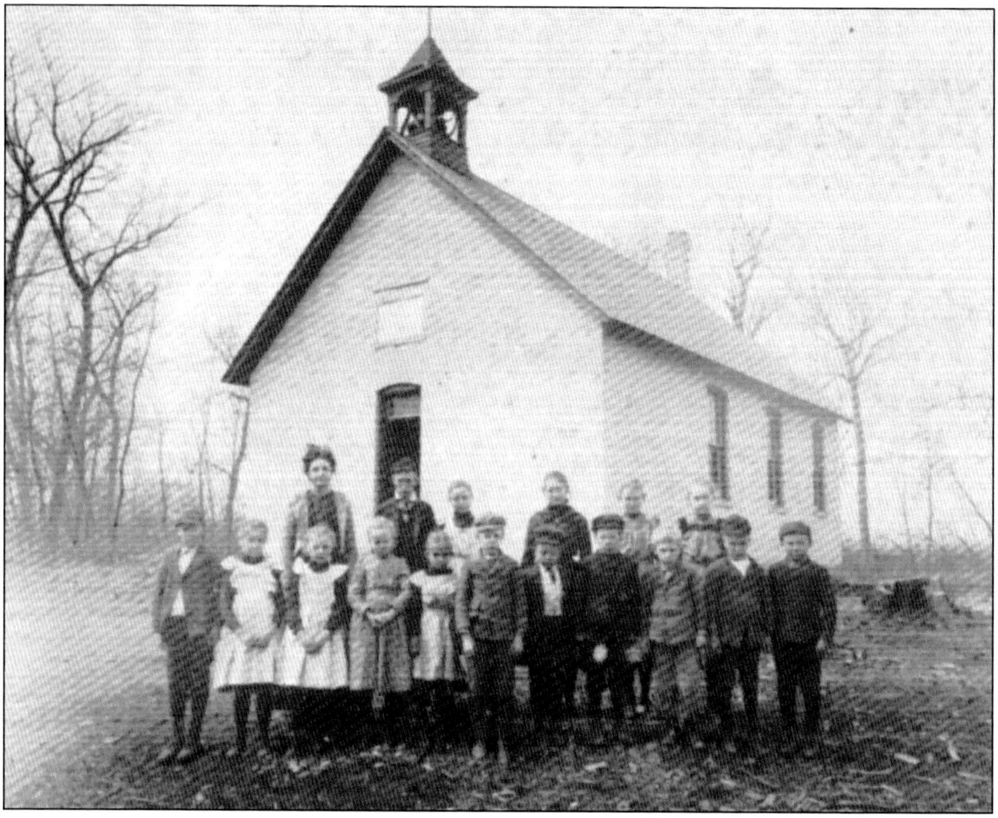

Carter School, District # 15, in 1910.

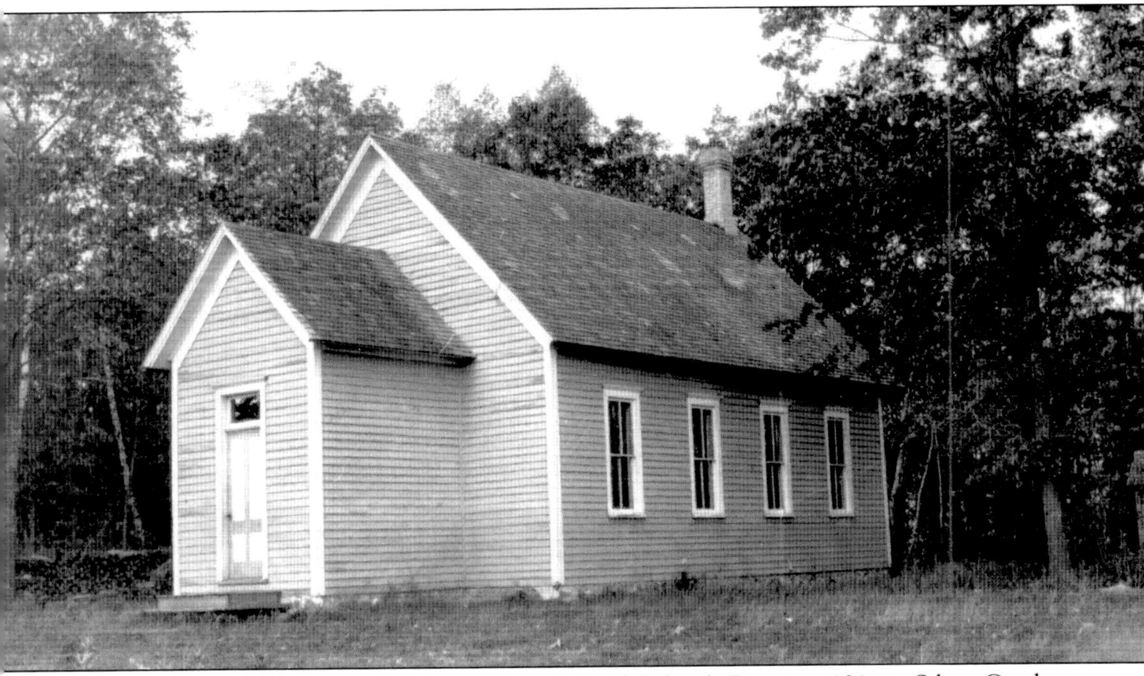

SORENSEN SCHOOL, DISTRICT # 95, c. 1920. Enfield School, District #121, in Silver Creek Township Section 23, was the last school to be established in the community, in July 1892. The Enfield school district included farms that were previously in Districts #8, #13, and #95. The 1910 census reported 57 school-age children (ages 5 to 20) in the Enfield School district.

1893	Miss Carrie Trogen	1923-26	Miss Evelyn Trogen
1893	Miss Gertrude Sheldon	1926-30	Miss Lydia Swanson
1894	Miss Carrie Trogen	1930-32	Mrs. Evelyn Trogen Abrahamson
1895	Miss Gertrude Sheldon	1932-34	Miss Mona Bryant
1896	Miss Carrie Trogen	1934-37	Lois Stubbs
1896-97	Mr. Andrew Ezra Trogen	1937-38	Anne Ness
1898-99	Mr. J.C. Grant	1938-39	Lois Stubbs
1899-00	Miss. Lilliam M. Ferris	1939-41	Erma Gordon
1900-01	Mr. Andrew Ezra Trogen	1941-42	Mrs. Catherine Claseman
1902-03	Miss Grace Beede	1942-43	Harrietta Frank
1903-08	?	1942-43	Frances Pinneo Anderson
1908-09	Miss. Edith Parker	1943-44	Marian Piram
1909-10	Miss Mryle Northrup	1944-45	Theresa Hudek
1911-12	Miss Francis Pinneo	1945-46	Marcela B. Nokk
1912-13	Miss Eva Gaunt	1946-47	Elsie O. Johnson
1913-14	Mrs. M.E. Carlson	1947-48	Mrs. Alice R.O. Johnson
1914-15	Sabina ZumBrunnen	1948-49	Gladys Christensen
1915-21	?	1949-50	John Wentland
1922-23	Miss Lydia Swanson	1950-51	Glorene Swanson

ENFIELD SCHOOL TEACHERS, 1893–1951.

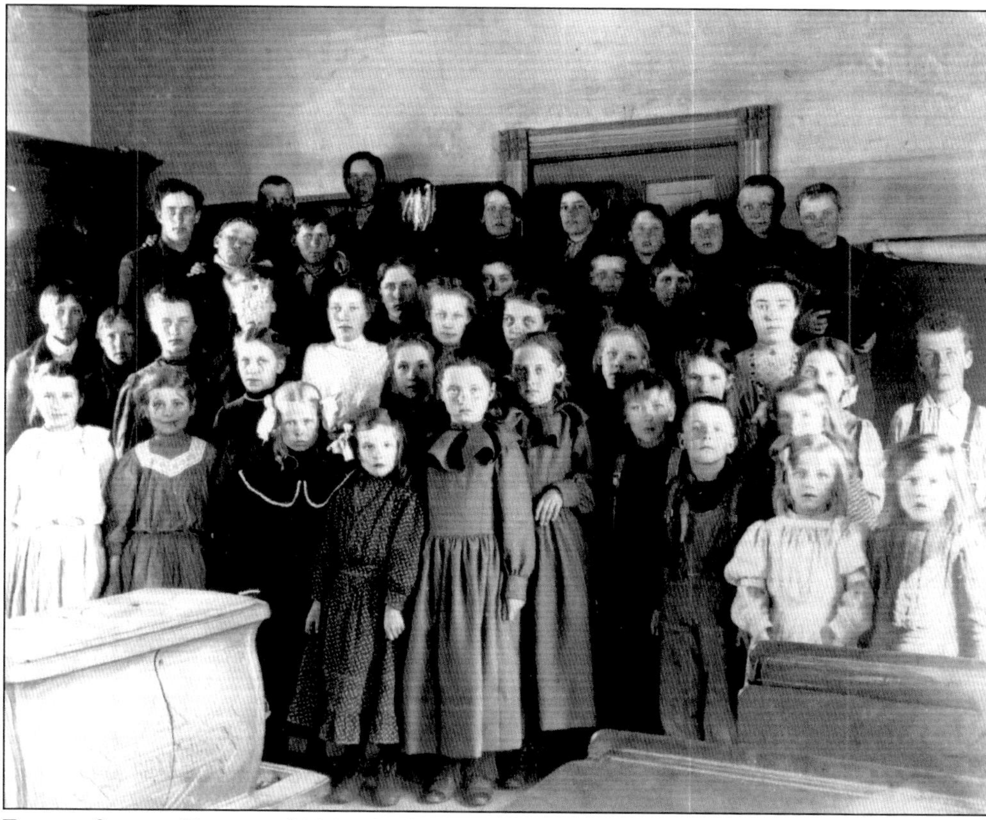

ENFIELD SCHOOL DISTRICT #121, 1905.

Opposite: ENFIELD SCHOOL BUILDING, 2001. The Trogen family figured heavily in the history of the Enfield School. Erick Trogen Johnson and his son, Andrew E. Trogen, were involved with its organization. Erick Trogen's brothers, Andrew J. Trogen and Jonas Johnson, and Erick's wife's brother, Olof Anderson, were school treasurers. Carrie Trogen was the first teacher. Carrie's older brother, Andrew Ezra Trogen, taught for several years in the 1890s. Evelyn Trogen Abrahamson taught in the Enfield school from 1923 to 1926 and again from 1930 to 1932. The younger Trogen children were students at the Enfield school as was the author's father, Edwin Abrahamson, and his siblings. The author's brother, Bruce, and sister, Mavis, were students in the Enfield school from 1948 until the school closed in 1951.

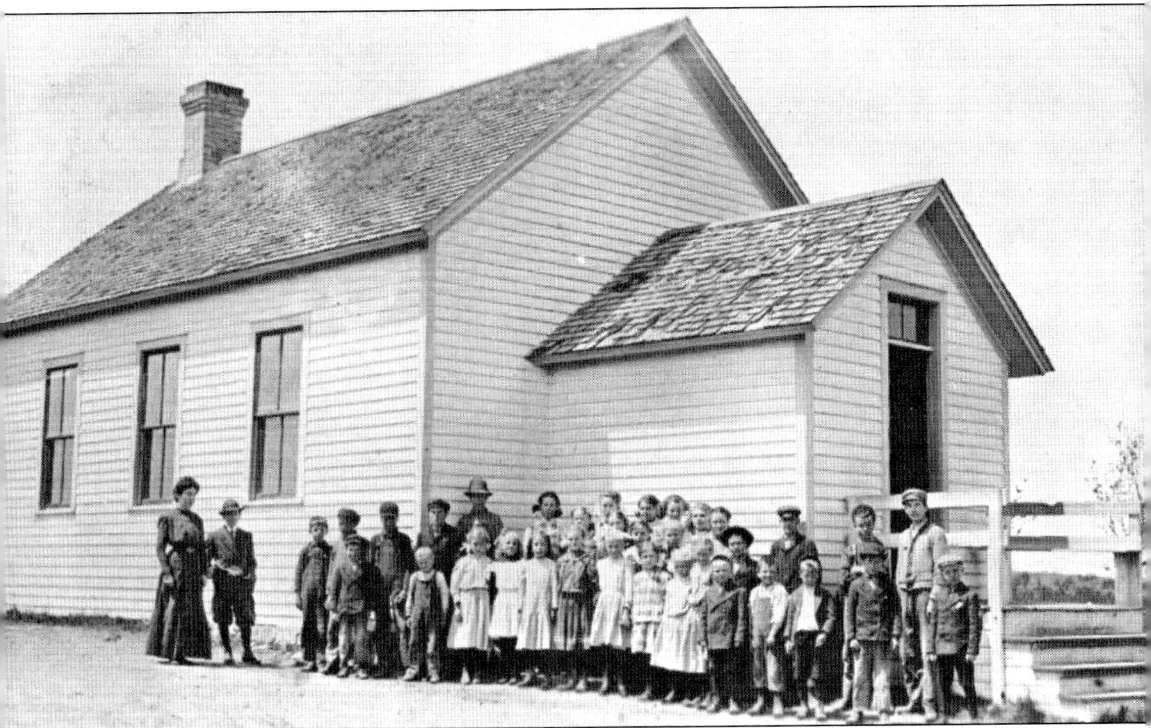

ENFIELD SCHOOL AND STUDENTS, 1910. The Enfield School building was moved to Monticello when the school closed in 1951. It became, and remains, the clubhouse for the Monticello Rod and Gun Club. The author's father, Edwin Abrahamson, is the boy at far right in the front row.

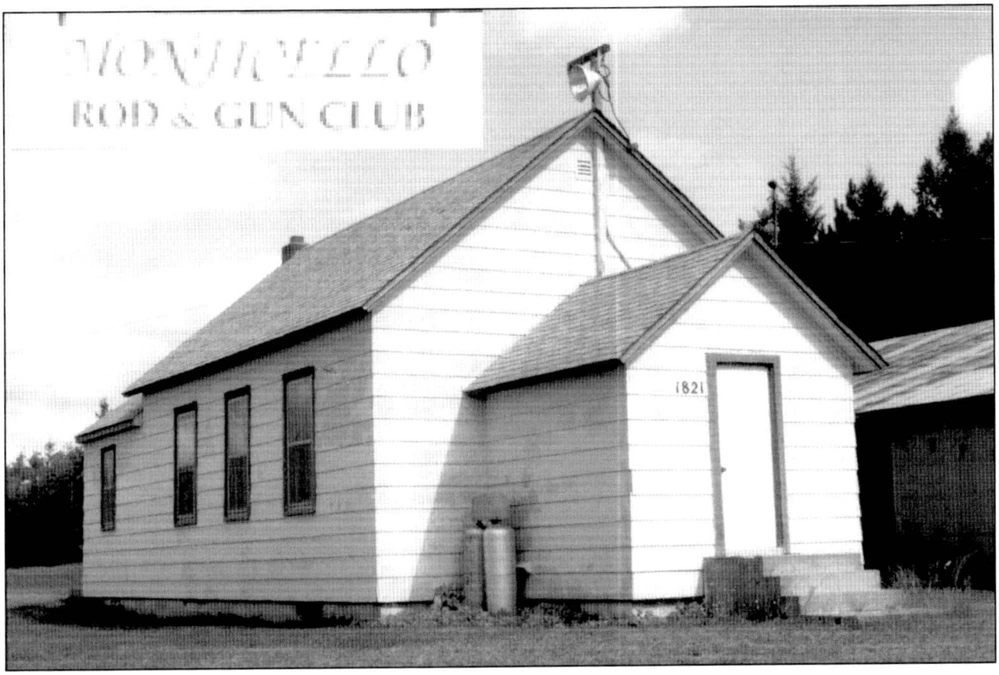

You will not marry during the term of your contract.
You are not to keep company with men.
You must be home between the hours of 8 p.m. and 6 a.m. unless attending a school function.
You may not loiter downtown in any of the ice cream stores.
You may not travel beyond the city limits unless you have the permission of the chairman of the school board.
You may not ride in a carriage or automobile with any man unless he be your father or brother.
You may not smoke cigarettes.
You may not dress in bright colors.
You may not under any circumstances dye your hair.
You must wear at least two petticoats.
Your dresses must not be any shorter than two inches above the ankle.
To keep the schoolroom neat and clean, you must sweep the floor at least once daily; scrub the floor at least once a week with hot soapy water; clean the blackboard at least once a day; and start the fire at 7 a.m. so the room will be warm by 8 a.m.

-- Polk County Historical Society

RULES FOR TEACHERS, C. 1910. These kinds of rules were common in the Polk County, Minnesota area at the time.

Five

Churches and the Cemetery

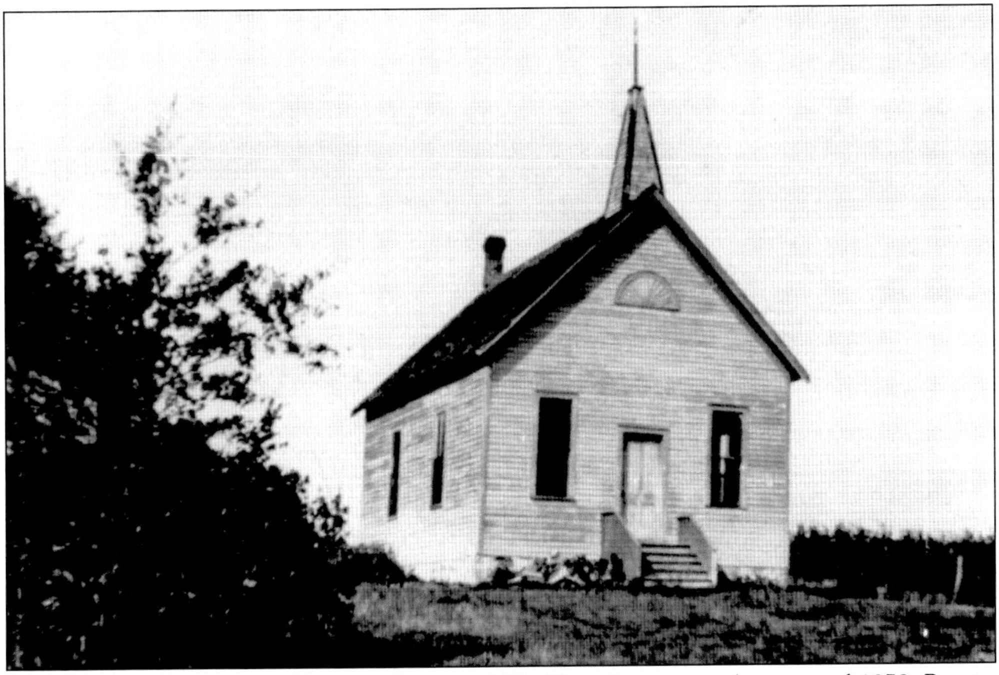

Enfield Swedish Baptist Church, Built 1877. This photo was taken around 1878. Baptist churches were central to the Swedish emigration of the 1860s and 1870s. The early Swedish settlers organized a Baptist congregation soon after they arrived in Silver Creek Township in the late 1860s and early 1870s. They had left Sweden so that they would be free to practice their religion without persecution.

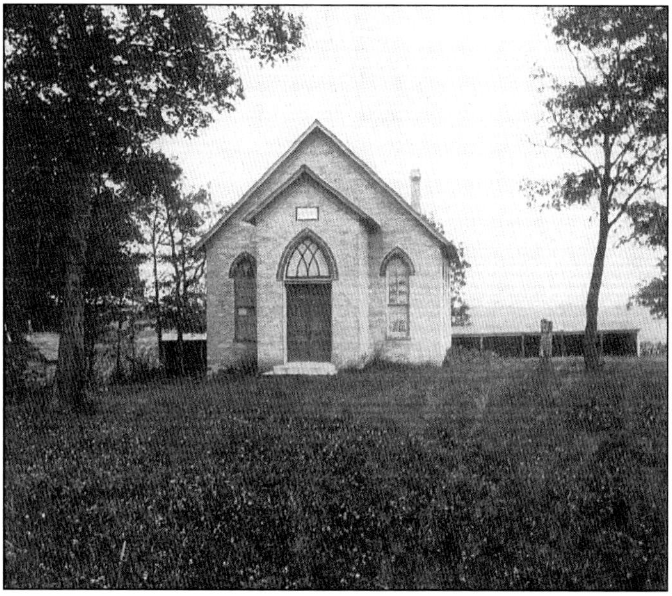

Enfield Swedish Lutheran Church, Built in 1891. Note the horse barn, privies, and woodshed in the rear of this c. 1910 photo. All Swedes were at that time required to be members of the Swedish Lutheran Church. Baptists were being fined, imprisoned, and otherwise harassed by the Swedish authorities—king's sheriffs and the priests of the State Lutheran Church.

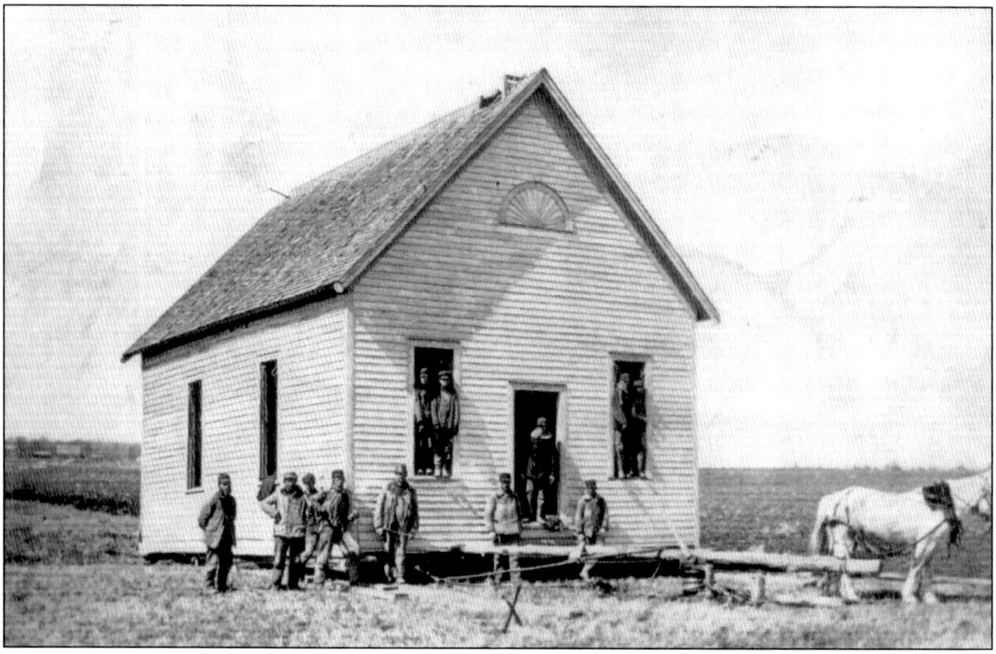

Moving Baptist Church Building, c. 1905. The various recording secretaries mentioned in the annual reports of the North American Baptist Congregations in the early years of the Enfield Baptist Church included O.B. Olson, P.O. Swenson, A. Anderson, Andrew Ezra Trogen, John Lindgren, Fred Wagner, Anna Oswald, Jennie Mild, and O.W. Hellerstedt. Jacob Peterson, Kestin (Mrs. Erick) Trogen's half-brother, was, in 1876, the first person baptized into the Enfield Baptist congregation. The congregation met in parishioners' homes until the church building was built in 1877, just north of what is now the junction of Crofoot Ave. and 127th St. NW.

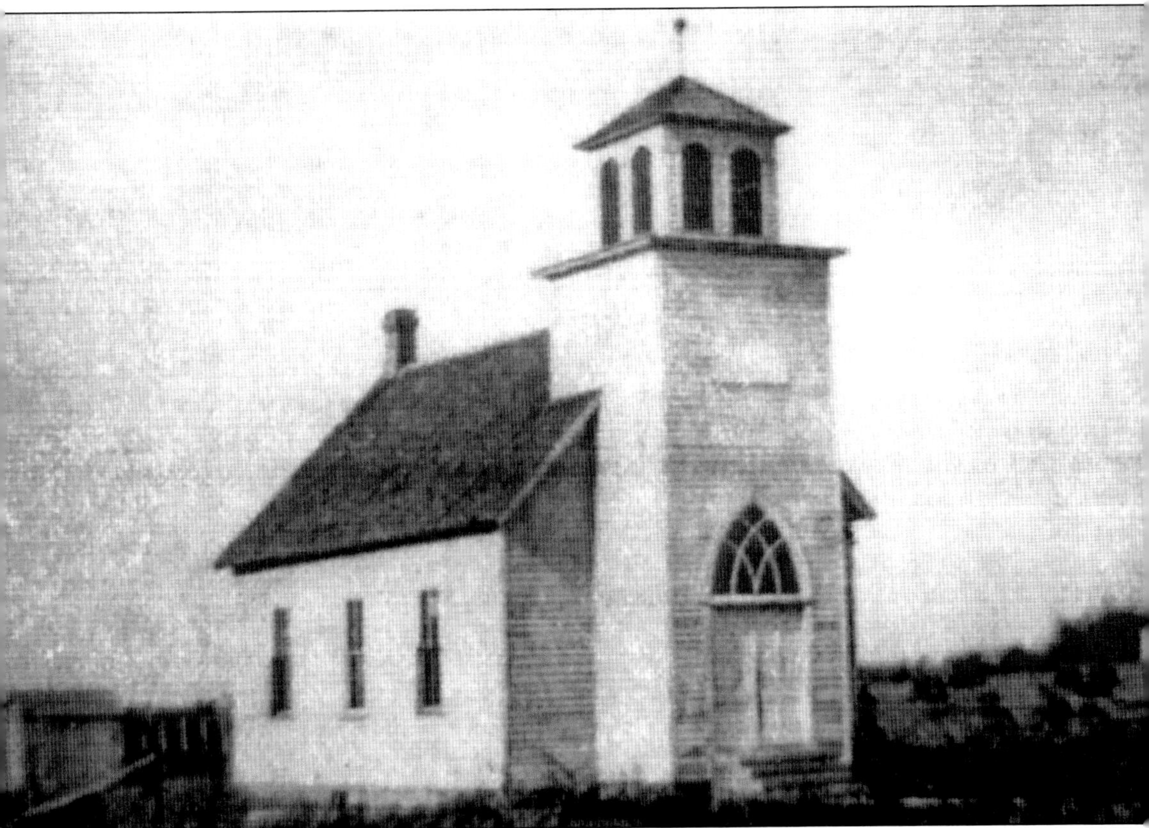

Baptist Church in Enfield Village, c. 1910. The building was moved to Enfield village in the spring of 1905. It was then remodeled and an entry and bell tower were added. The last recorded service in the Baptist church was the funeral of Edward Trogen in October 1935. The building was sold to Enoch Anderson in the early 1940s for use first as a granary and was then later moved to his farmstead for use as a garage. A Silver Creek Township Swedish Lutheran congregation began to form in the 1880s, meeting first in members' homes. Founding and early members included Johan and Maria Anderson, Charles Abrahamson, Aron Benson, Edina and Myrtle F. Berg, Carl Broman, J. Victor Carlson, Charles Felien, Frank Gustafson, Svan and Sabina Hammerstrom, John O., Florence, George, and Isaak O. Hoglund, C., Hilda, C.F., and A.P. Johnson, Carl and Rudolph Lundquist, John B. Magnuson, A. Nord, John and Walter Olson, C.A., Edward, and Anton Peterson, Anton Pearson, Ida (Mrs. Olaf) Swanson, John and Nellie Sorgensen, and J.H. Tonrnell. P.A. Wagner from Buffalo began to conduct services in 1889. A church congregation was formally organized on April 24, 1890 at a meeting in the home of Jens and Anna Sorensen. The 24 founding members elected to call their new church the Scandinavian Evangelical Lutheran Church of Silver Creek and to associate with the Augustana Lutheran Synod. The synod requested, however, that the Scandinavian designation be dropped.

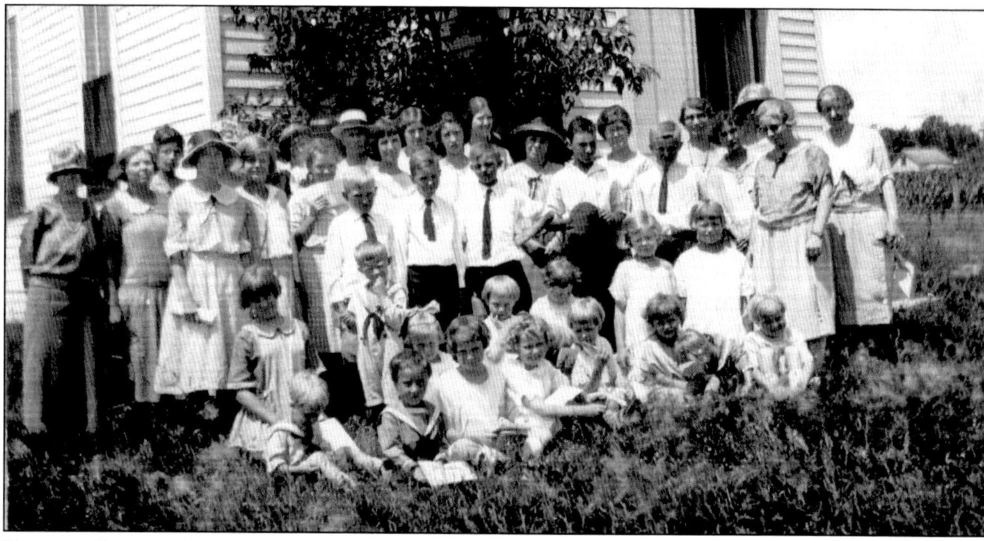

Baptist Church Sunday School, c. 1910. There were between 40 and 50 members of the Sunday school in the 1910–1920 period, so the entire congregation was probably well over 100 persons. The church had a regular pastor during some years, but pastors sent from Bethel Seminary served most often. One of them, an Ole Larson, worked as a hired man for Frank Abrahamson in about 1910. Larson later became the Bishop of Swedish Baptist churches in the Pacific Northwest.

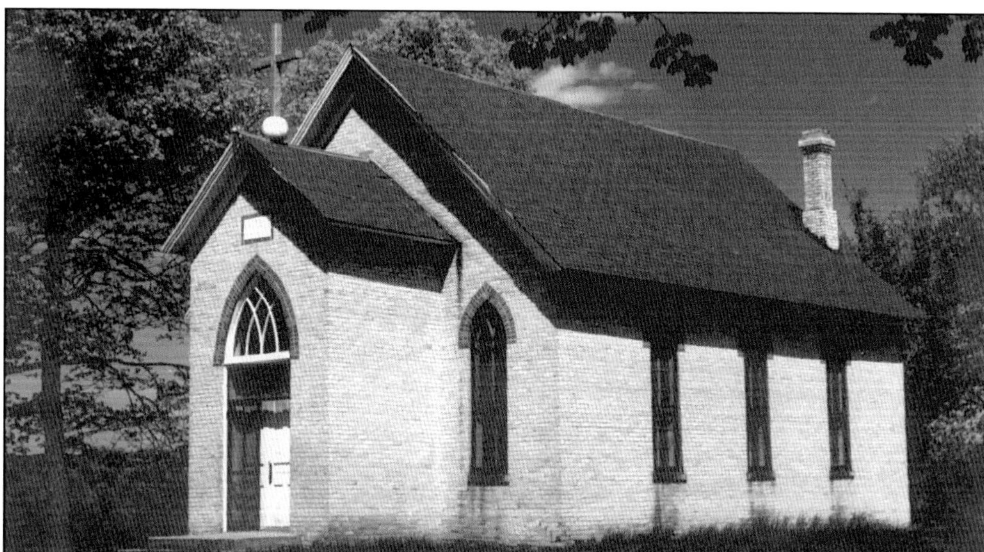

Faith Lutheran Church, Built in 1891. (Photo 1947.) The brick church building was built on land purchased from Jens Sorensen in 1891. Jens Sorensen was a bricklayer in addition to being a farmer; he built the church building. The building was expanded by the addition of a social room in 1956 and again expanded in 1986. The Enfield Lutheran Church membership began to decline after the Trinity Lutheran Church, also affiliated with the Augustana Synod, was organized in Monticello in 1947. The Enfield congregation membership, which had included 73 adult members in 1906, had only 70 communicant members and 12 children in 1965. The congregation recovered, however, and in 2001 has well over 200 members with a full-time pastor, a church nurse, and a secretary.

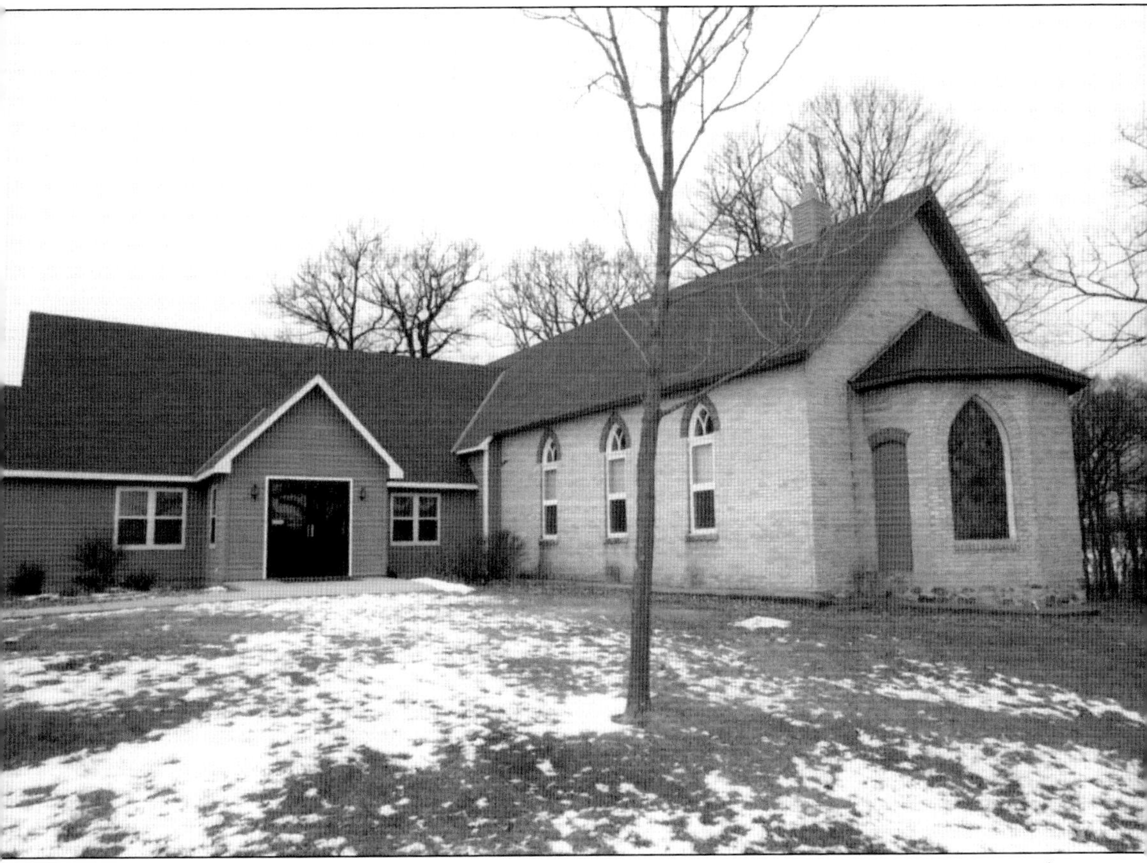

FAITH LUTHERAN CHURCH, 2002. The non-denominational Lake Side Cemetery was organized on February 11, 1889. Land was purchased from Jens Sorensen. The cemetery land extends from the top of the hill to the shore of West Lake. Families often used the cemetery lakeshore for picnics on Memorial Day or on other visits to the cemetery. The original cemetery had 96 lots, each eight by sixteen feet—the space for four graves. Several lots at the south edge of the cemetery were set aside for single burials and as a potters' field. Only full four-grave lots were sold until 1984. The cemetery was expanded in 1914 by adding 24 lots. Cemetery maintenance was neglected for a number of years beginning in the 1940s. Descendants of several of the original families reconstituted the cemetery association in 1983. This group organized cemetery work days during which the land was leveled, new grass was planted, the old fence, gate, and brush were removed, and a new flagpole and wrought iron sign were installed. Contributions were solicited to establish a cemetery maintenance fund large enough so that the interest should pay for routine maintenance in perpetuity. The cemetery land along the shore of West Lake has been allowed to grow up in brush, but will soon be cleared so that families can again enjoy the lakeside of the Lake Side Cemetery.

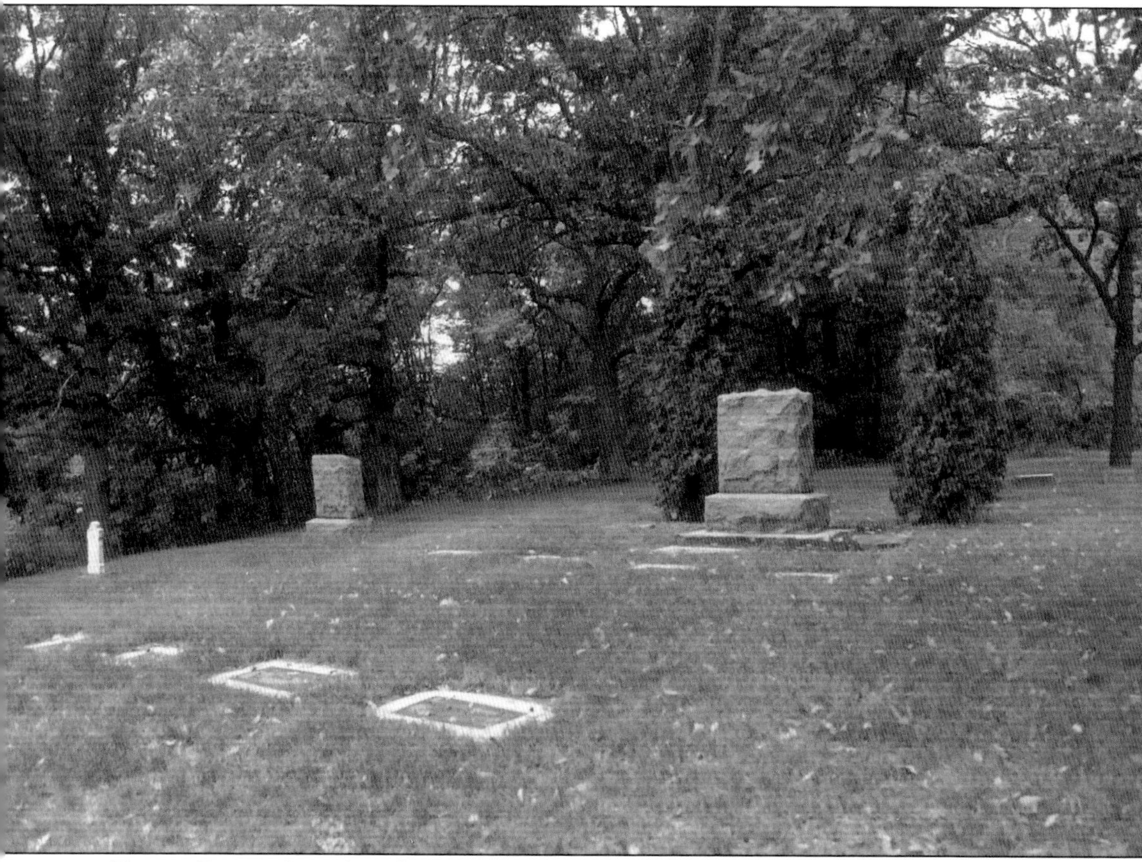

TROGEN PLOT AT LAKE SIDE CEMETERY, 2001. The new Lake Side Cemetery Association expanded the cemetery by adding more lots both to the north and to the east of the old lots and began to sell individual grave sites. No burials are permitted in the 1889 or 1914 lots except for descendants of the original families. While Lake Side Cemetery remains non-denominational, the neighboring Faith Lutheran Church has assumed some responsibility for the cemetery, but the independent Lake Side Cemetery Association retains fiscal control and operates as a public cemetery. The original cemetery records are in the archives of the Wright County Historical Society.

Six

Rails, Roads, and Wires

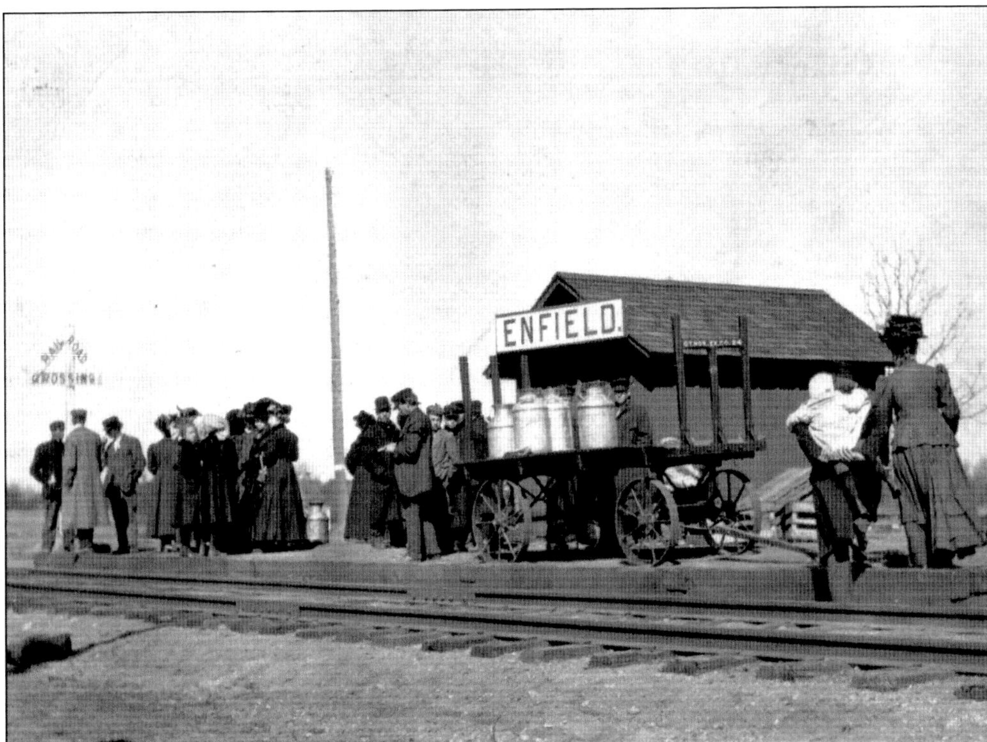

Enfield Railroad Siding, 1910. Railroad trains first ran through the community in December of 1882 when the Minneapolis & St. Cloud Railroad Company built its line and a siding. The Minneapolis & St. Cloud Railroad Company was chartered in 1855. Its charter was taken over by James J. Hill's Great Northern Railway Company in 1889. Hill is known as the Empire Builder, and, among other things, is quoted as saying, "give me Swedes, snus, and whiskey, and I can build a railroad through hell." The place was called Silver Creek Siding. The village name was changed from Silver Creek Siding when Enfield got its own post office in 1910. The first depot was a small cream station on a cinder platform. A more formal depot, a used freight car, was installed in 1910. It is not known who selected the name Enfield for the village.

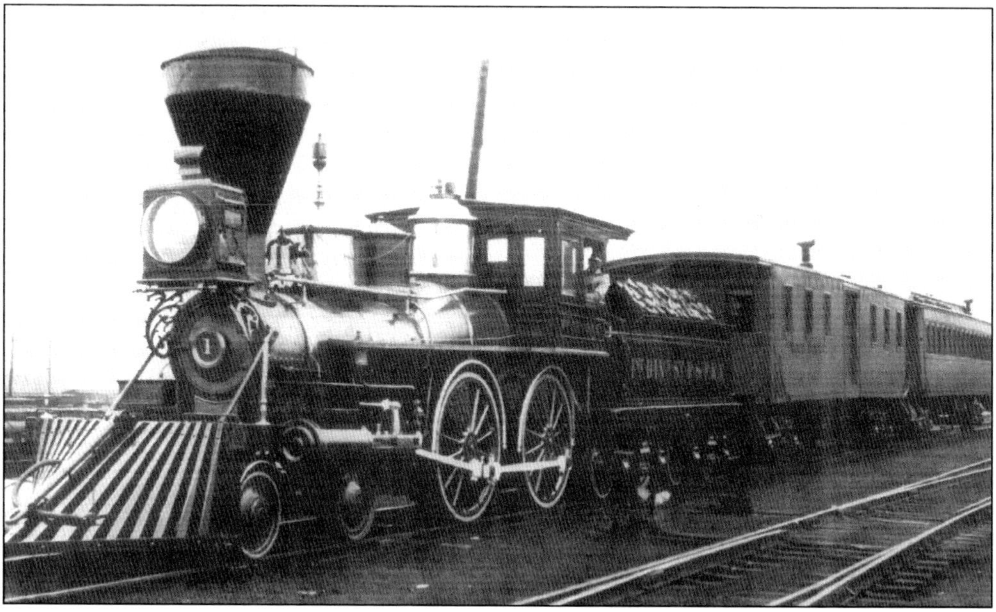

The Locomotive William Crooks. This train is identified in *Clearwater Remembers* as the First Locomotive through Enfield in 1882. There were four passenger trains each way each day in the early 1900s, two of which were local trains that stopped at every village. The through trains and the Winnipeg Flyer stopped for water in Monticello and other larger towns.

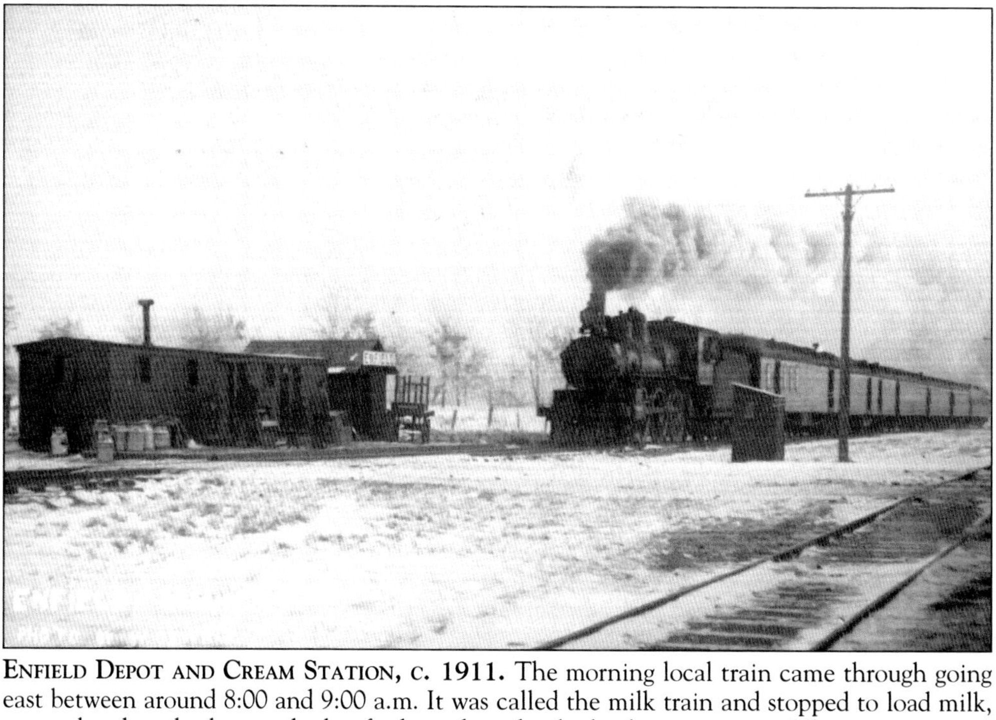

Enfield Depot and Cream Station, c. 1911. The morning local train came through going east between around 8:00 and 9:00 a.m. It was called the milk train and stopped to load milk, cream, butchered calves, and other fresh produce that had to be sent express. This train returned about 6:00 in the evening. The second daily local train came going west at around 7:00 p.m. and went as far as Fargo.

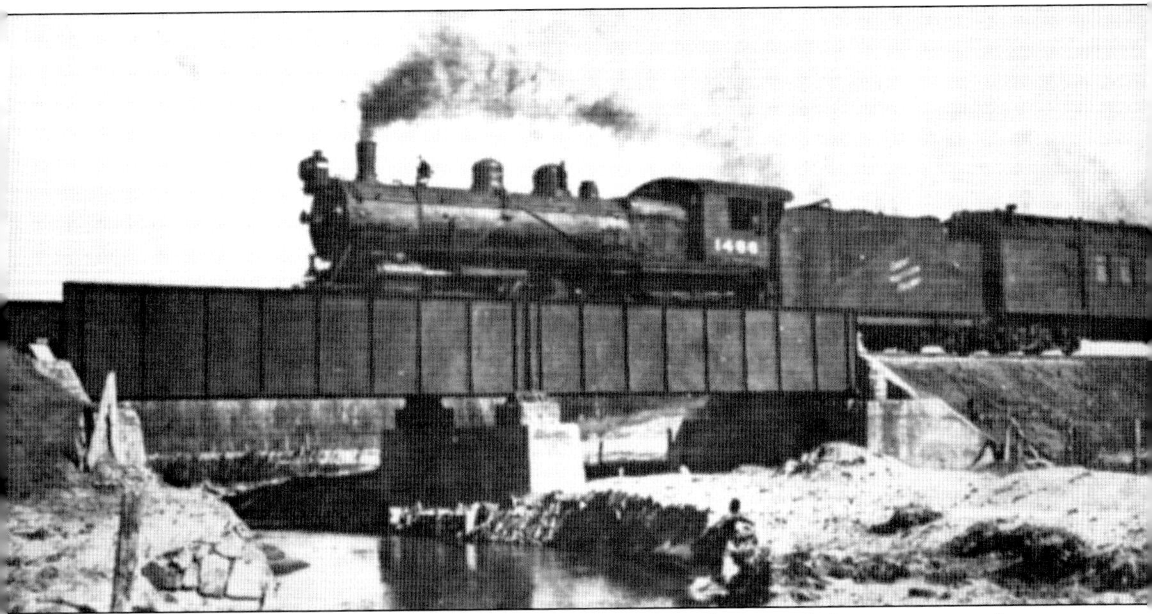

TRAIN CROSSING SILVER CREEK, C. 1910. There were two freight trains daily, one going each way. They dropped off and picked up cars at the siding and had cattle cars for outgoing and incoming livestock. There was also a train going through one way around midnight and returning at about 6:00 a.m. The boxcar depot was sold in 1931 to Art Post; he used it as a chicken house. Trains quit running in the early 1970s. The signals along the Great Northern track were taken down in 1977, the telegraph lines and poles were removed in 1979, and the track and ties were torn out in 1982. The roadbed is now a trail used by noisy machines, cyclists, and hikers.

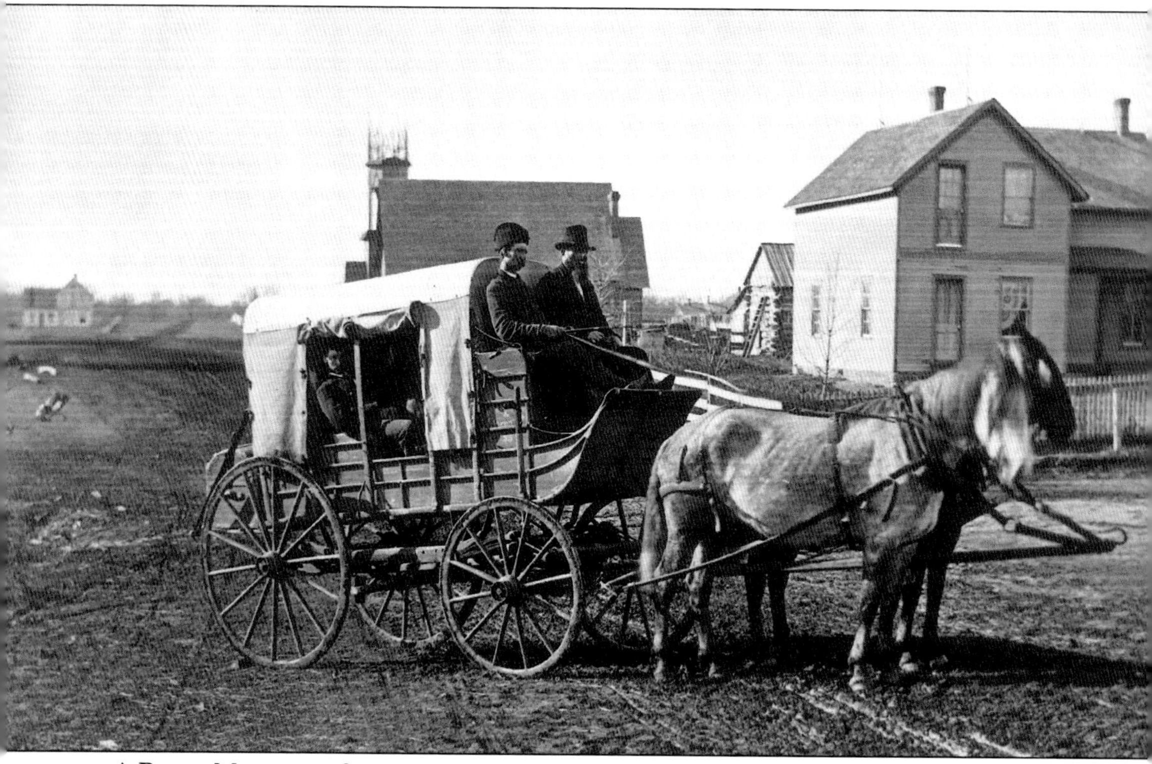

A Rural Minnesota Stagecoach, 1876. Roads began with the Red River Trail along the north edge of Silver Creek Township serving as the stagecoach road at the time of settlement. Other early roads probably more or less followed ancient trails. New roads began to penetrate the township by the 1890s, aligned more or less on rectilinear coordinates, but winding around wetlands. Roads were added and others abandoned until the present configuration of township and county roads was somewhat stabilized by the 1940s with the construction of what is now Wright County Road #111 from Enfield south past North Lake at the boundary of Sections 34 and 35.

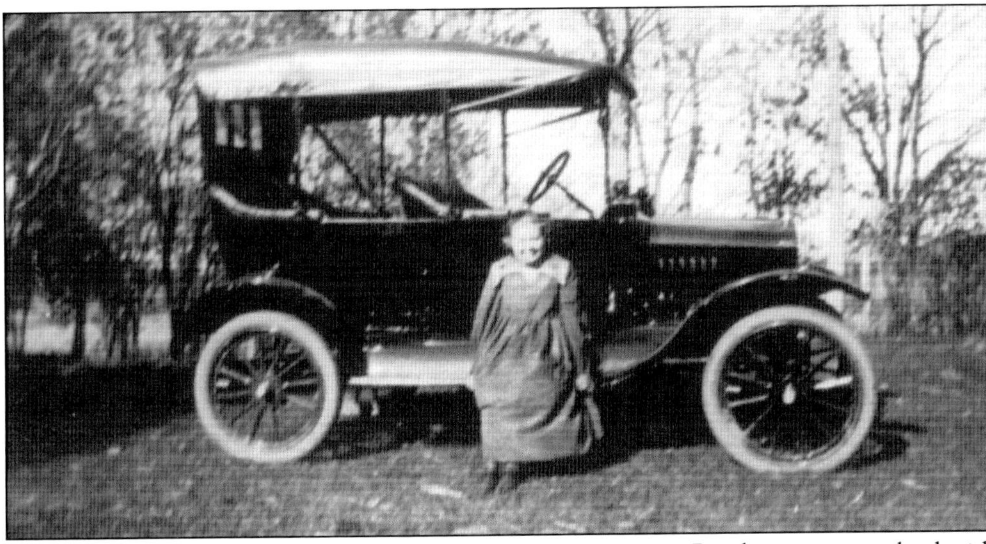

EVELYN TROGEN AND HER FAMILY'S MODEL-T FORD, C. 1916. Road transport evolved with the times. Buggies and sleighs were the everyday vehicles until automobiles and trucks began to appear in the Enfield community between about 1905 and 1915. The sleighs and buggies had been put into a shed by the 1920s, but they were brought out regularly—probably for the enjoyment of the children. The heavy bobsleds, however, continued to be used well into the 1950s, primarily to bring in timber from the woods or to haul milk to the cheese factory when there was too much snow on the road for the family pickup truck.

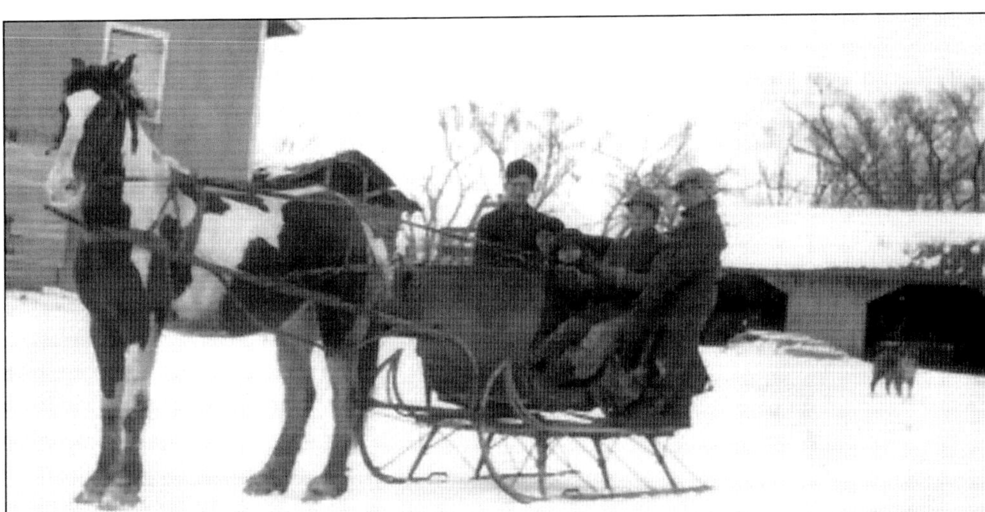

BOB BREVIK, MAVIS, BRUCE, AND DEAN ABRAHAMSON, C. 1946. The first highway through the community was Minnesota Trunk Highway #152, completed in 1935. This highway provided a direct route northwest through Clearwater to St. Cloud and southeast through Monticello to Minneapolis. Enfield Village then began to decline, transport began to shift from rail to highway, and local commerce shifted to Monticello. The 1930s also saw significant consolidation of farms, with old 40- and 80-acre farms being combined into larger units.

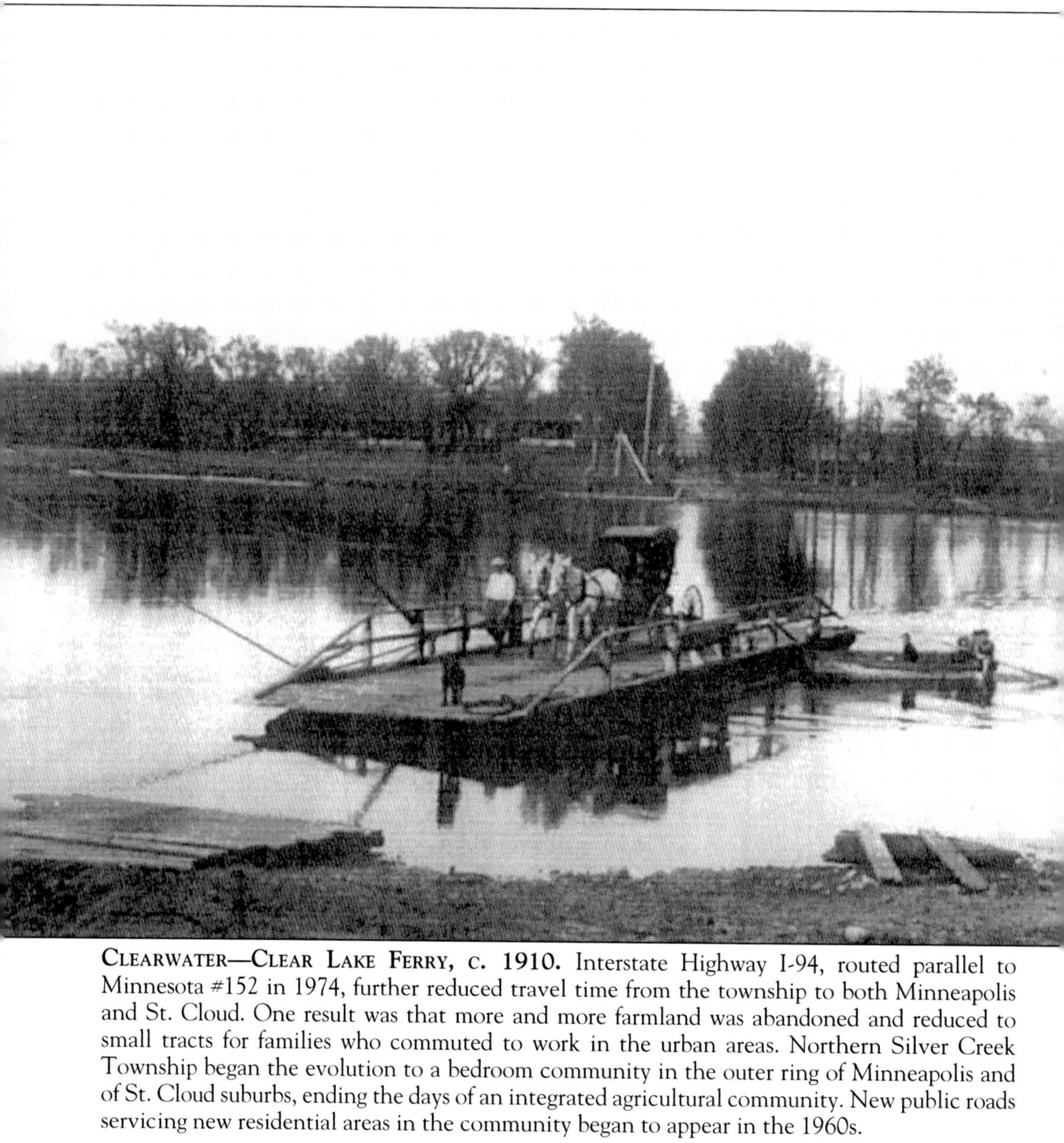

Clearwater—Clear Lake Ferry, c. 1910. Interstate Highway I-94, routed parallel to Minnesota #152 in 1974, further reduced travel time from the township to both Minneapolis and St. Cloud. One result was that more and more farmland was abandoned and reduced to small tracts for families who commuted to work in the urban areas. Northern Silver Creek Township began the evolution to a bedroom community in the outer ring of Minneapolis and of St. Cloud suburbs, ending the days of an integrated agricultural community. New public roads servicing new residential areas in the community began to appear in the 1960s.

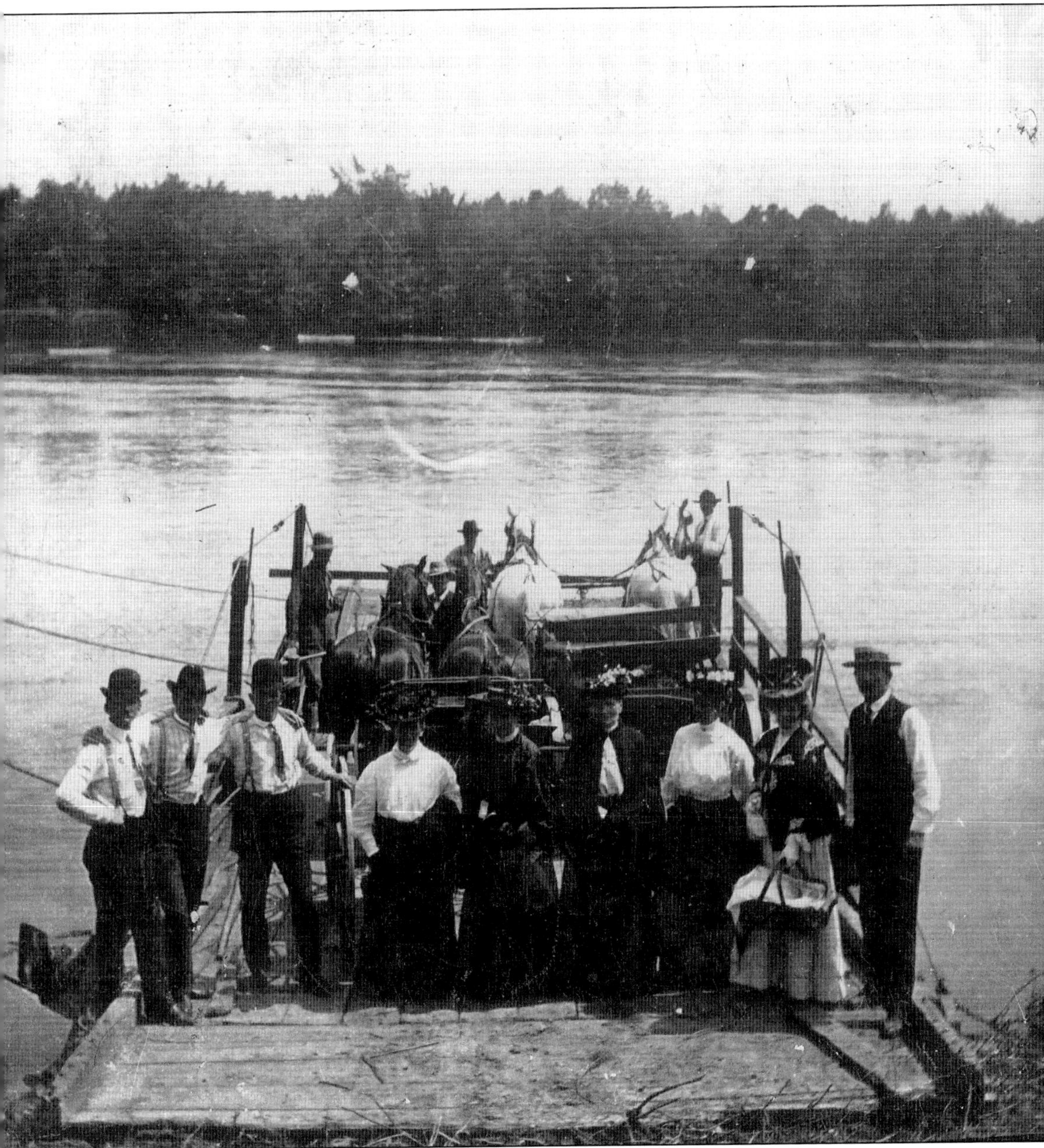

Enfield–Becker Ferry, 1910. Cable ferries provided communities with access to other Swedish-American families who had settled across the Mississippi River. There were ferries between Clearwater and Clear Lake, between Monticello and Big Lake, and between Enfield and Becker. The Monticello–Big Lake ferry began operation in 1855 and operated until the first wooden bridge was built in 1891. The center section of the Monticello–Big Lake bridge was mounted on a pier with apparatus so that the middle of the bridge could be rotated to permit passage of the stern-wheeled steamboats operated by the Mississippi & Rum River Boom Company that drove logs down the river. The Enfield–Becker ferry was operating in the 1890s and early 1900s. It broke loose during a spring flood, washed downriver, and lodged on Boom Island. It was not reinstalled.

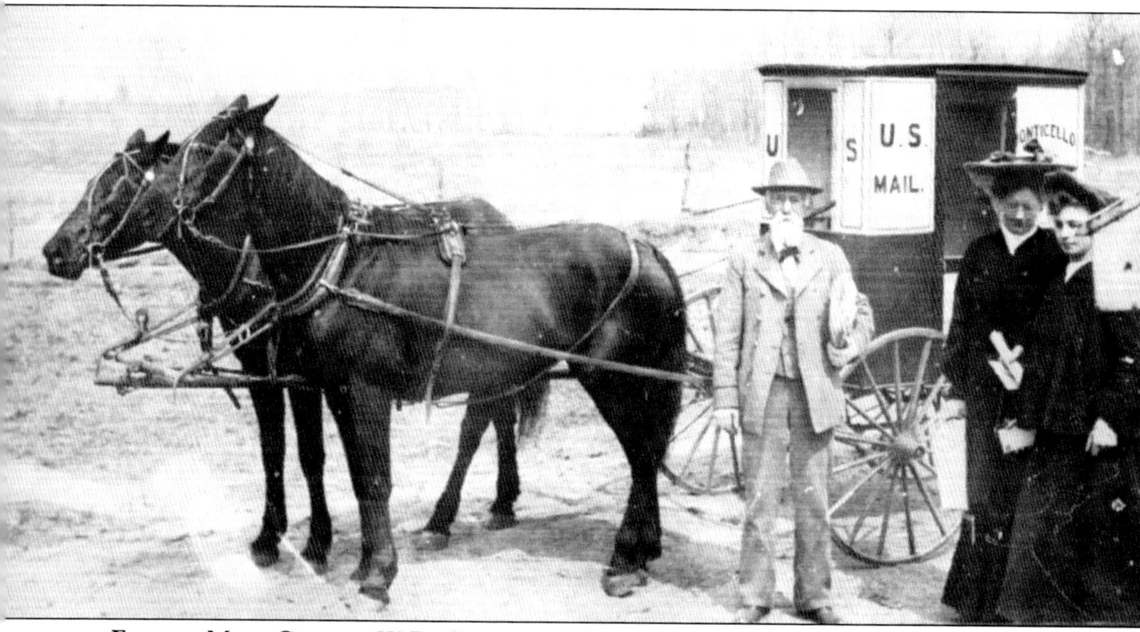

ENFIELD MAIL CARRIER W.B. SAWYER, A CIVIL WAR VETERAN, C. 1910. Mail began to be delivered in 1905 to Enfield families on Monticello Rural Route #1. There were rows of mailboxes, one at the junction of the road going north from Enfield and the schoolhouse road and another across the road from the schoolhouse. Prior to this, mail had to be picked up in Monticello. The Enfield post office was established in 1910 and housed in the Louis P. Berglund Store. The first postmaster was Charles P. Weston. L.P. Berglund became postmaster in 1911. The Post Office was moved to the Gustafson Store c. 1927. The Enfield Post Office closed in 1954 and a rural mail route out of Monticello was again initiated. The mail trains did not stop, or even slow down. The incoming mailbag was tossed from the train as it passed through the village; the outgoing mailbag was hung on an apparatus located by the track and was grabbed with a hook as the train passed.

Seven

THE VILLAGE

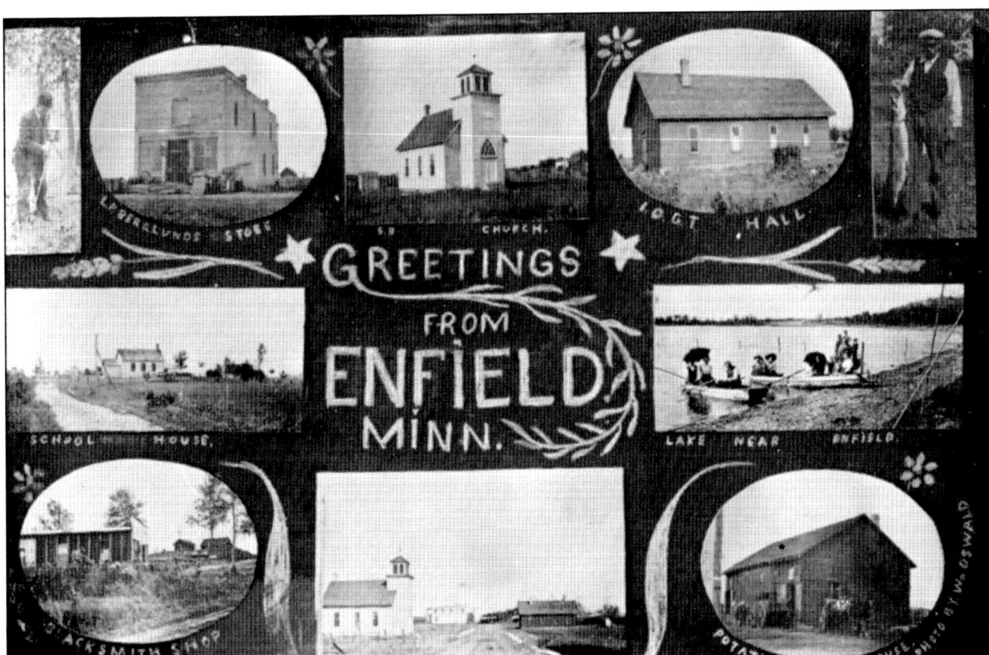

GREETINGS FROM ENFIELD, 1910. Pictured clockwise are Wm. Oswald, the community photographer, L.P. Berglund General Store, Baptist Church, IOGT Hall, Wm. Oswald and Pike from Mississippi River, Picnic on Locke Lake, Healy Potato Warehouse, View down Main Street Looking North, Gust Okerman's Blacksmith Shop, and Enfield School.

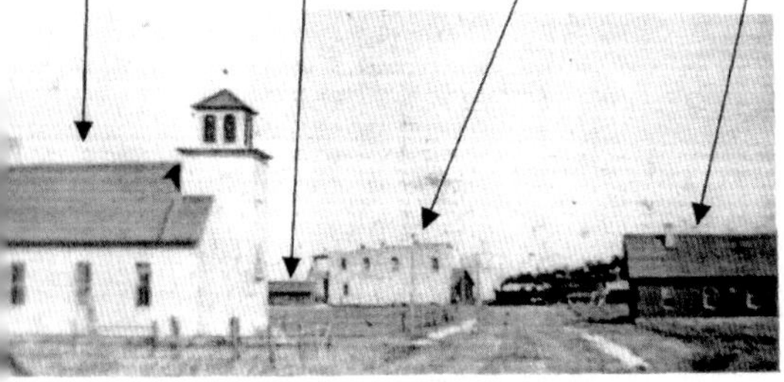

VIEW DUE NORTH WITH GREAT NOTHERN TRAIN IN BACKGROUND

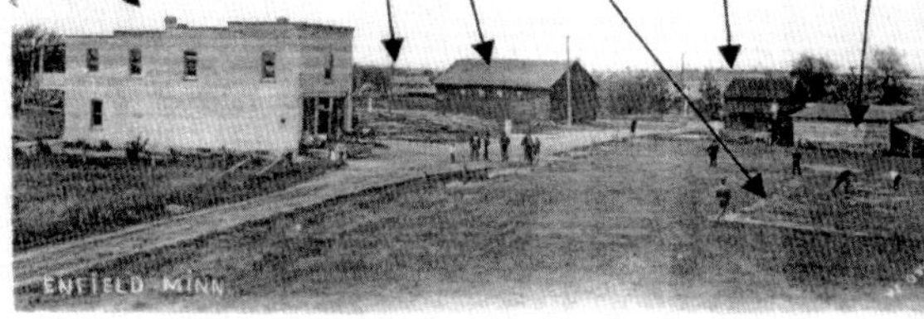

PROBABLY TAKEN FROM ROOF OF THE I.O.G.T AND ENFIELD TOWN HALL

Photographs About 1910

ENFIELD VILLAGE. Enfield village began as Silver Creek Siding when the Minneapolis & St. Cloud Railroad Company built its line through the community in 1882. Prior to the arrival of the railroad, the settlers had to tote their products and purchases to and from the nearest established town on their backs or with oxen or horse-drawn wagons. Verner Abrahamson relates being told by Kestin Trogen, who, with her husband Erick, homesteaded in 1871, that she walked carrying a sack of flour seven miles from Monticello on the trail near Melrose Lake.

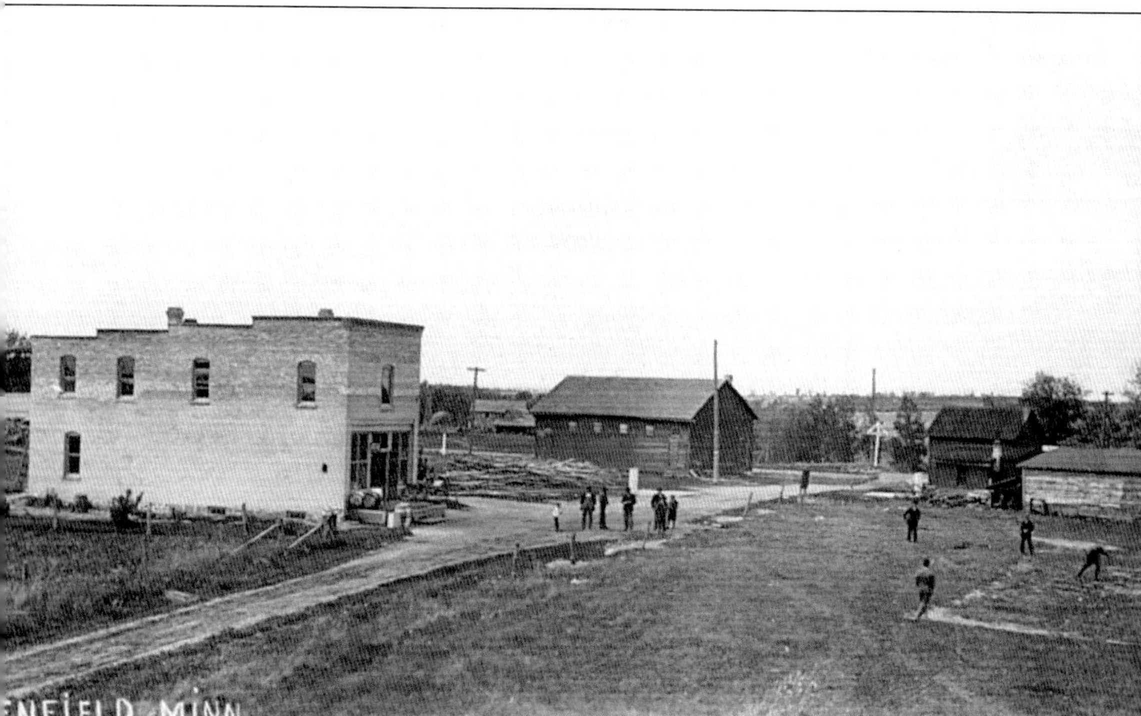

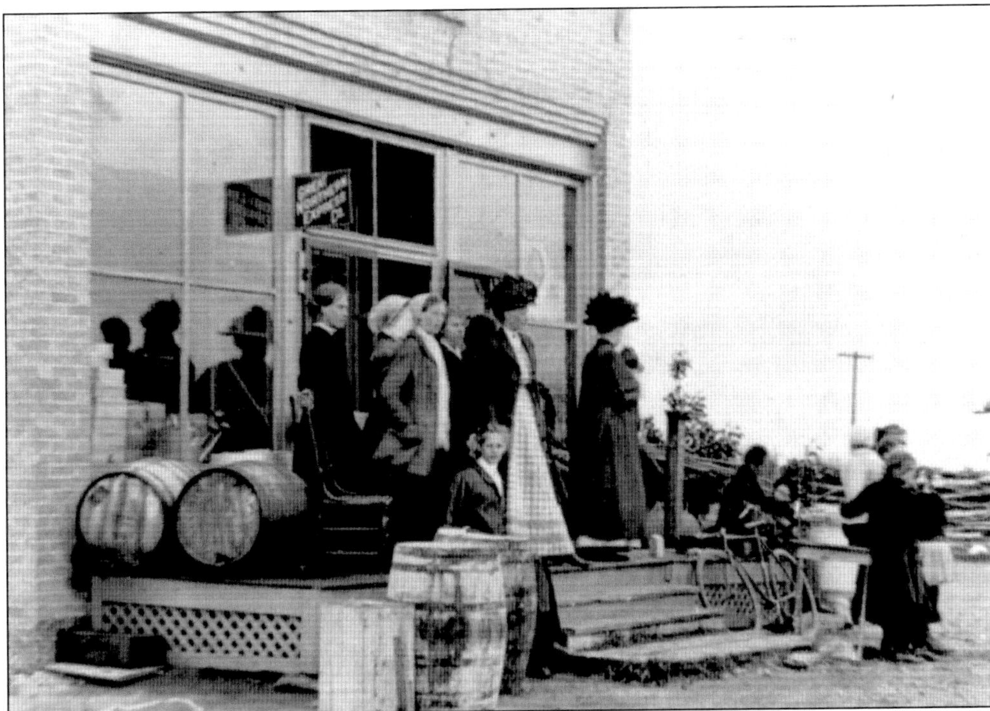

Berglund Store, c. 1910. Louis P. Berglund moved to Silver Creek Siding in 1905 and built a substantial general store; a second floor, with living quarters, was added later. Berglund had a complete line of groceries, hardware, nails, bolts, dry goods, overalls, shoes, and the Minnesota Line of farm machinery that was manufactured at the State Reformatory in St. Cloud and the State Prison in Stillwater. L.P. Berglund was also the Great Northern Railroad depot agent and the postmaster for a number of years. Berglund sold the store and its contents in about 1913 to John Hoglund from Hasty and Hoglund's son, Martin. Hoglund's son-in-law, Sig Tornvig, ran the store. Tornvig left after a year or two and was replaced by Ed Coombs, another of John Hoglund's sons-in-law. The store was again sold in about 1920 to Clarence Berglund, L.P. Berglund's son. The younger Berglund ran it for a few years until he died, after which it was run by his widow, Dora, and her brother, Rudolph Hokanson. It was next sold to Martin Johnson and then passed through the hands of Mr. and Mrs. Myron Styles, and a Mr. and Mrs. Henneman.

Opposite: **Enfield Village Looking NW, c. 1910.** Berglund store is in the left foreground, with the potato warehouse and lumber yard left to right in the background. General stores in the community began with the sale of flour, sugar, salt, coffee, and other staples out of the Aleck Swanson farmhouse probably in the 1880s. The Swanson farmstead was located just south of the Enfield School. Farmers bartered eggs for groceries; Swanson, in turn, sold the eggs to Louis P. Berglund and his wife, Anna, the daughter of Kestin Trogen's brother Olof Anderson, who then operated a store in Minneapolis.

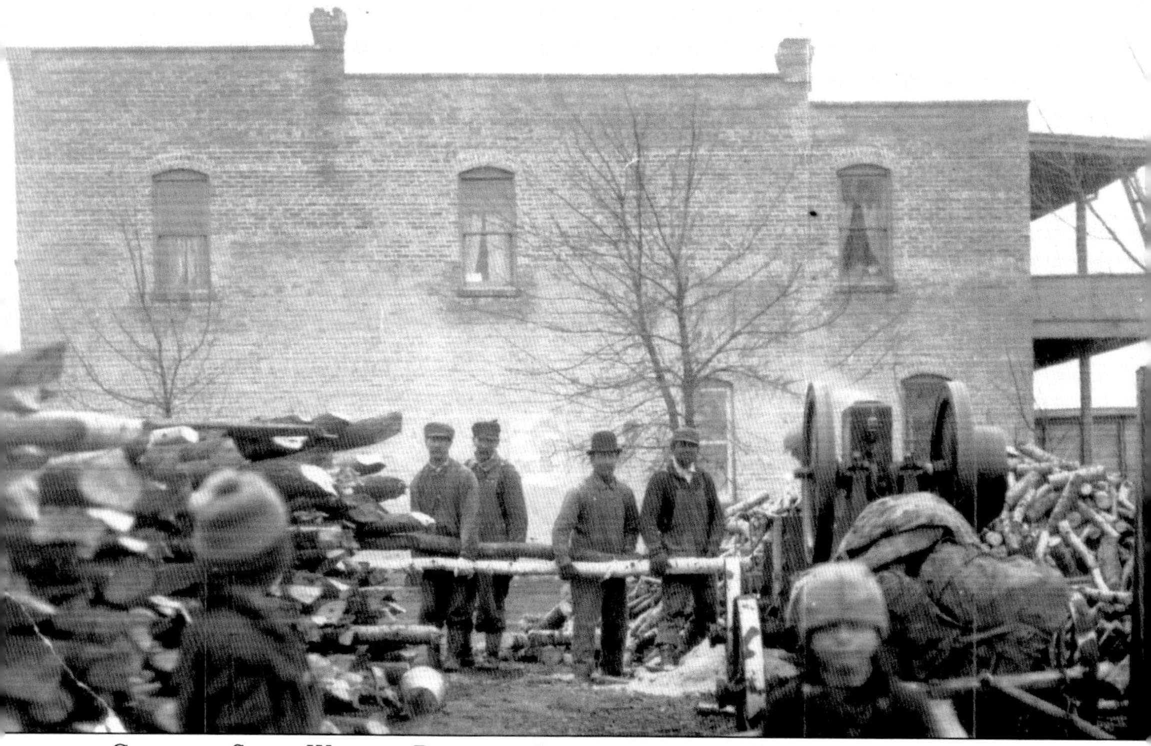

CHUNKING STOVE WOOD BY BERGLUND STORE, C. 1910. Mel Platten operated the store from 1935 to 1940 and Carl Swanson was operating it in about 1943. The building was then sold to a Mr. Kelly who operated a tavern. A Mr. and Mrs. Clarence (Red) Stevens continued operation of the tavern from 1962 until 1974. The building has since been used as a residence. The Farmers' Co-op built a second general store in 1919, the stucco store, located directly across the road from the Berglund store. The Co-op did not open or operate the store, but sold it to Alfred Gustafson, a nearby farmer, in the early 1920s. All of the merchandise was sold when Gustafson died in the 1930s and the store stood empty for a while. During this period Myron and Mrs. Styles were operating the Berglund store. The Farmers' Co-op helped John "Buzz" Lyrenmann reopen the Gustafson store when Styles left. The village was not without a general store from 1905 to 1957. Lyrenmann installed a freezer room in the store basement when the REA brought electricity to Enfield in 1944. There were sets of locked drawers, each about four cubic feet, rented to individual families. Most of the farmers by then had stopped butchering their meat animals on the farm, but had them slaughtered, cut, wrapped, and frozen at the Clearwater, Monticello, or Maple Lake slaughterhouses.

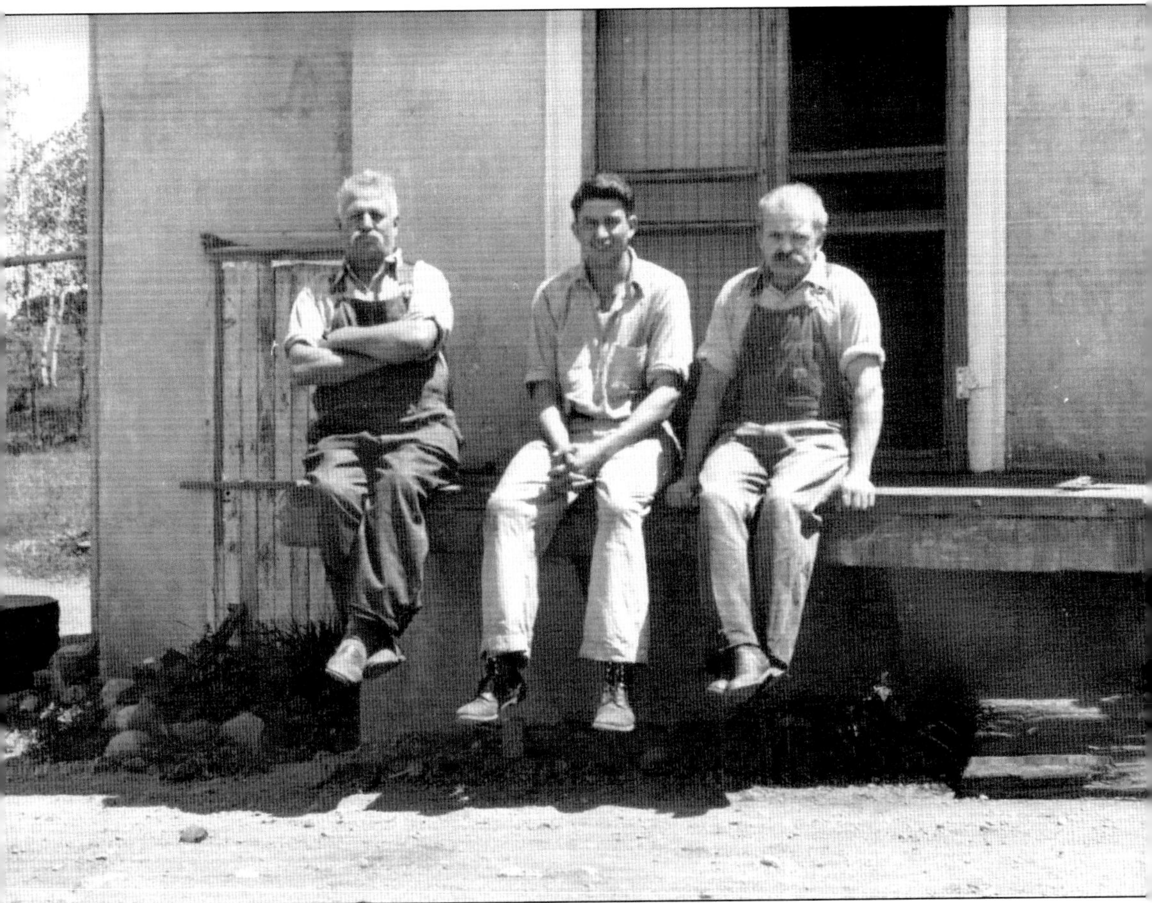

Enfield Cheese Makers Carl Frehner, John Frehner, and August Wirz in 1934. The Post Office was also moved to the Lyrenmann store. The building burned to the ground in 1953. The site was sold to Kenneth Adams who rebuilt on the site in 1954, the year that Enfield lost its post office and rural mail delivery again began. The cheese factory had then closed and there was no need to go to the store to pick up mail, and the Adams store closed in 1957. The building is now the residence of Jeff Hoglund, who operates a semi-tractor service facility across the road from the old store. Milk and cream supplied cash income for most of the farms. Milk and cream were shipped on the milk train to the Twin Cities Milk Producers' Association in Minneapolis until the Association decided in about 1920 not to buy milk produced more than 35 miles from Minneapolis. The farmers then again had to separate the milk and cream with the cream sold to make butter at the creameries in Monticello or Silver Creek. Some farmers sold home-churned butter. A cheese factory was built in Hasty in the early 1920s and the milk from Enfield farms was then taken there for a few years before the Enfield Cheese factory opened. Cheese began to be made in Enfield in 1927 when the Farmers' Co-op built the cheese factory. The farmers brought their milk to the cheese factory twice a day during the summer and once a day during the winter. Whey, the liquid left after the milk solids had been transformed into cheese, was taken back to the farms and fed to the pigs. Limburger and brick cheeses were produced.

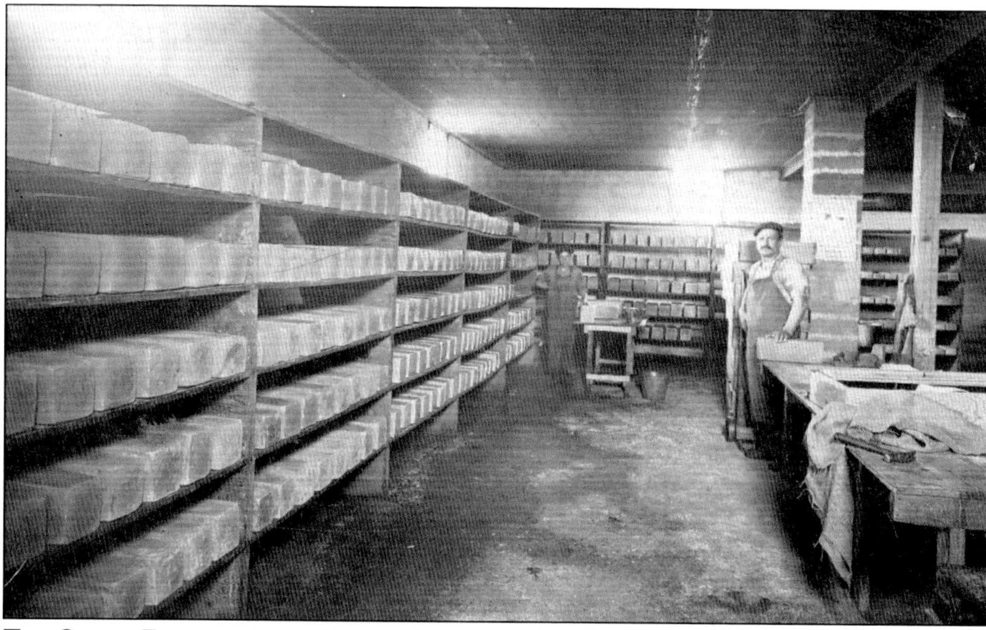

The Cheese Factory Aging Room, John and Carl Frehner. The first cheese maker was August Martini, soon replaced by a Mr. Widmer. Carl Frehner came from Wisconsin to be the Enfield cheese maker in 1934. His brother-in-law, August Wirz, assisted him. Carl's son, John, took over in 1939 and remained as cheese maker until the Enfield cheese factory closed. Land O'Lakes built a large milk-drying plant in Monticello and drove the cheese factory out of business in August 1950. The Hasty cheese factory was also forced to close and John Frehner then bought the Hasty building from which he operated a cheese retail store.

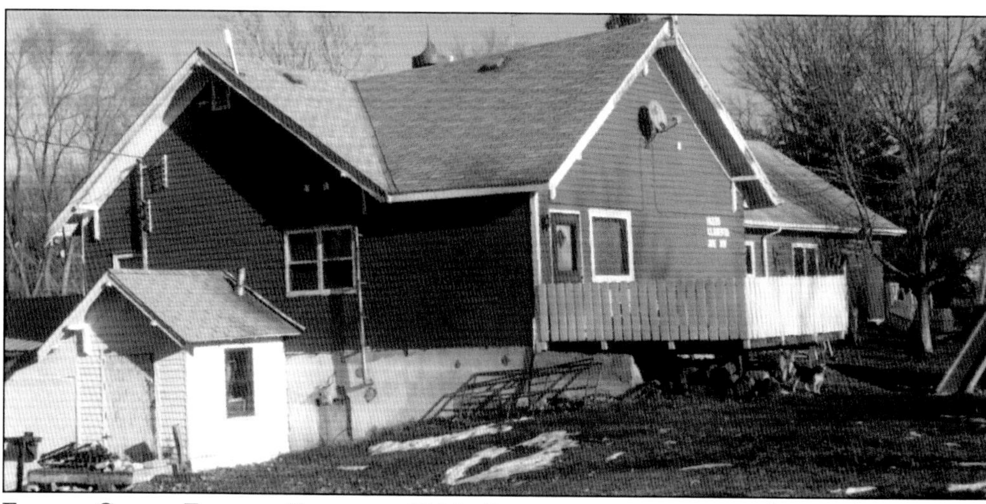

Enfield Cheese Factory Building, 2001. Potatoes were a major cash crop from the late 1800s until about 1930. Potatoes were grown on freshly broken land. Rebecca Barnett recalls that a couple of acres were cleared each year and, when the stumps had been blown out using dynamite, her father broadcast cast rutabaga seeds sometime in or around July. Potatoes were planted on the new land early the next spring. Rutabagas were not regarded as a delicacy on the Swedish farmers' tables—perhaps they brought too many memories of the Old Country and semi-famine food. Most Enfield rutabagas were cooked up for winter pig feed.

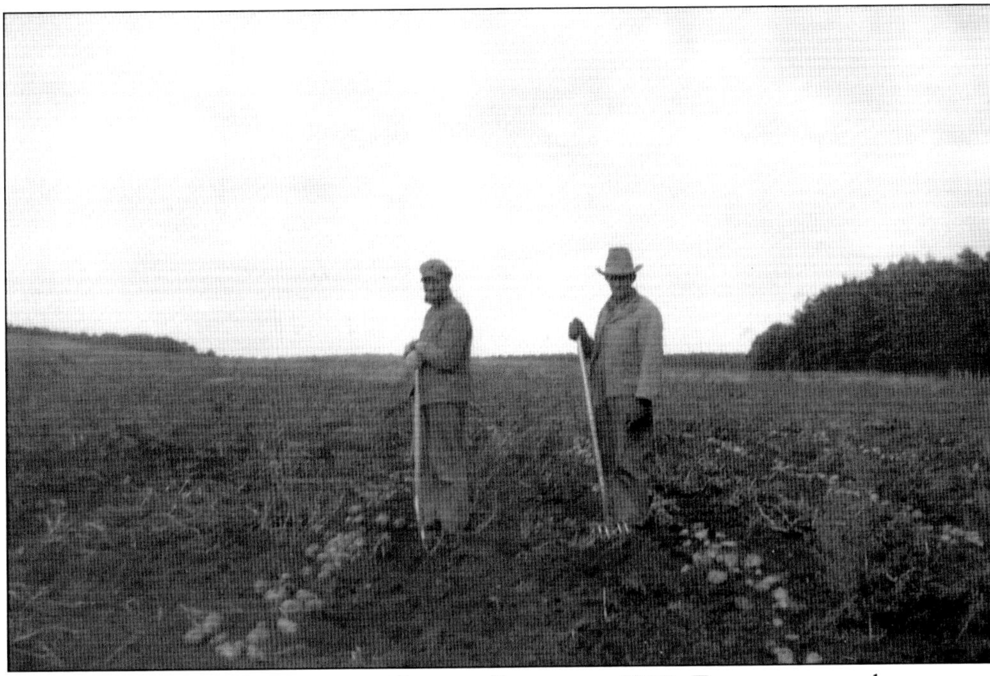

VERNER AND FRANK ABRAHAMSON DIGGING POTATOES, 1922. Two potato warehouses were established along the south side of the railroad siding. Aleck Swanson ran the Healy Company warehouse. The building was sold in 1936 to Leon Abendroth, a farmer north of Hasty, for use as an icehouse. Andrew Westling emigrated with his family from Gagnef in 1893 and operated the Farmers' Co-op potato warehouse in Enfield for a couple of years before he moved his family to southeast Minneapolis, where he later became general manager of the Concrete Elevator Company in southeast Minneapolis.

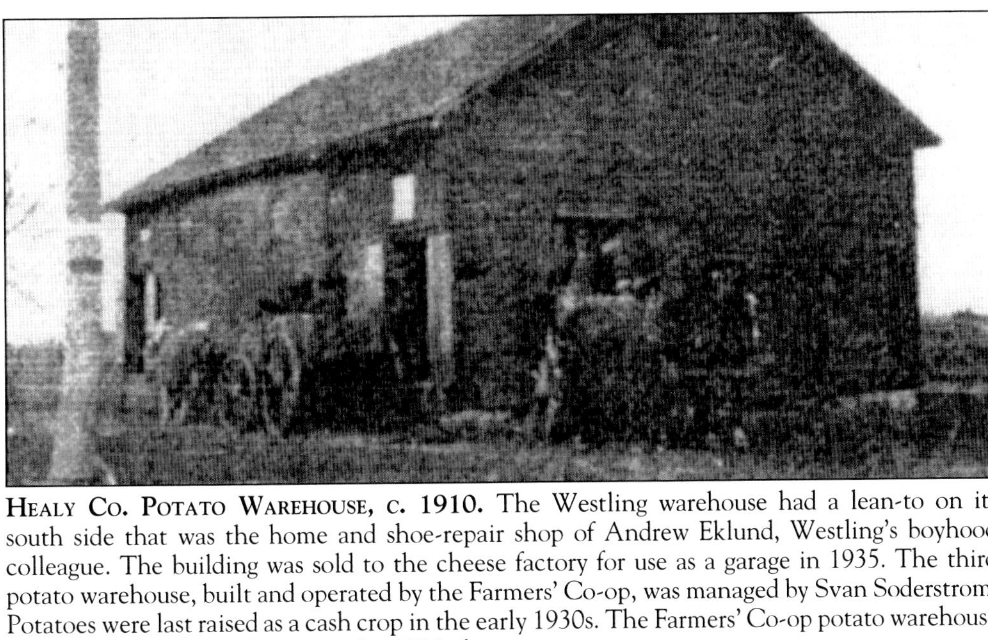

HEALY CO. POTATO WAREHOUSE, C. 1910. The Westling warehouse had a lean-to on its south side that was the home and shoe-repair shop of Andrew Eklund, Westling's boyhood colleague. The building was sold to the cheese factory for use as a garage in 1935. The third potato warehouse, built and operated by the Farmers' Co-op, was managed by Svan Soderstrom. Potatoes were last raised as a cash crop in the early 1930s. The Farmers' Co-op potato warehouse was sold to the cheese factory in the 1930s for use as a garage.

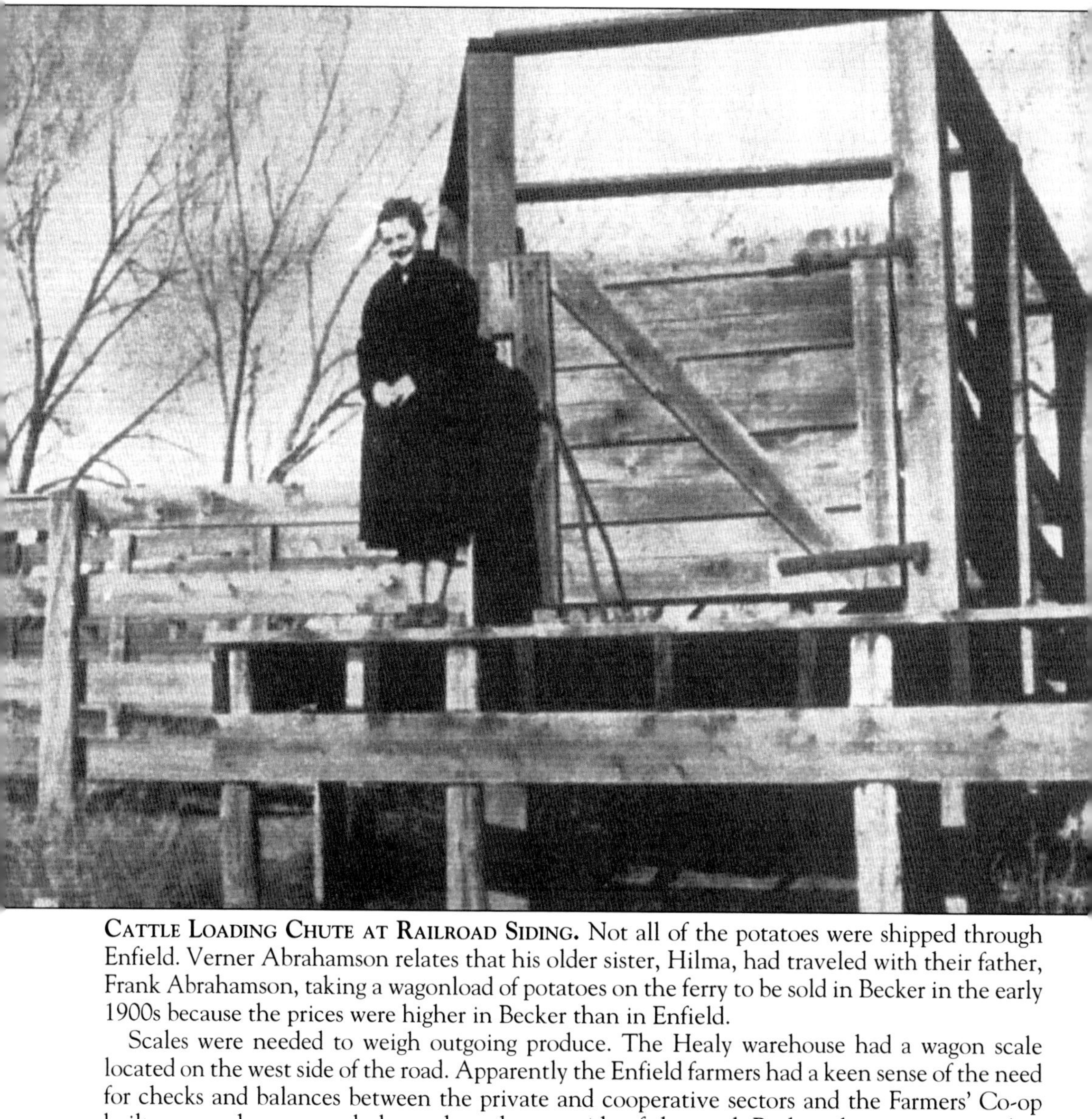

Cattle Loading Chute at Railroad Siding. Not all of the potatoes were shipped through Enfield. Verner Abrahamson relates that his older sister, Hilma, had traveled with their father, Frank Abrahamson, taking a wagonload of potatoes on the ferry to be sold in Becker in the early 1900s because the prices were higher in Becker than in Enfield.

Scales were needed to weigh outgoing produce. The Healy warehouse had a wagon scale located on the west side of the road. Apparently the Enfield farmers had a keen sense of the need for checks and balances between the private and cooperative sectors and the Farmers' Co-op built a second wagon scale located on the east side of the road. Both scales were removed in 1935 when the highway came through the village.

Shoes need regular repair in farm communities. A shoe-repair shop was located in a lean-to addition on the south side of the Westling potato warehouse. There were two cobblers, Andrew Eklund and later Andrew Hero. Hero later established a shop in Silver Creek village.

Livestock being shipped out were held in a little stockyard located just to the east of the Farmers' Co-op potato warehouse. C. Rupert Hagerstrom managed the stockyard.

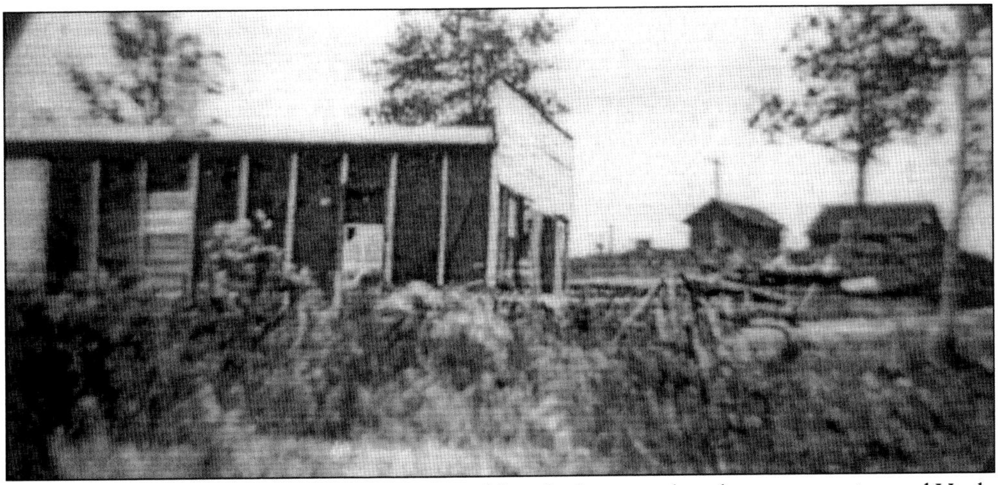

Gust Okerman's Blacksmith Shop, c. 1910. View looking south—the cream station and Healy Potato Warehouse are in the background. Blacksmiths were essential to a farming community. A few of the larger farms had their own blacksmith shops, such as the ZumBrunnen brothers farm in Section 28 and the Frank Abrahamson farm in Section 23. Olof Anderson built Enfield's first commercial blacksmith shop. The blacksmith, Gust Okerman, later built his own shop to the north of the railroad track and also installed a feed-grinding mill. This blacksmith shop and feed mill ceased operation c. 1915 when Okerman moved back to St. Cloud. The buildings were removed in 1927 when the cheese factory was constructed on the site.

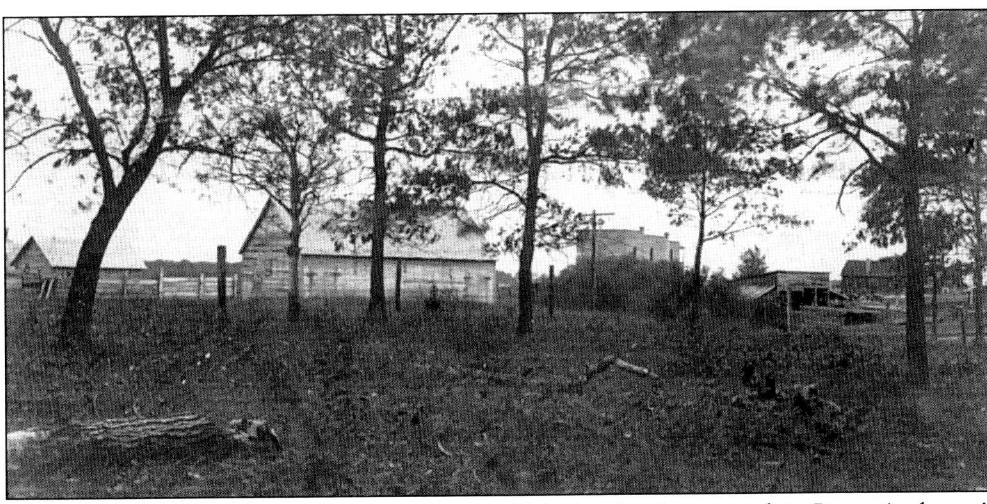

Enfield Village Looking Southwest, c. 1910. In the foreground is Peter Anderson's Farmstead. In the background from left to right are Berglund Store, Lumber Yard Building, and Healy Potato Warehouse. Lumber was sold from a yard in Enfield for a few years. The stock was sold in 1910 to the Hasty yard of the Central Lumber Company that was managed by Andrew G. Nord. The Hoglund family was also involved with the Hasty lumberyard. The lumberyard was most remembered for a tragic accident that happened when the lumber was being moved to Hasty by horse-drawn wagons. Verner Abrahamson, who was then six years old, recounted: "One of the younger Hoglund boys (Rudolph Austin Hoglund—born May 29, 1898) fell off a load of lumber, the wagon ran over him, and he was killed instantly. This happened just north of the schoolhouse road (on November 3, 1910) and the next morning on the way to school we could see quite a bit of blood where it had happened."

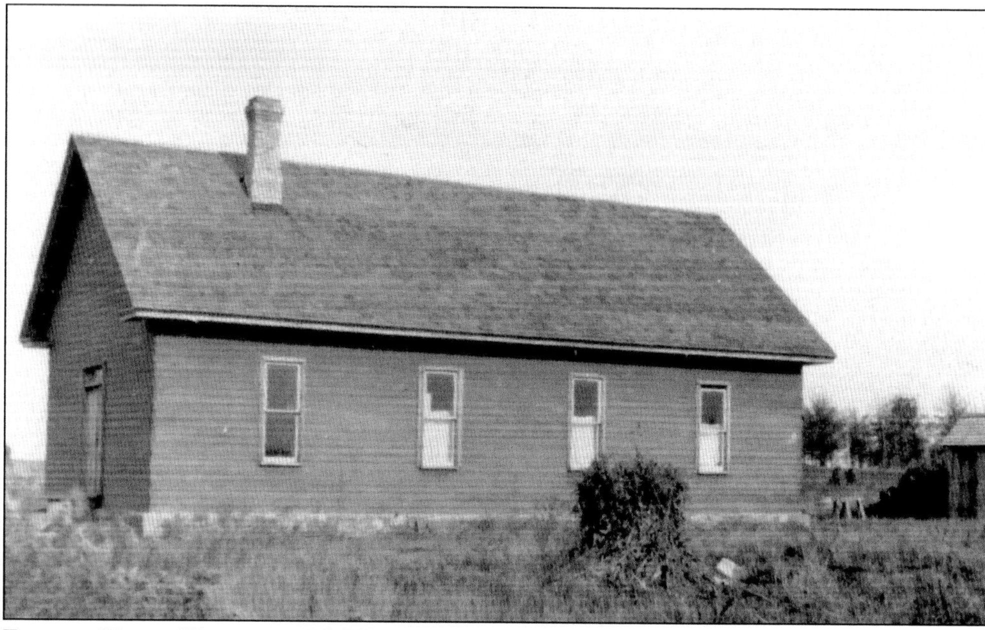

ENFIELD TOWN HALL AND IOGT HALL, 1910. The Enfield town hall was built by the Farmers' Co-op in 1910. It served as the lodge for the International Order of Good Templars (IOGT), a temperance society, and for community social events. IOGT meetings continued through the 1920s.

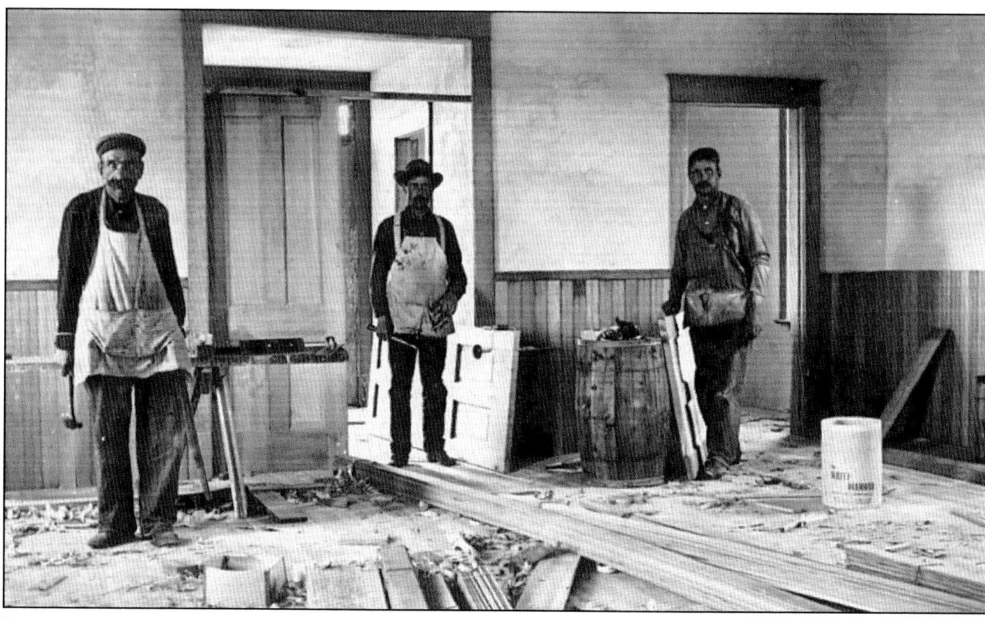

INTERIOR WORK IN THE IOGT HALL, 1910.

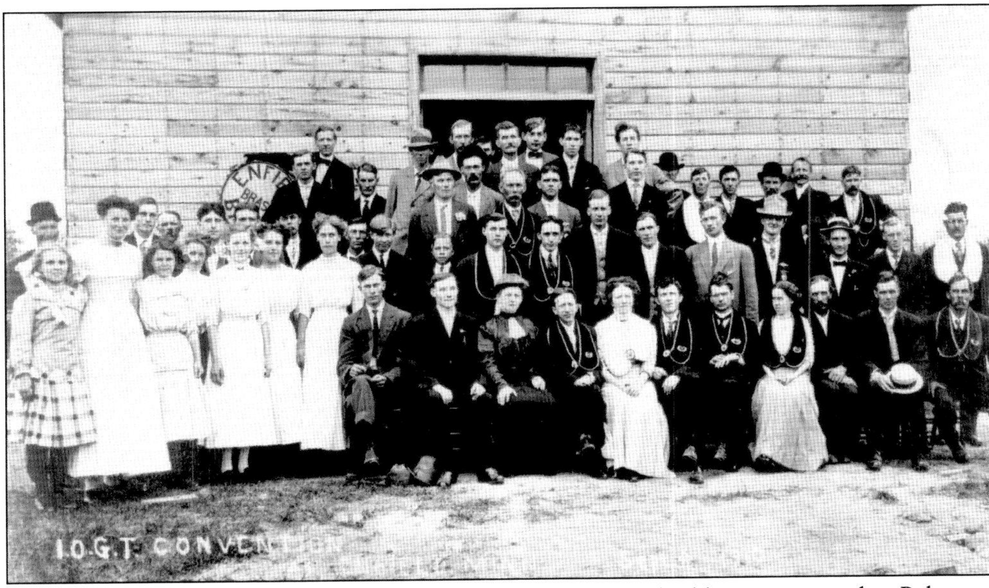

ENFIELD IOGT HALL DEDICATION, SEPTEMBER 4, 1910. The building was moved to Palm and East Fourth Streets in Monticello in 1941 and became the sanctuary of the new Assembly of God congregation. It then became the sanctuary for the St. Michael's and All Angels' Episcopal congregation in 1961. The building was converted into a residential duplex in 1999.

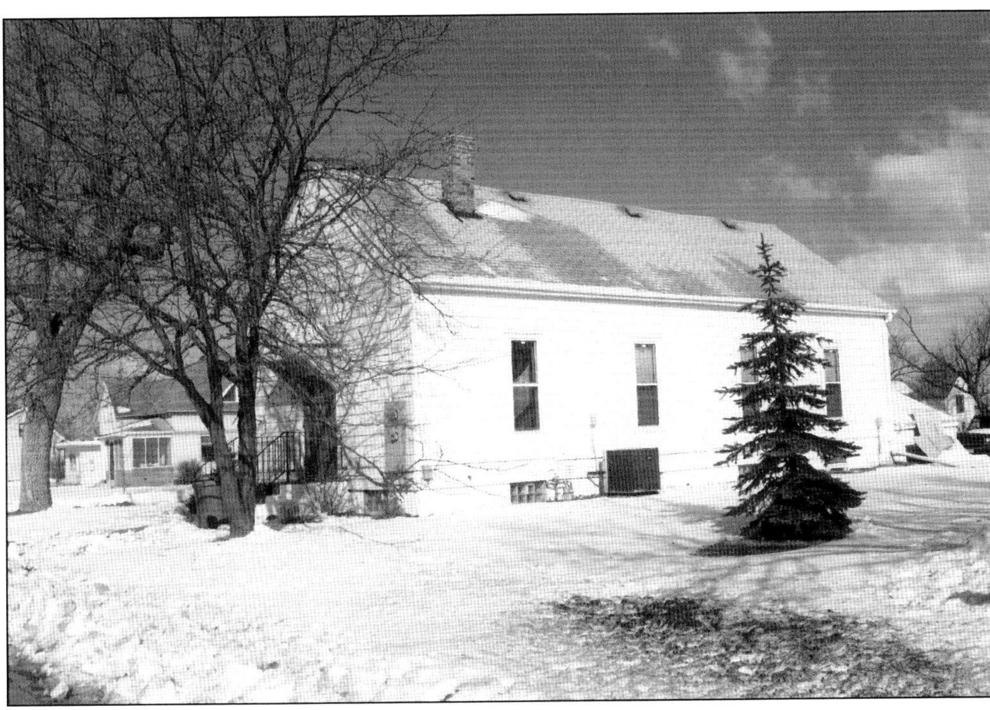

ENFIELD IOGT HALL BUILDING, 2002.

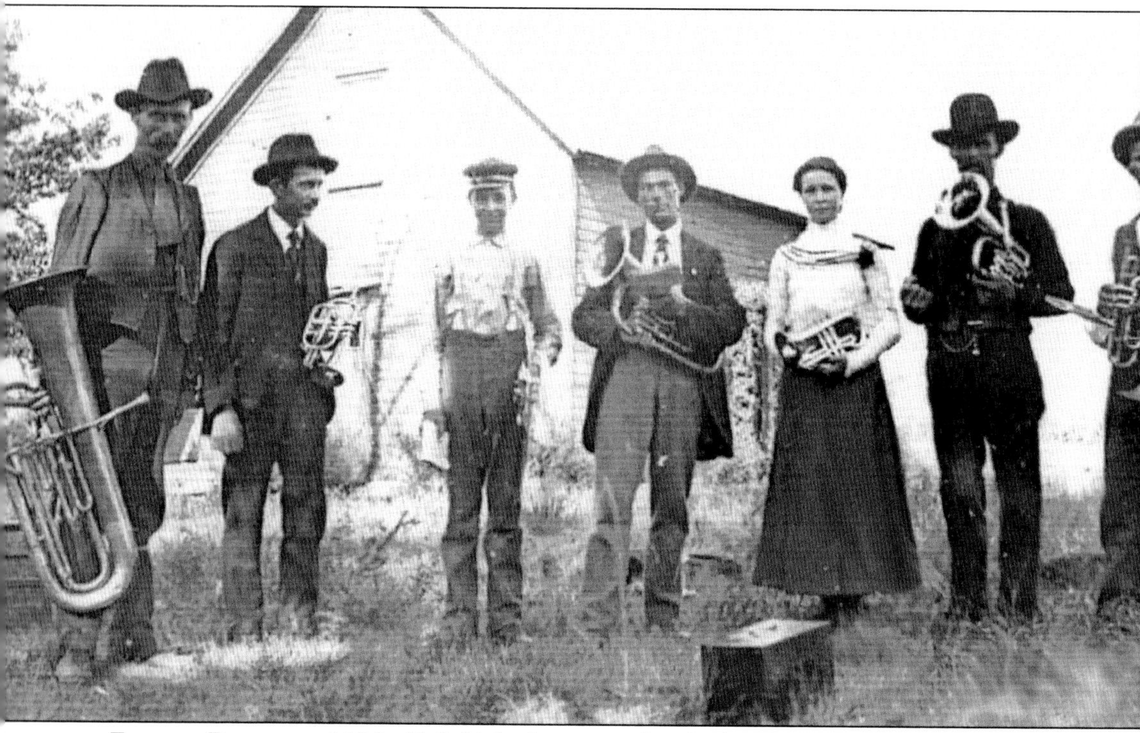

ENFIELD BAND, C. 1900. Enfield had a town band. Art Larson was the band director and played cornet. Nils Hokanson played a bass drum emblazoned with "Enfield Brass Band." Clarence Berglund had the snare drums. Other members included Carl Swanson, Emmanuel Swanson, several of the Oswald girls, and the Oswald brothers, Frank, William, and John. The band played for Fourth of July celebrations held in the Enfield Park, at parties, occasionally to meet the passenger trains, and on other special occasions.

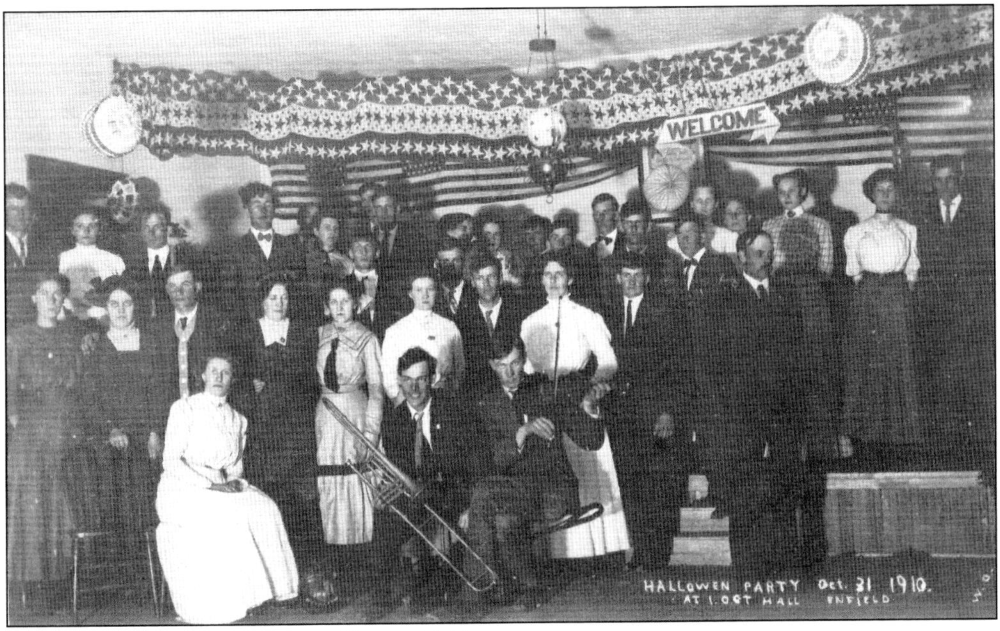

HALLOWEEN PARTY AT ENFIELD HALL, 1910.

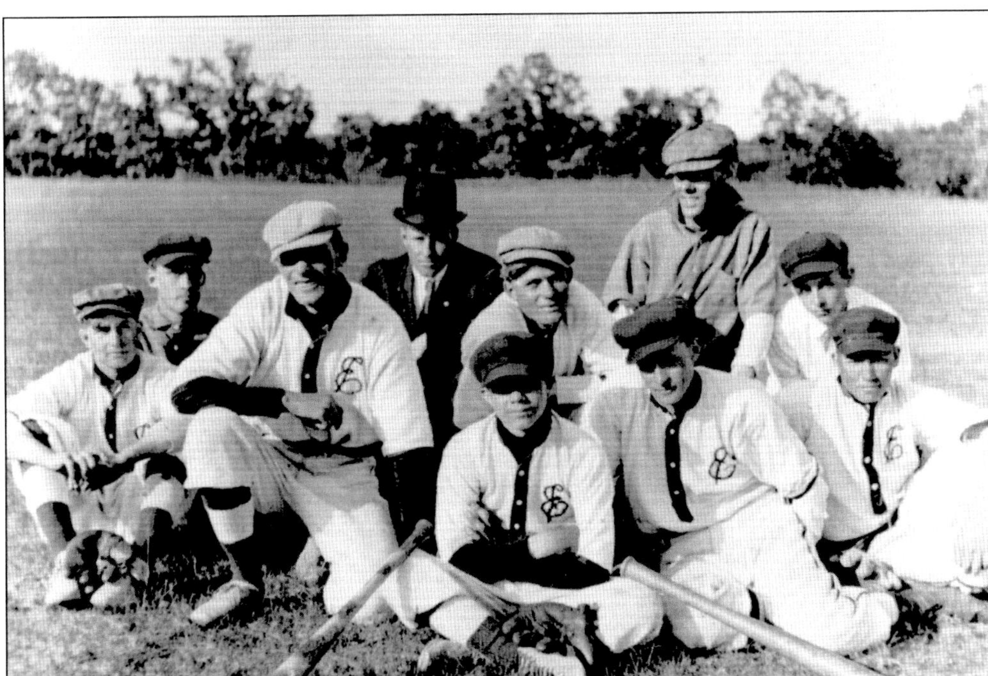

ENFIELD BASEBALL TEAM, JUNE 1912. Baseball was taken seriously in early twentieth century Enfield. This is the earliest extant photograph is of the S(ilver) C(reek Siding) Grays.

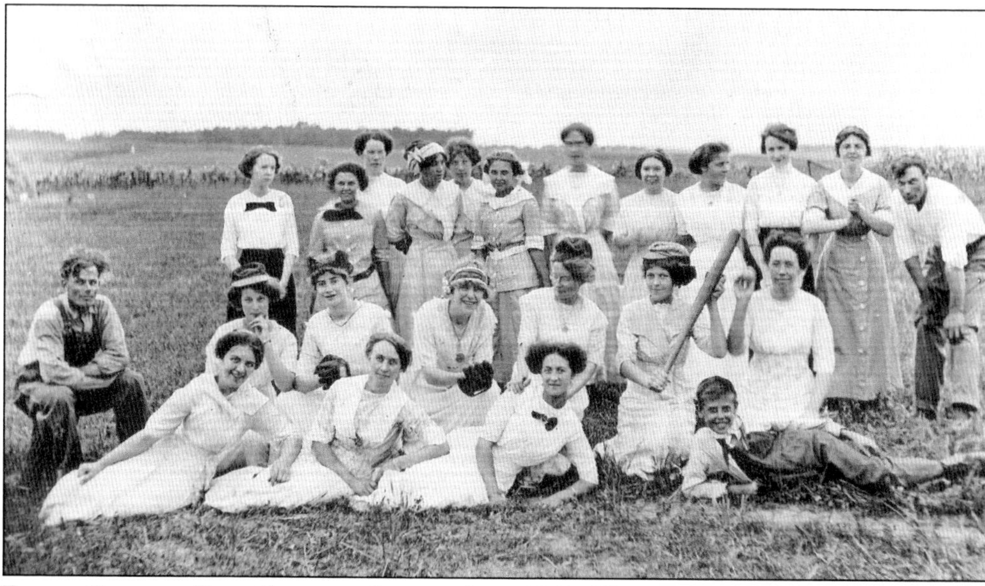

ENFIELD BASEBALL TEAM CHEERING SECTION, JUNE 1912. There was a joint Enfield-Hasty team in 1933, with one regular, Ray Fretchell, who came from Robbinsdale to pitch. Glenn Abrahamson played on the local team in the early 1940s—it then had players from Hasty, Enfield, and Silver Creek villages. The author went with him to a game against the Clear Lake team in about 1941—crossing the river on the Clearwater-Clear Lake ferry.

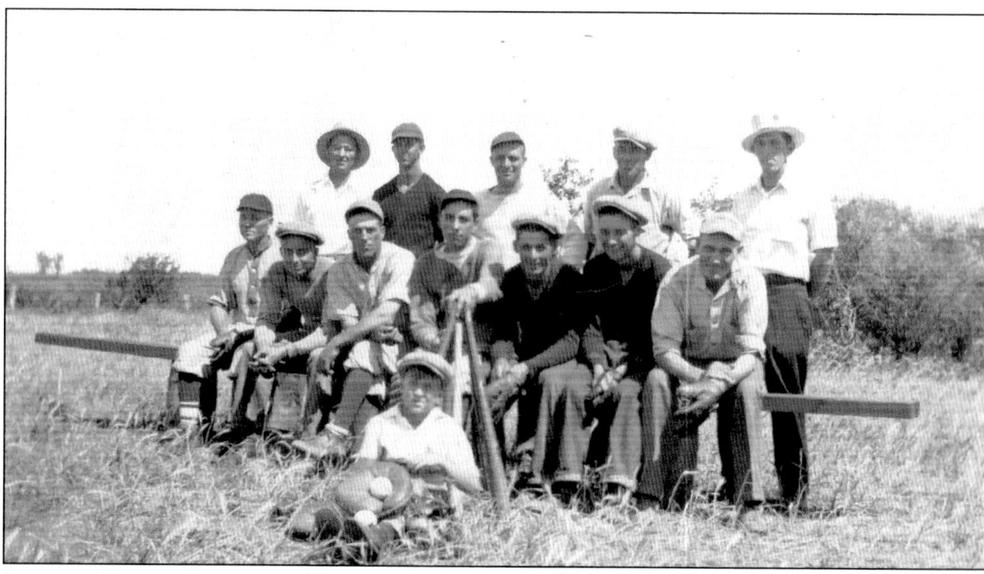

ENFIELD-HASTY BASEBALL TEAM, 1933. Pictured from left to right are: (front row) Donald Swanberg (Mascot); (middle row) George Haight, Ray Fretchell, Jack Starry, Virgil Dearing, Melvin Platten, Gordon Everson, and Emmanuel Swanson; (back row) Harry Swanberg (Secretary-Treasurer), Alvin Abrahamson, Clifford Berglund, Percy Schmidt, and Ray Adamson (Manager).

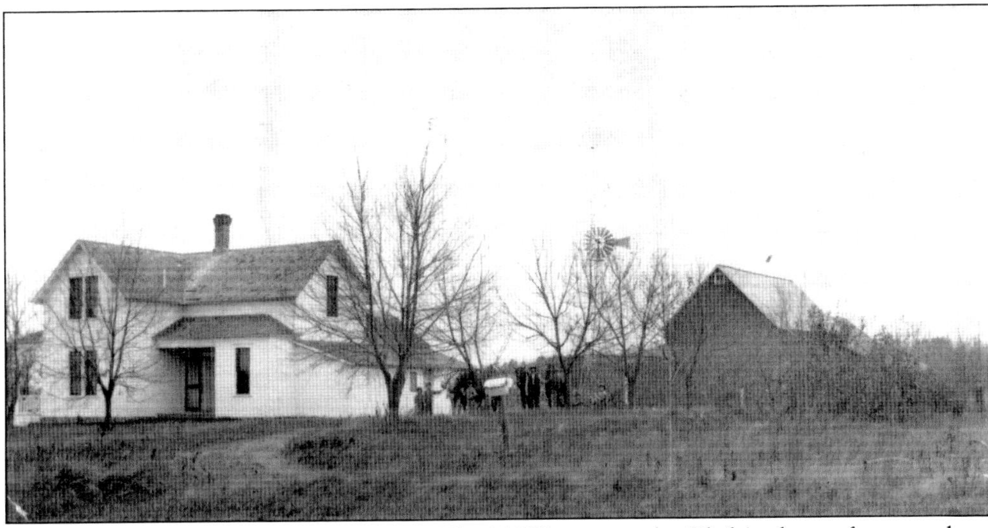

Olof Anderson House, Built c. 1897. The 1897 house on the Olof Anderson farm may have been the first residence in what became Enfield Village. This house was later moved about a quarter mile south to the Enoch and Esther Anderson farmstead. The Svan Ahl farmstead and house were located just north of the west end of the railroad siding. Pete Anderson built a house just north of the east end of the siding in 1916; the Chamberlain and the P.O. Swenson families later occupied this house. The Louis P. Berglund house was built in 1905 at the west end of the village, just across from the Enfield Park.

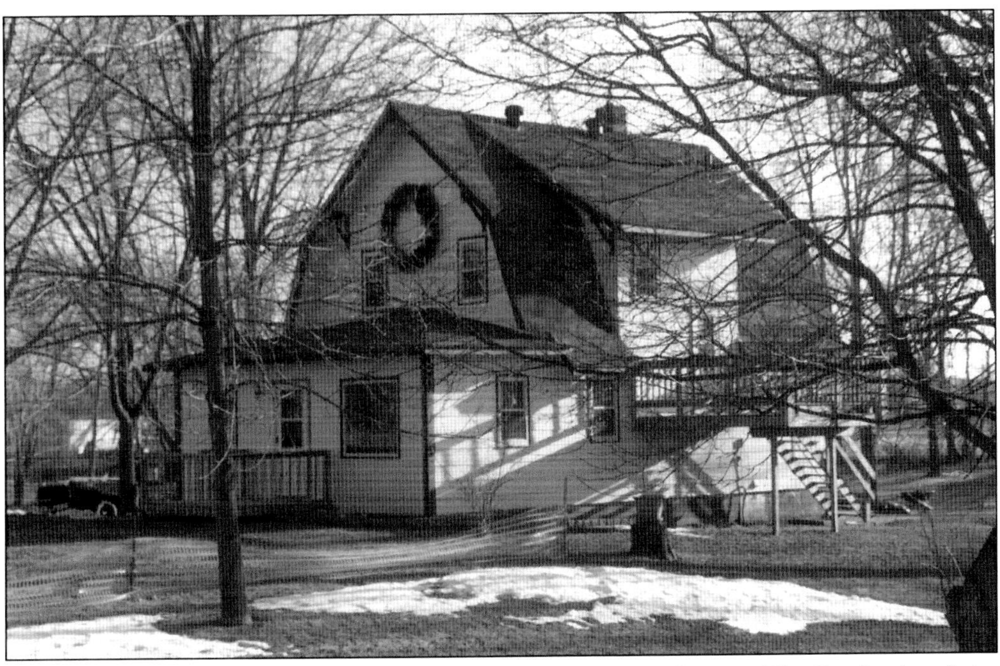

L.P. Berglund House, Built 1905, Seen Here in a 2001 Photo. The Berglund and the Gustafson general stores had residential quarters on their second stories, as did the cheese factory. The L.P. Berglund, the P.O. Swenson, and the Pete Anderson houses are still occupied in 2002, as are the residential quarters in the Berglund store, the Kenneth Adams store, and the cheese factory.

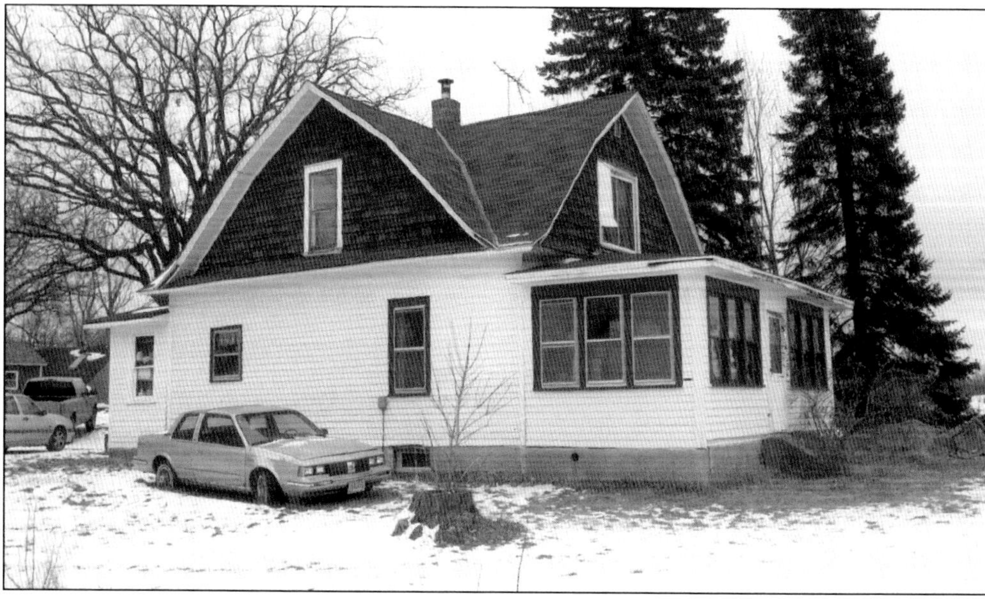

Pete Anderson House, Built 1916, Seen Here in a 2002 Photo. Cooperative associations were central to the establishment of Minnesota rural communities in the late nineteenth and early twentieth centuries. The Enfield farmers, through their Co-op, built a town hall, a town park, and, indirectly, organized their school. The Co-op also built a potato warehouse, a livestock yard, a second general store, and even a second wagon platform scale to provide some competition with the private-sector businesses in the community. The last major initiative by the Co-op was to build a new cheese factory in 1927 after the Twin City Milk Producers froze the outlying farmers out of the Minneapolis market. The Co-op and its activities survived the Great Depression, but could not survive the pressures from Land O'Lakes, Inc. and from Highway #152.

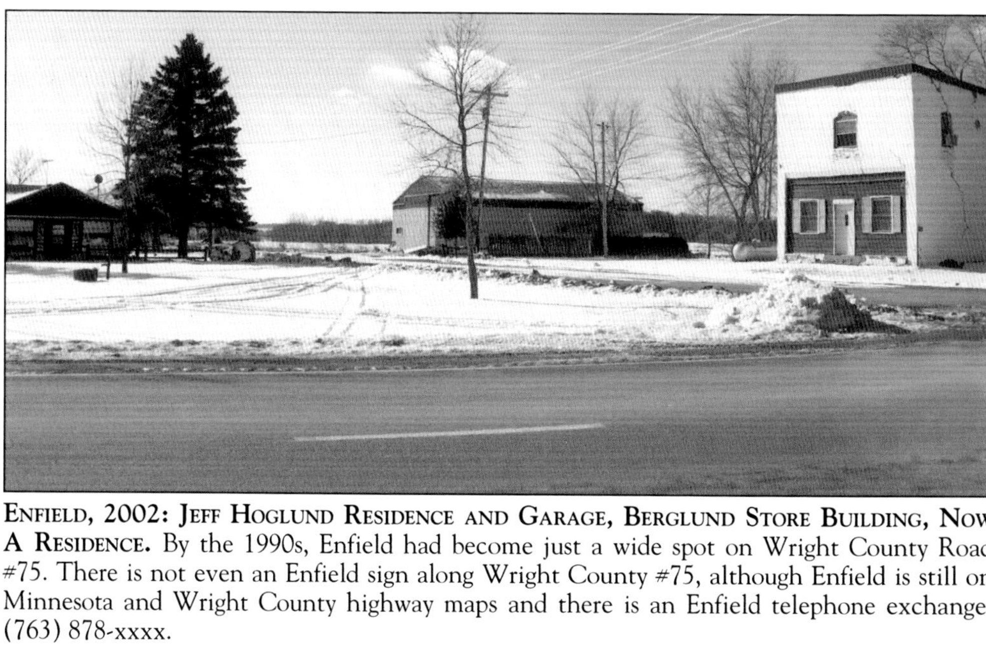

Enfield, 2002: Jeff Hoglund Residence and Garage, Berglund Store Building, Now A Residence. By the 1990s, Enfield had become just a wide spot on Wright County Road #75. There is not even an Enfield sign along Wright County #75, although Enfield is still on Minnesota and Wright County highway maps and there is an Enfield telephone exchange: (763) 878-xxxx.

1855	Monticello post office & Wright County established
1871	Erick and Kestin Trogen Homestead in Section 26
1877	Baptist Church building built in Section 27
1882	Railroad built: Silver Creek Siding established: First train in December
1897	Olaf Anderson House Built in what was to become Enfield village
1889	Lake Side Cemetery established; Anna Anderson is first burial
1891	Swedish Lutheran Church built
1900	Frank & Amanda Abrahamson start farm in Section 23
1905	Monticello-Silver Creek Telephone Company established
1905	L.P. Berglund builds brick general store & frame house
1905	Baptist Church moved to Silver Creek Siding village
Early 1900s	Three potato warehouses in Enfield
1910	Post office established & village name changed to Enfield
1910	I.O.G.T. hall built in Silver Creek Siding
1910	Enfield lumber yard moved to Hasty
1910	Enfield depot installed (an old box car)
1912	Blacksmith shop and feed mill established
1916	Pete Anderson & Chamberlin houses built
1919	Local farmers's Co-Op general store built [the Gustafson store]
1927	Farmers's Co-Op builds cheese factory
1931	Depot sold to Art Post for use as chickenhouse
1935	Minnesota Highway #152 built through Enfield village
1936	Healy potato warehouse moved to Hasty
Late 1930s	Baptist Church congregation stops meeting
1940	Baptist Church building becomes Enoch Anderson's granary
1941	I.O.G.T. hall moved to Monticello for use as a church
1944	Rural Electrification (REA) comes to Enfield
1950	Cheese factory bought by Land O'Lakes and is closed
1951	Wright County District School #121 closes
1953	Gustafson store, built in 1919, burns
1954	Post Office closes & rural mail delivery again begins
1957	The last general store closes
1973	Interstate I-94 built
1977	Signals along Great Northern track taken down
1979	Telegraph lines along Great Northern railroad track taken down
1982	The Great Northern railroad tracks removed
2002	Enfield is wide spot on County Road #75 without even a road sign

ENFIELD CHRONOLOGY.

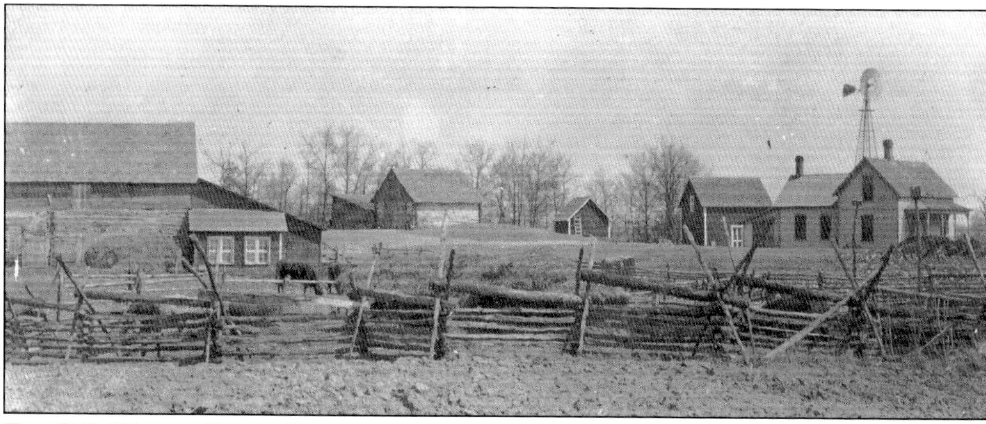

THE C.P. WESTON FAMILY FARMSTEAD, C. 1905.

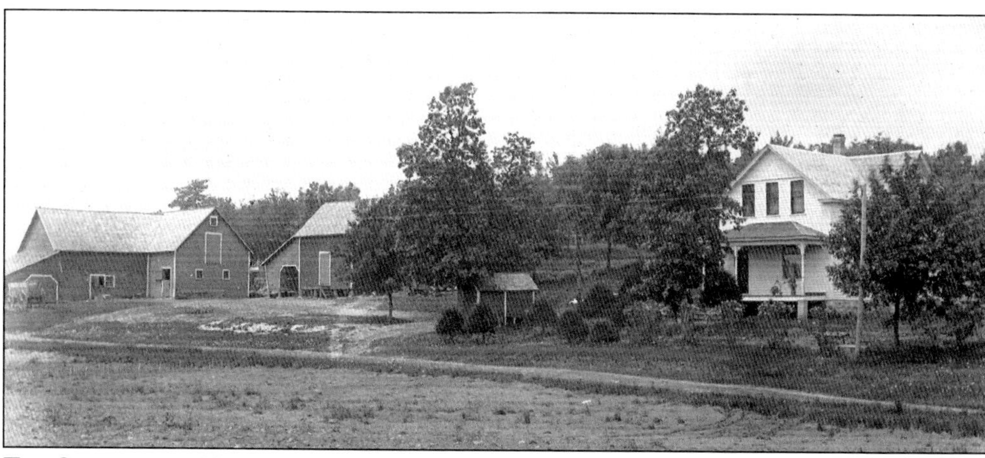

THE CHARLIE AND HANNA ABRAHAMSON FARM, C. 1905.

Eight

The Water

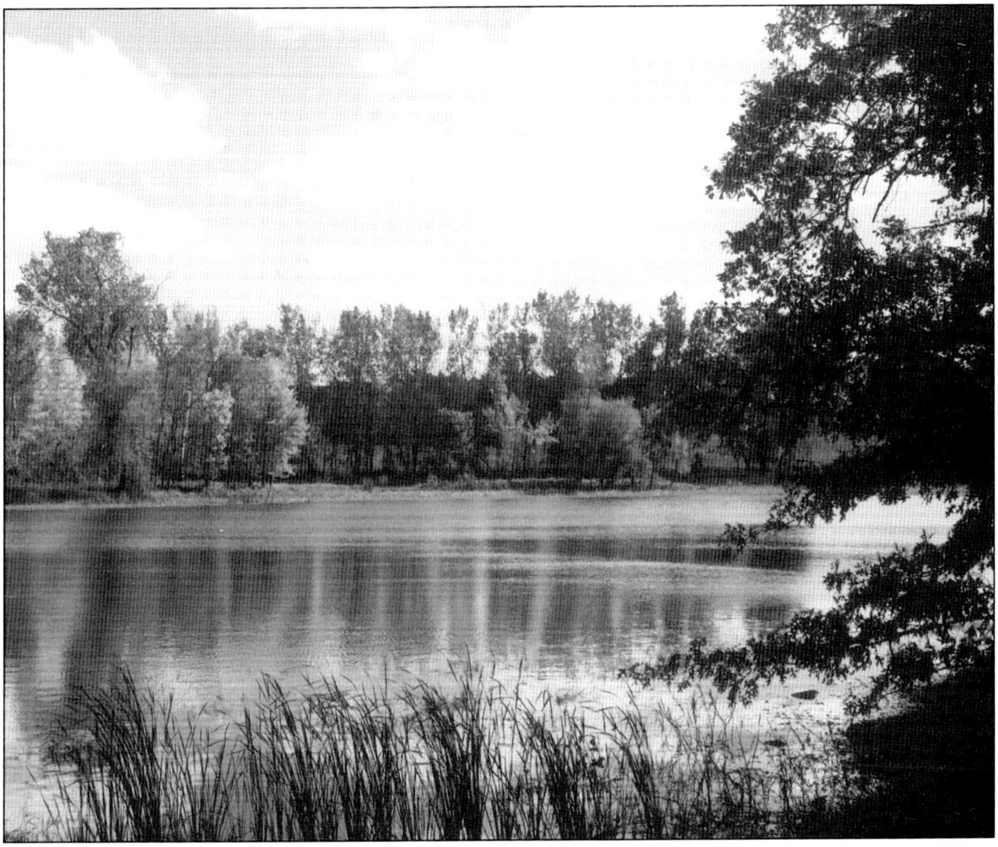

Pond Overlooked by Andrew Ezra Trogen Farmstead in Section 26. Water did not play a major part in the lives of Enfield community farmers other than how wetlands and rainfall affected farming. Many of the wetlands and other low places were tiled and drained. Silver Creek was dredged, eliminating more wetlands. Other than a little sport fishing and picnics on Sundays and holidays, the lakes played but minor roles. At least one or two farmers around each of the larger lakes had a boat or two that they would rent to neighborhood families or kids for fishing trips.

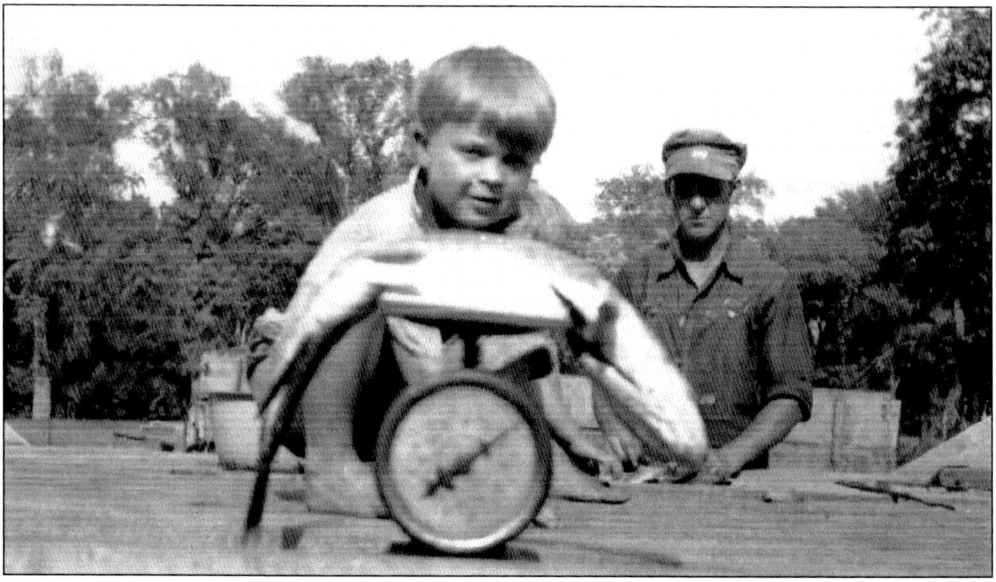

Dean and Ed Abrahamson with Dean's First Big Fish, 1940. There were a few summer cabins on a couple of these lakes—some owned by former community residents who had subsequently moved to Minneapolis, but by and large the lake shores and banks of the Mississippi River were undisturbed farmland.

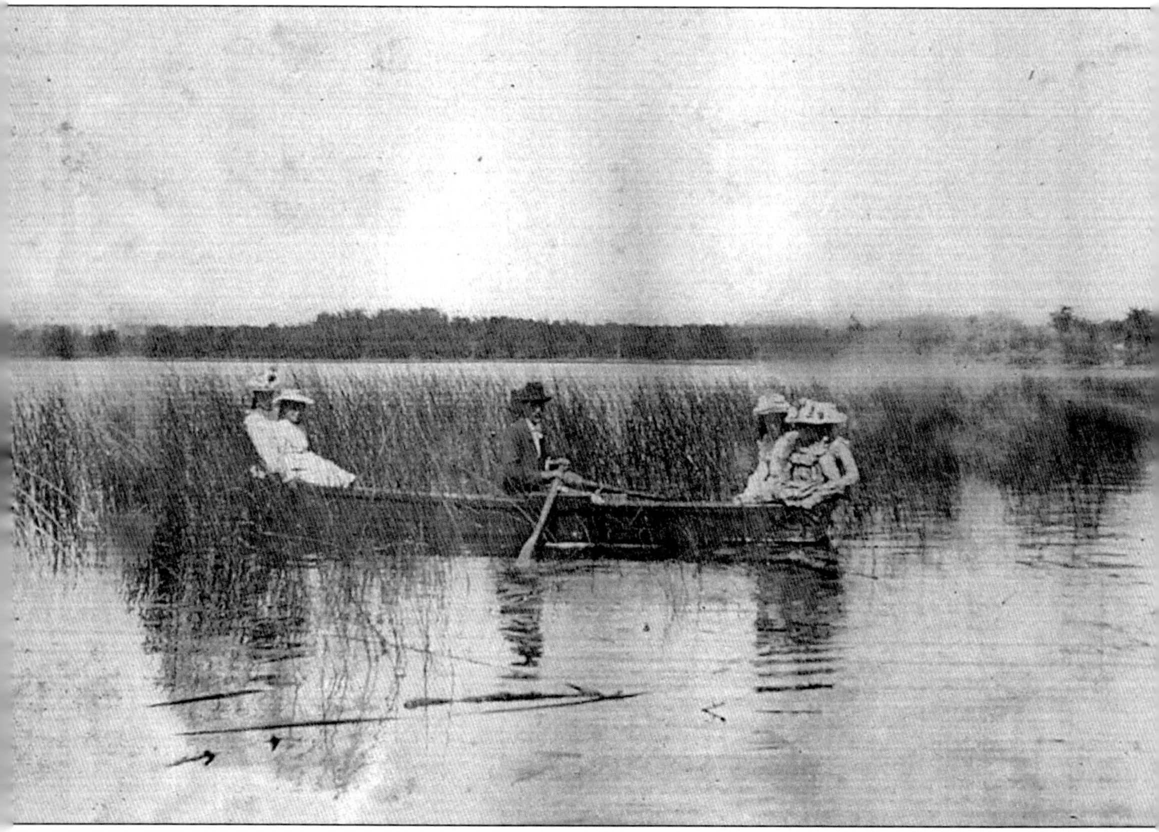

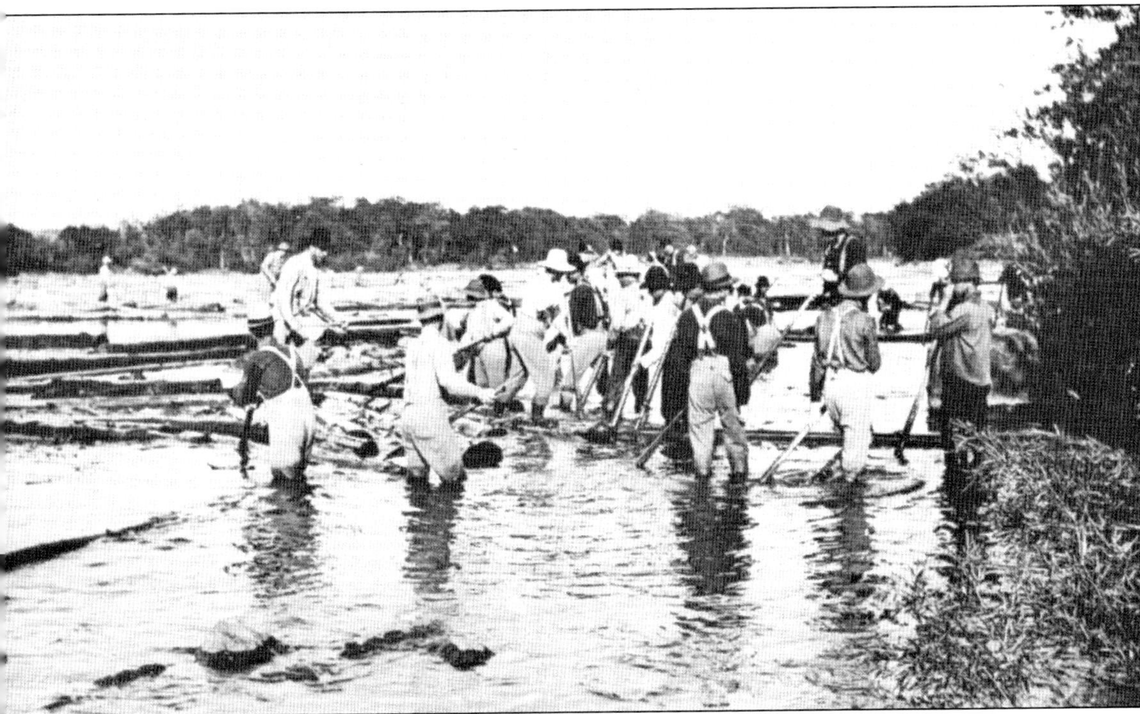

Driving Logs Near Mouth of Silver Creek, c. 1910. Swedish farmers built their farmsteads overlooking water wherever practicable. Many Swedish-American cemeteries, including Enfield's Lake Side Cemetery, were on hills overlooking lakes following a tradition dating from the Viking era. Water took its toll of life. Ernest Felien, the 13-year-old son of Charles and Hilda Felien, drowned in the Mississippi River on the 6th of July in 1919. His father spent several days looking until he found Ernest's body. John Bell of Monticello drowned while hunting ducks in North Lake on October 23, 1938.

Opposite: **Picnic on Locke Lake, c. 1910.** The many ponds and other wetlands were a welcome home to ducks, geese, and, in the early days, swans—many of these fowl graced family tables in the fall. Swans have now returned to Enfield lakes.

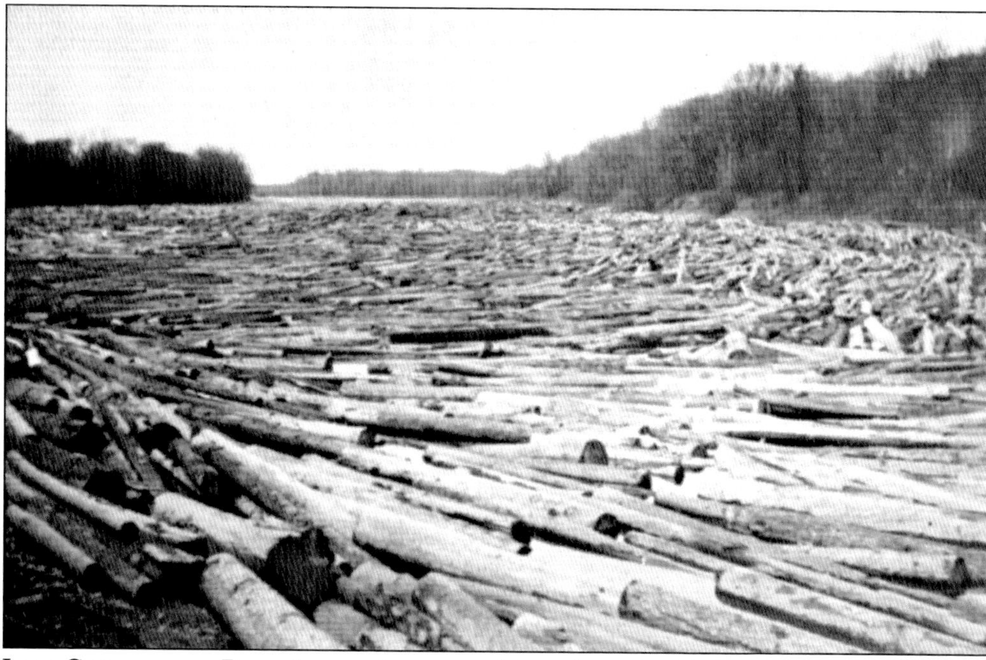

Logs Collected at Boom Island. Logs were driven down the Mississippi River until the last drive in 1916. The logs had been cut in the extensive pine forests to the north and floated to downstream sawmills in Minneapolis and elsewhere during the high water of the spring and early summer. Enfield folks watched the drives, but did not participate—although oral history has it that now and then a log found its way into community barns and other buildings. This photo was taken on the Mississippi River by a present-day nuclear power plant.

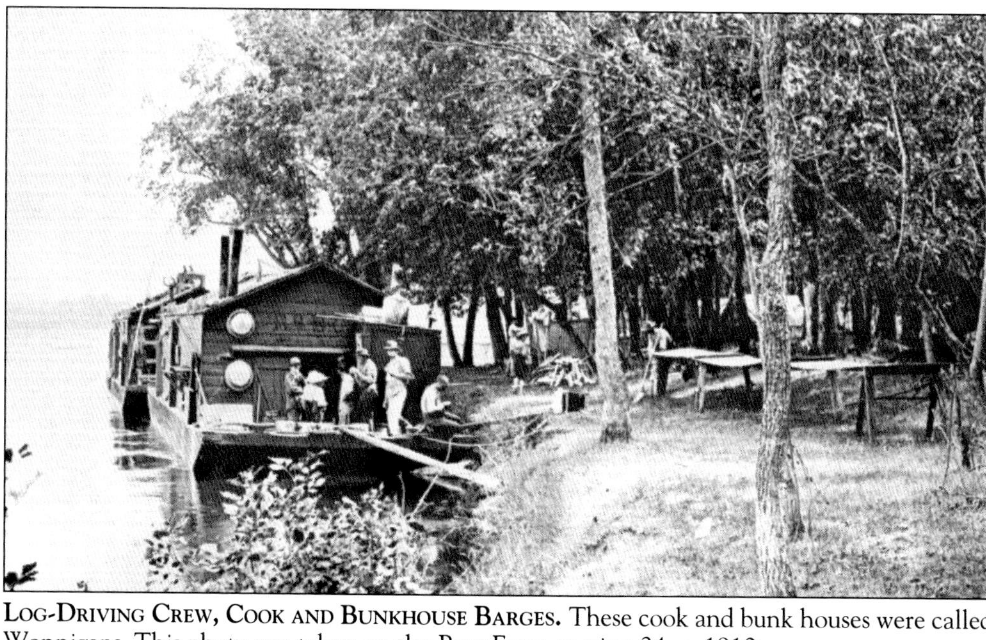

Log-Driving Crew, Cook and Bunkhouse Barges. These cook and bunk houses were called Wannigans. This photo was taken on the Berg Farm, section 24, c. 1910.

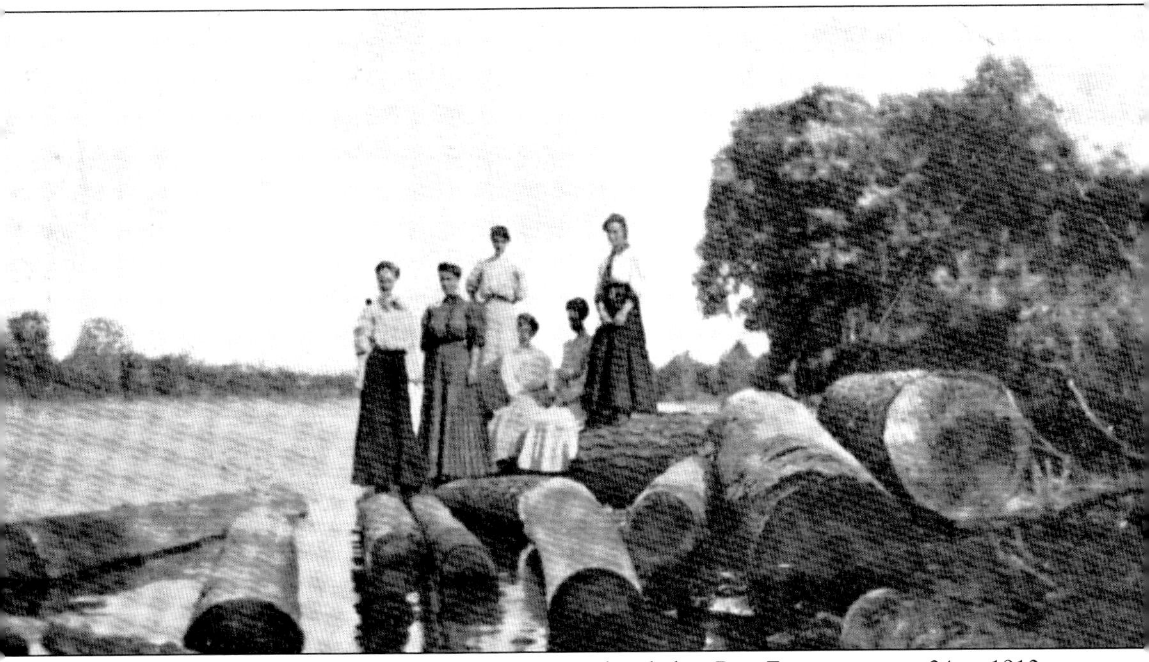

LOCAL LADIES ON STRANDED LOGS. This photo was taken below Berg Farm in section 24, *c.* 1910.

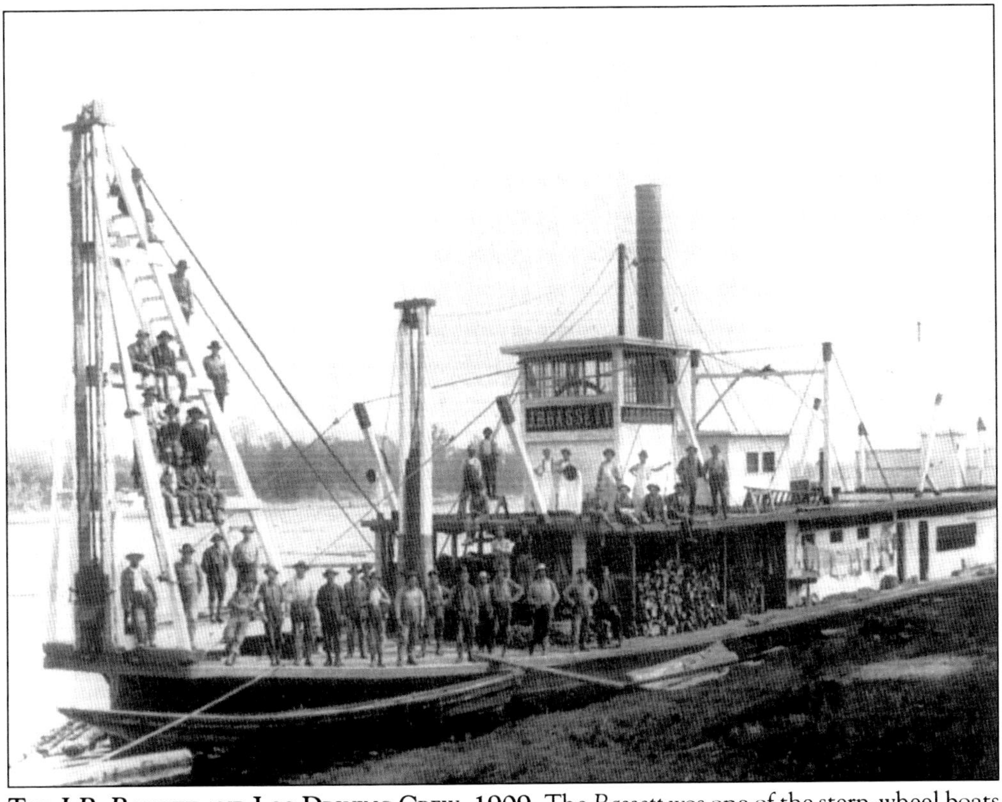

THE *J.B. BASSETT* AND LOG DRIVING CREW, 1909. The *Bassett* was one of the stern-wheel boats of the Mississippi and Rum River Boom Company. The photo was taken in Clearwater.

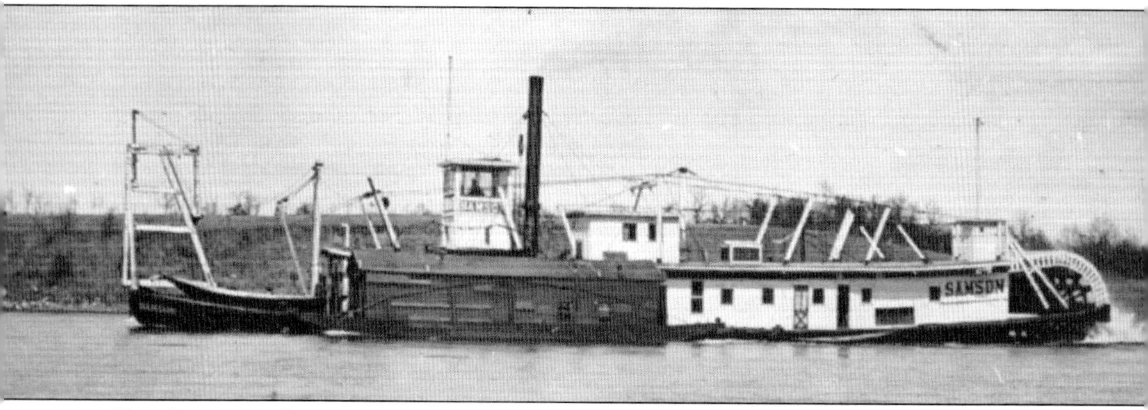

THE SAMPSON, ONE OF THE MISSISSIPPI AND RUM RIVER BOOM COMPANY STERN WHEELERS. This photo was taken on the Mississippi River north of Enfield, *c.* 1915. Note the Wannigan tied to her side.

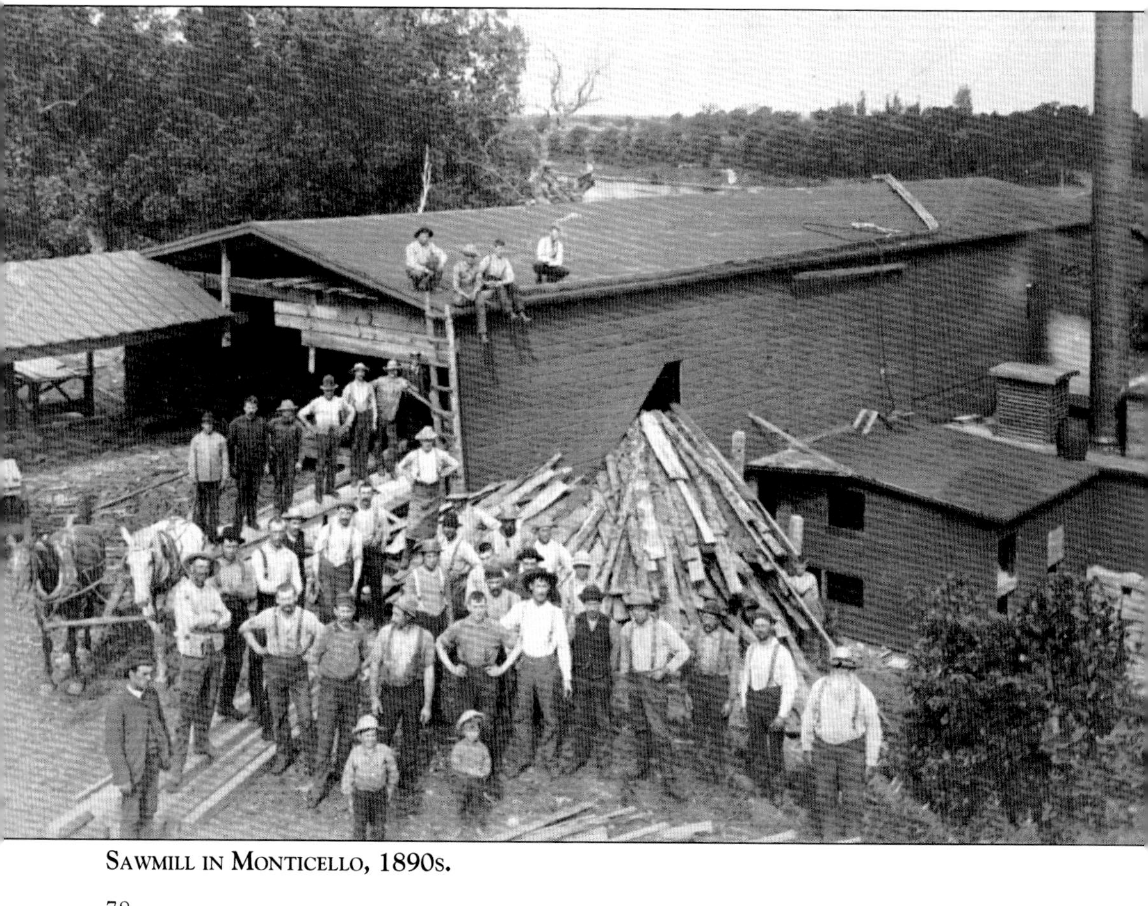

SAWMILL IN MONTICELLO, 1890S.

Nine

THE LANDS AND THE FARMS

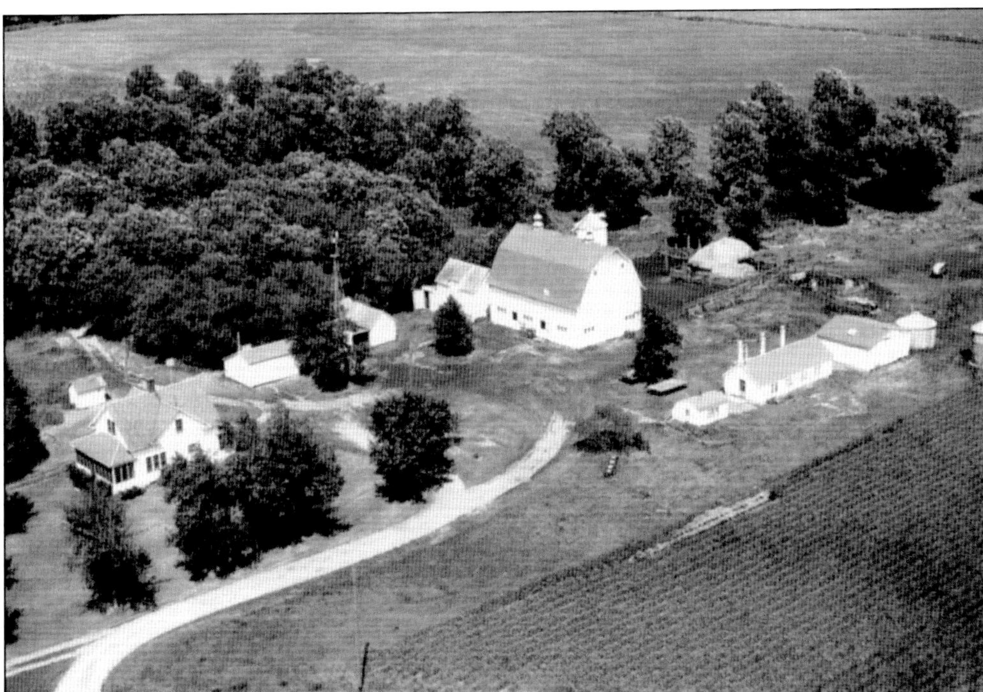

A MATURE ENFIELD FARMSTEAD. This 1950 photograph shows the Ruth Westing and B. Ernest Berg Farm in section 24. The families, the land, and the farms were the heart of the Enfield community. The homesteaders came to a northern Silver Creek Township that was part of the extensive mixed-hardwood forest known as Minnesota's Big Woods. Remnants of the Big Woods are preserved in the Harry Larson Memorial Forest and the Lake Maria State Park. The region, situated on a glacial moraine, is hilly with many wetlands and small lakes. Soil type varies, sometimes within the confines of a single field. The farmers were fairly aggressive about draining wetlands and laying drainage tiles, as was common in early twentieth century Minnesota.

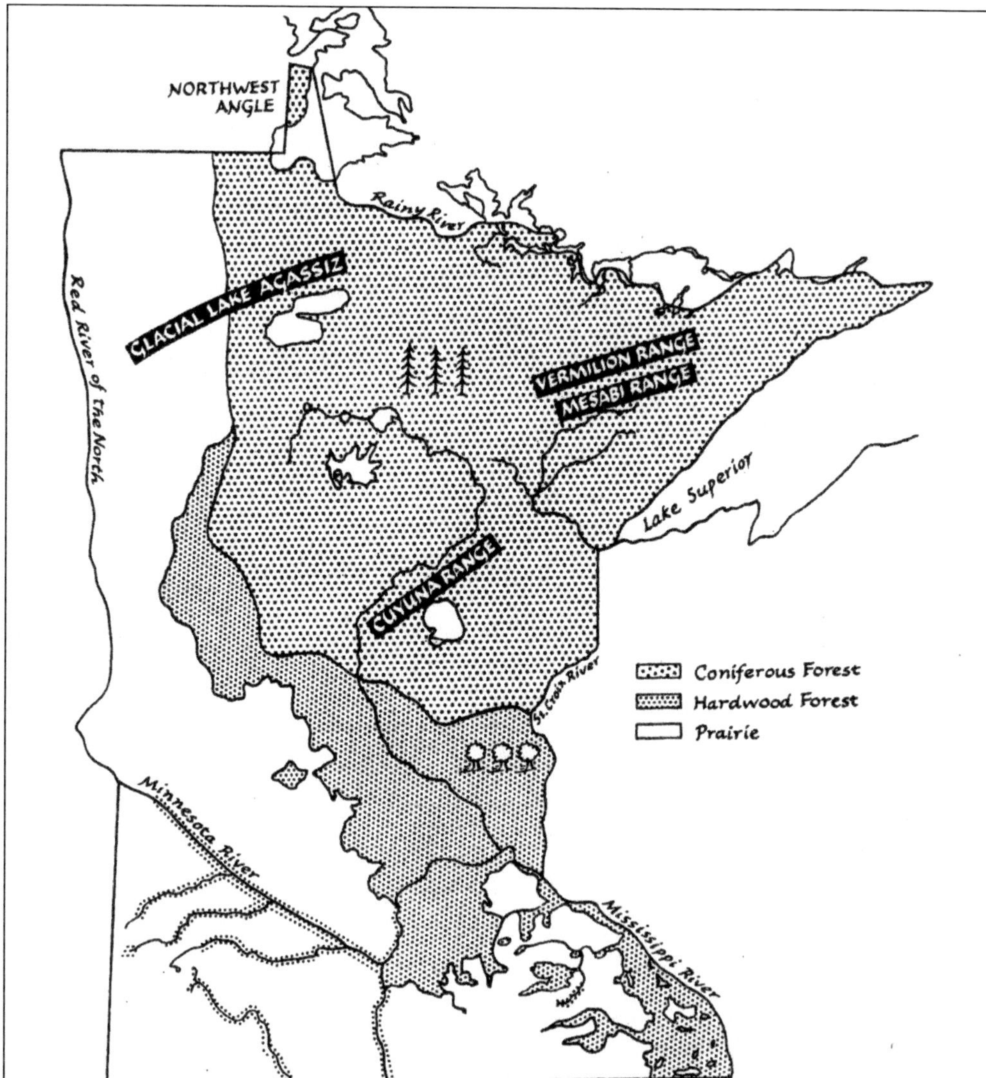

Major Pre-Settlement Land Areas of Minnesota. While all of Wright County was part of the Big Woods, there were patches of prairie: Clearwater Prairie, about six square miles; Monticello Prairie, also known as the West Prairie, about 18 square miles; and the three square mile Mooers's Prairie south of Cokato. The only patch of prairie in Silver Creek Township was Moody's Prairie, also known as Sandborn's Prairie, about one square mile in Sections 22 and 27 south of Locke Lake. Verner Abrahamson's memoirs note that there were only small trees in the woods extending to the Mississippi River in Sections 14 and 15 in the early 1900s. He speculated that this had been a patch of prairie before the first settlers began to suppress fires. Wright County land-ownership plat maps are published from time to time. Early maps show ancient trails giving way to modern roads, the coming and going of the railroad, schools and churches being built, land passing from parents to children, foreclosures, and sales to persons not previously associated with the community. They also show the consolidation of the original 40- and 80-acre farms into larger units, and, more recently, the division of the farms into small tracts as the Enfield area is passing from an integrated farm community into a bedroom suburb in the Minneapolis-St. Cloud urban corridor.

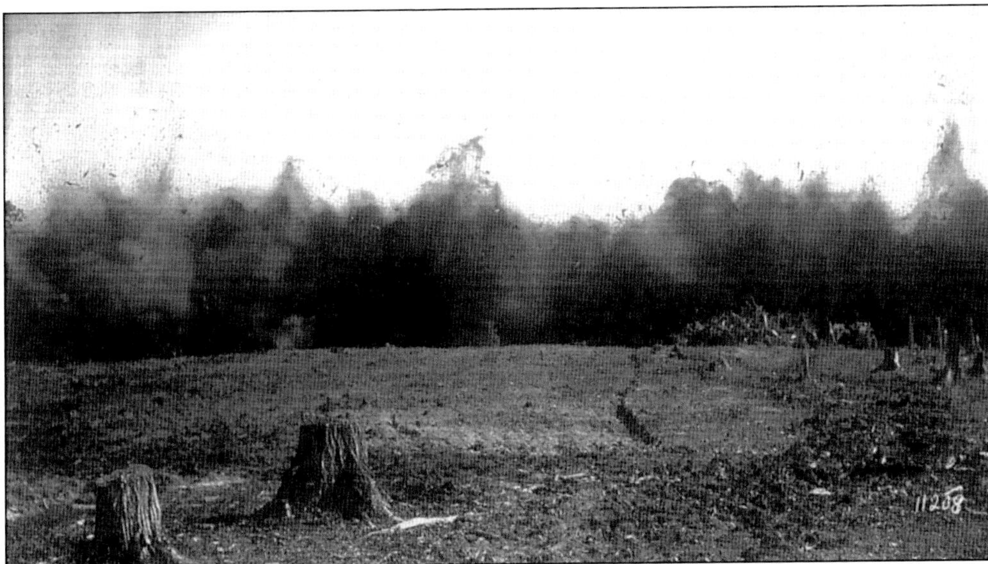

Blasting Stumps When Clearing Land. The first settlers came to the Big Woods with the contents of their emigrant chests—an axe, a saw, a grub hoe, and some other iron tools. They usually had enough cash to buy an oxen or two and perhaps a milk cow—those that were especially well-endowed bought a team of horses. Their first task was to build a house and a barn and to break enough land for the crops to sustain them through the first winter.

Few first-hand written records of the experiences of the first homesteaders in Silver Creek Township have been found, but their circumstances are described in graphic detail in Vilhelm Moberg's four-volume emigrant historical novels. Erick and Kestin Trogen related that bands of Indians came through their farm in Section 26 in the 1870s and of their clearing land with their team of oxen with Kestin wielding the grub hoe. Dynamite, patented by the Swede Alfred Nobel in 1867, soon found good use on Minnesota homesteads.

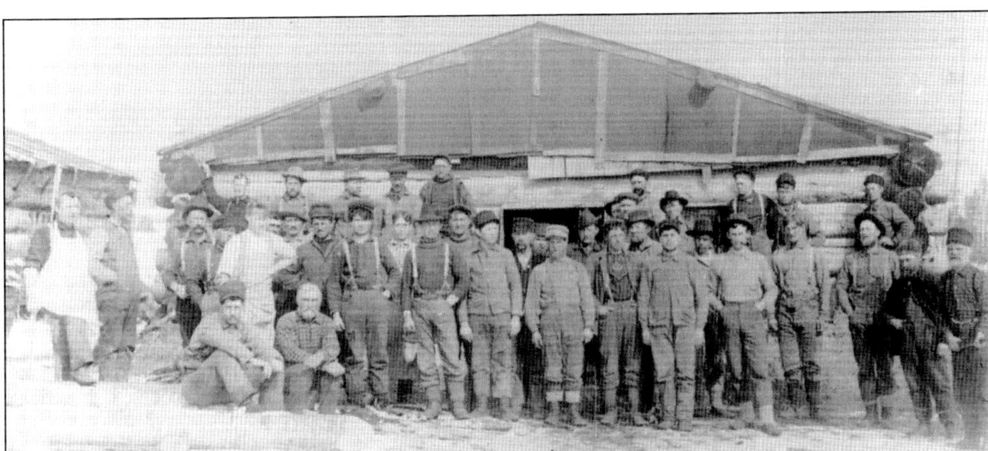

Silver Creek Township Logging Crew, c. 1890. Some of the timber from the Big Woods was cut and sawn into lumber locally. There was a logging operation and sawmill at Silver Creek in the late 1800s. It probably included some of the land in what was to become the Enfield community. There were also small sawmills operated by a single family or a group of neighbors in Section 3, another in Section 24, and probably others as well. Many an Enfield house and barn was made of locally-sawn White Oak.

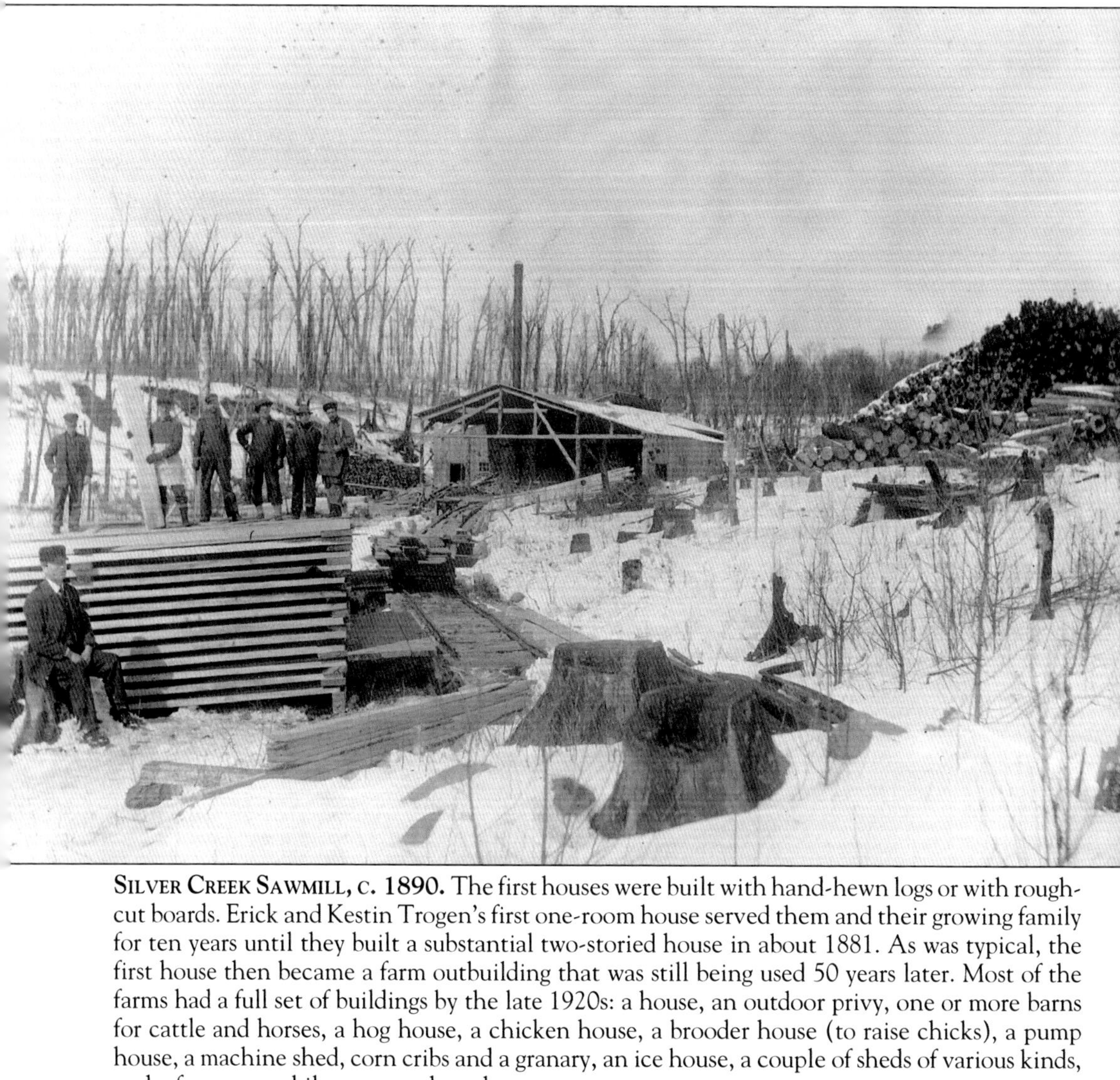

SILVER CREEK SAWMILL, C. 1890. The first houses were built with hand-hewn logs or with rough-cut boards. Erick and Kestin Trogen's first one-room house served them and their growing family for ten years until they built a substantial two-storied house in about 1881. As was typical, the first house then became a farm outbuilding that was still being used 50 years later. Most of the farms had a full set of buildings by the late 1920s: a house, an outdoor privy, one or more barns for cattle and horses, a hog house, a chicken house, a brooder house (to raise chicks), a pump house, a machine shed, corn cribs and a granary, an ice house, a couple of sheds of various kinds, and, after automobiles appeared on the scene, a garage.

The author's grandmother, Amanda Johanessdotter Felien Abrahamson, kept a small diary recording the building of their farm and their family. Frank and Amanda Abrahamson did not settle in the Enfield community until they married in 1900—so they were able to use buildings that had been erected by homesteaders who had departed. A very similar account could be rendered for each of the old Enfield families. I have incorporated a few notes into Grandmother's record:

> Frank Abrahamson was born 14 February 1871 at Bysättra, Knutby, Uppland. He came to Minnesota in May 1889 at the age of 18. *[Frank's brother, Charlie, had come to Silver Creek Township a few years earlier and had sent money for Frank's passage. Frank and Charlie later helped pay for the passage of two of their sisters who later came to the community.]* Frank worked making railroads in Montana, Idaho, and Washington and later on the crews building lighthouses on the Great Lakes. He saved his money and bought his first 40 acres *[in Section 23 just south of Silver Creek Siding]* in 1896.

Frank and I were married in the Minneapolis Court House on 2 April 1900. I was born 1 January 1874 in Förlångsö, Wissefjärda, Småland and came to Minnesota in June 1892 at age 18. *[Amanda's two brothers, Charles and John Felien, had earlier settled near Melrose Lake; they paid for her passage. Amanda contracted either typhoid fever or typhus on the ship and spent about six weeks in the immigrant hospital before travelling on to Minnesota.]* I worked as a housemaid in Minneapolis and in Chicago and used the time to save some money and to learn English. We bought the 40 acres where the buildings now stand when we married. There was a 12 by 12 foot log house on the forty, but no other buildings when we moved there the spring of 1900.

We built a log barn for Flora and Nig, our first two horses, the two cows, and the two calves that we bought when we got married. In the fall of 1900 we moved the 12 by 16 foot sawn lumber house that was on the NE corner of Dad's first 40 acres. It became what is now the dining room of our house. The L.P. Anderson family had lived in the house—nine children and two adults. The men slept in the unheated attic and got into it with an outside ladder.

We bought the Leffler forty between our other two forties in 1901. It had a set of buildings on the hill west of Fox Lake. *[The Wm. Leffler building site and road to it can be seen from the soil color on the 1940 aerial photographs.]* On 9 February 1901 our daugher, Hilma, was born. *[Hilma, Edwin, and Verner, their first three children, were born in the old log house. Mrs. Martin Carlson neé Pearson, a.k.a. Pierson or Person, was the community midwife who assisted with bringing Amanda's and Frank's first six children into the world.]*

We got the well made in the spring of 1902. Before that I carried drinking water from Gubbe Ahl's place. *[The Svan Ahl family's farm was immediately northwest of Enfield village nearly a half-mile from Frank's and Amanda's farmstead. It is now the Harold and Charlotte Langanki farm.]* Edwin Theodore was born on 10 September 1902. Verner Fredolf was born on 4 February 1904. That summer we added the sitting room and bedroom and tore down the log house. The windmill was put up in 1905.

On 23 May 1906 the twins, Martin Clarence and Authur Lawrence were born. That fall we bought another 40 acres just northwest of the home place.

The buildings were built and rebuilt as needed. We built the cow barn and tore down the log barn in 1907. In the summer of 1910 we added the kitchen, bathroom, pantry, and back porch to the house. Alvin Richard was born 2 May 1911. We bought the 80 acres just north of the home place in Section 14 from *[Nils]* Hokanson and sold the forty we had bought in 1906. The old wood silo was built in 1913. The horse barn was built in spring of 1914 and the present chicken house was built in 1915. We added the front porch and two bedrooms and storage room above it in the summer of 1916. Helen Pauline was born on 29 June 1917.

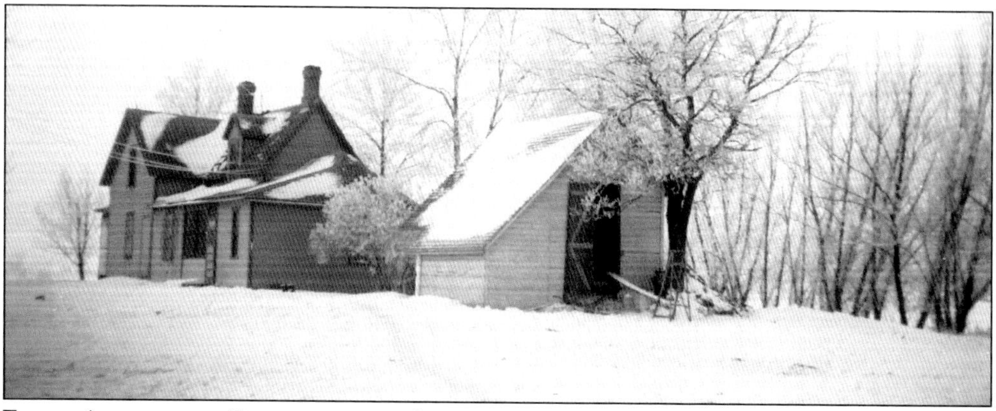

Frank Abrahamson Farmhouse and Icehouse. From Amanda's diary: "We had the upstairs bedrooms plastered in the spring of 1918 and also put in running water in the bathroom and a *[wood-fired]* boiler and hot-water central heating that summer. The 32-Volt Delco electric light system with a wind generator was added in 1920. *[A carbide gas light system had been installed in the house a few years earlier.]* The granary was built in 1917 and the pig house in 1919. We also built the ice house just north of the house; it had the room for the cream separator, the scales, and the other milk equipment.

Kenneth Raymond was born 21 January 1921. The milk house and cement cooling tank were made that fall. The machine shed and cement silo were built in the summer of 1922. Glenn Everett was born on 22 June 1923. The addition on the east side of the cow barn, for youngstock, a feed room and feed grinder, was added in 1925. We had the house insulated and siding put on in 1943. In the spring of 1944 we got on the REA *[Rural Electrification Administration]* electricity. In 1944 we moved to the forty in Section 22 that we had bought in 1915 from Martin Carlson. The old log house on that place had been torn down in 1941 when our present little house was built. The farm was rented to *[their son]* Martin for three years. We had our farm auction on 25 November 1947 and Ed *[their eldest son, who had bought the farm]* moved there on 18 January 1948."

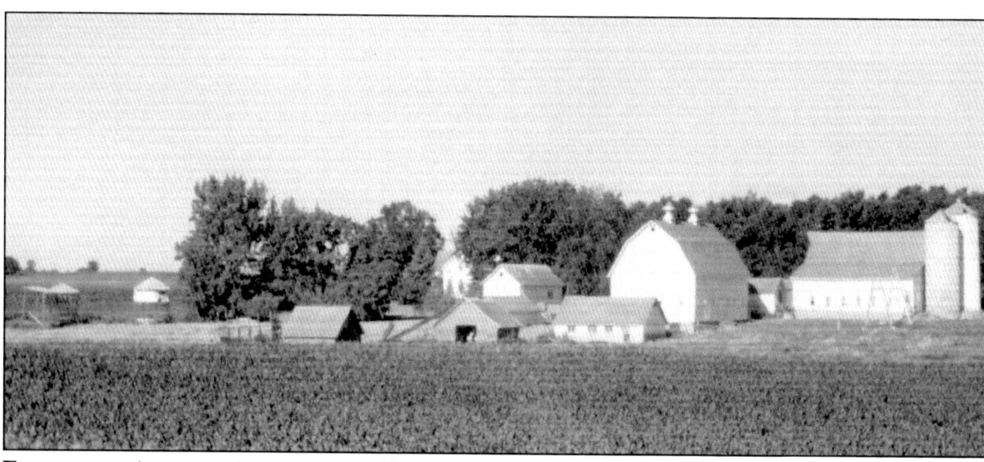

Frank and Amanda Abrahamson Farmstead. Enfield farmers, like farmers everywhere, had to sustain themselves and their animals and had to produce something that would provide cash income. Cash was needed for the staples of everyday life, for buildings, for livestock and machines, and for school expenses. Swedish families who immigrated to Minnesota tended to send their children to high school and college at least a generation earlier than did their siblings who remained in Sweden. The need for cash to pay the annual real estate taxes caused stress in many a pioneer farm household and the bank failures of the 1930s were devastating.

Frank and Amanda Abrahamson's Salebill, November 1947. Everyone in the family worked, children included. A careful search through the photograph collections of five Enfield families and through the relevant collections of the Wright County and State of Minnesota Historical Societies produced hundreds of photographs of men doing this thing or that—usually with either horses or machines—but virtually none of farm women or children at work. There are photographs of male children doing farm work—the context suggesting that it was the first time that they did something—and of children with their 4-H animals or projects.

Auction

Complete dispersal sale of all property on the Abrahamson farm, located 8 miles W. of Monticello on highway No. 152 to Enfield and then ½ mile N.

TUESDAY, NOVEMBER 25, 10:30 a.m.

Lunch—Silver Creek Lutheran Ladies' Aid

A herd of 35 head of Outstanding HOLSTEIN CATTLE—All T. B. and Bang's Tested

23 cows, 9 heifers. Papers furnished on all P. B's.

MACHINERY—Model B JOHN DEERE TRACTOR on rubber. Starter, lights, power lift. This tractor like new. 1946 Model. Power-lift cult. for same. No. 52 JD tractor plow; No. 5 JD trailer mower, 7 ft., used 1 season; McCDrg. power corn binder; 14-inch IHC ensilage cutter; McCDrg. side rake; JD hay loader used one week; 7 ft. McCDrg. grain binder; 8-ft. McCDrg. grain drill with grass seed attach.; JD 999 corn planter; Rubber tired trailer wagon with rack; 2 three-quarter size wagon running gears; hay rack; wagon box; 5 ft. McDrg. mower; 2-sec. spring tooth harrow; 3-sec. wood lever harrow; potato digger, corn sheller, 2 sets heavy work harness, 6 horse collars; 8-ft. field packer; mounted grindstone; new pump jack and ¾ hp motor; electric fencer; 2 six-ft. water tanks; 1 weeder; fanning mill; six-shovel cult.; oil burning brooder stove; forks, shovels, etc.

ONE 1946 CHEV. ½ TON PICKUP TRUCK, 4-speed trans., 6.50 six-ply tires, grain box for same.

SMALL LINE OF HOUSEHOLD FURNITURE.

DAIRY EQUIPMENT—1 DeLaval Milking Machine, complete with electric motor and pipeline to milk 27 cows. This machine has two single unit Surge pails. 13 ten-gallon milk cans, pails and other dairy equipment.

HAY & FEED—1200 bu. yellow corn in cribs; 300 bu. Ajax oats from certified seed; 300 bu. Marion oats; 600 bu. Vicland oats; 500 bu. succotash, oats and wheat; 200 bales second crop alfalfa; 35 tons of alfalfa and other tame hay in barn to be completely baled by day of sale; 2 stacks of alfalfa and timothy hay; 35 feet good corn ensilage in 13 foot silo.

USUAL AUCTION TERMS

FRANK ABRAHAMSON, Owner

Odegard & Nordwall, Auctioneers

Wright County State Bank, Clerk

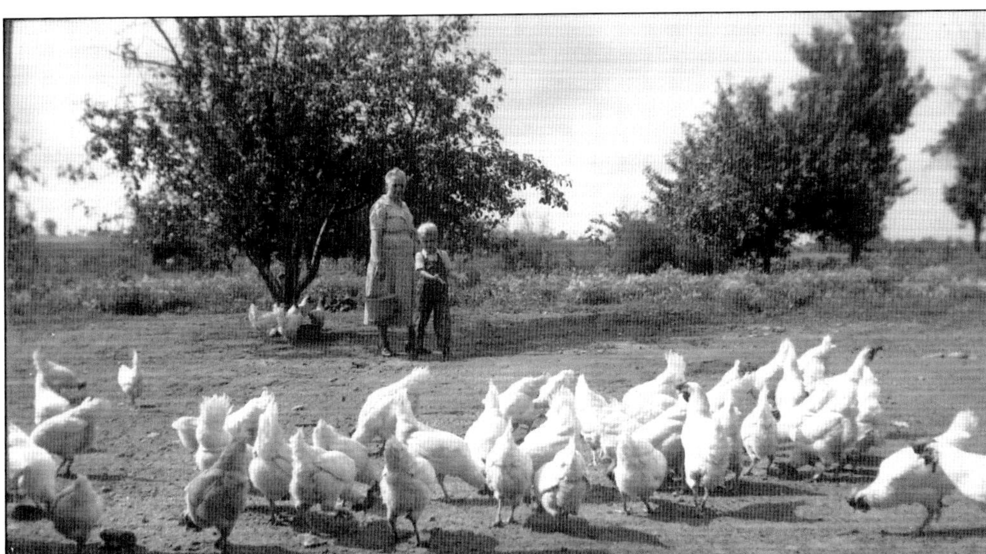

Amanda Abrahamson and Her Chickens, 1939. Generally, tending horses and hogs was men's work, tending chickens was often women's work with help from the kids, and, while everyone in the family often helped with milking, cattle husbandry was in the male domain.

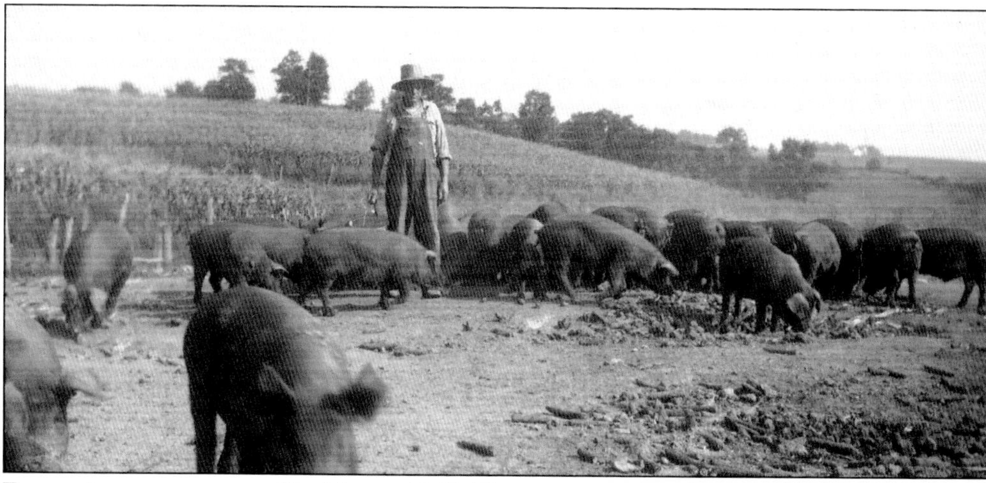

Frank Abrahamson and His Hogs, 1945. There are very few photographs documenting the day-to-day and season-to-season work of the farm women. The photographs of housewives' work reproduced here are from how-to brochures put out by the agricultural extension services.

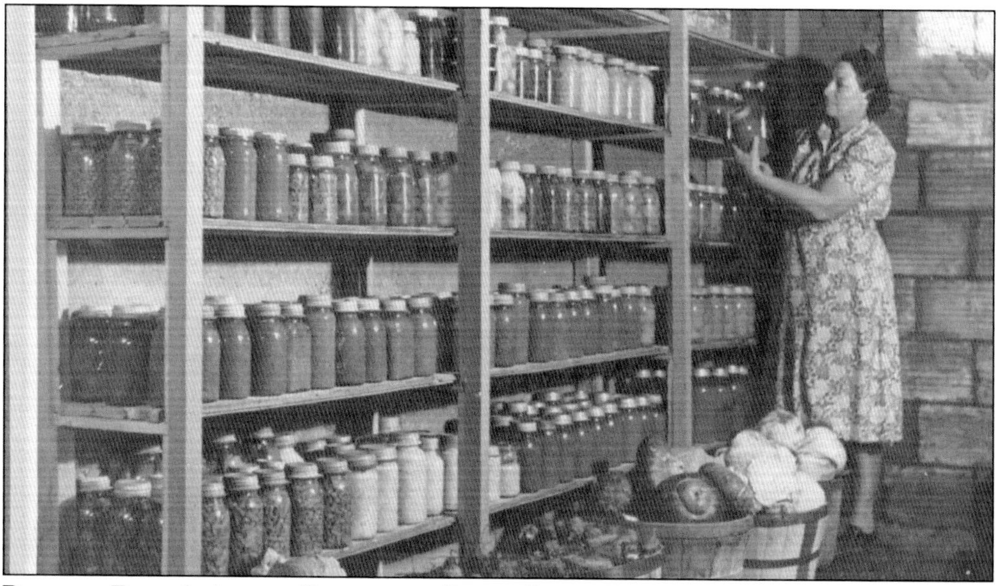

Part of a Family's Annual Canned and Cellar Goods. Farm women bore and took care of the children, maintained the house, sewed much of the family's clothing, did the cooking and baking, usually were in charge of the garden, and put up the food that would sustain the family through the winter. Putting up food meant preparing squash, apples, and root crops for storage, canning vegetables and fruits, and canning or otherwise curing meat. Eggs were commonly bartered for groceries that had to be bought—coffee, salt, sugar, flour, spices, and other staples—but most of the food was grown or raised on the farm. Amanda Abrahamson's diary records: "There was always a problem with fresh meat in the summer. Enfield stores did not sell fresh meat, only sausage and cheese that kept without refrigeration. Sometime the butcher in Monticello *[Fred Hitter, who also had land in the Enfield community]* would come around a couple of times a week, but was not too dependable. We ate a lot of chicken in the summer. We also had veal as it could be kept in the ice house for ten days or so. Calves were butchered when they were eight or ten weeks old."

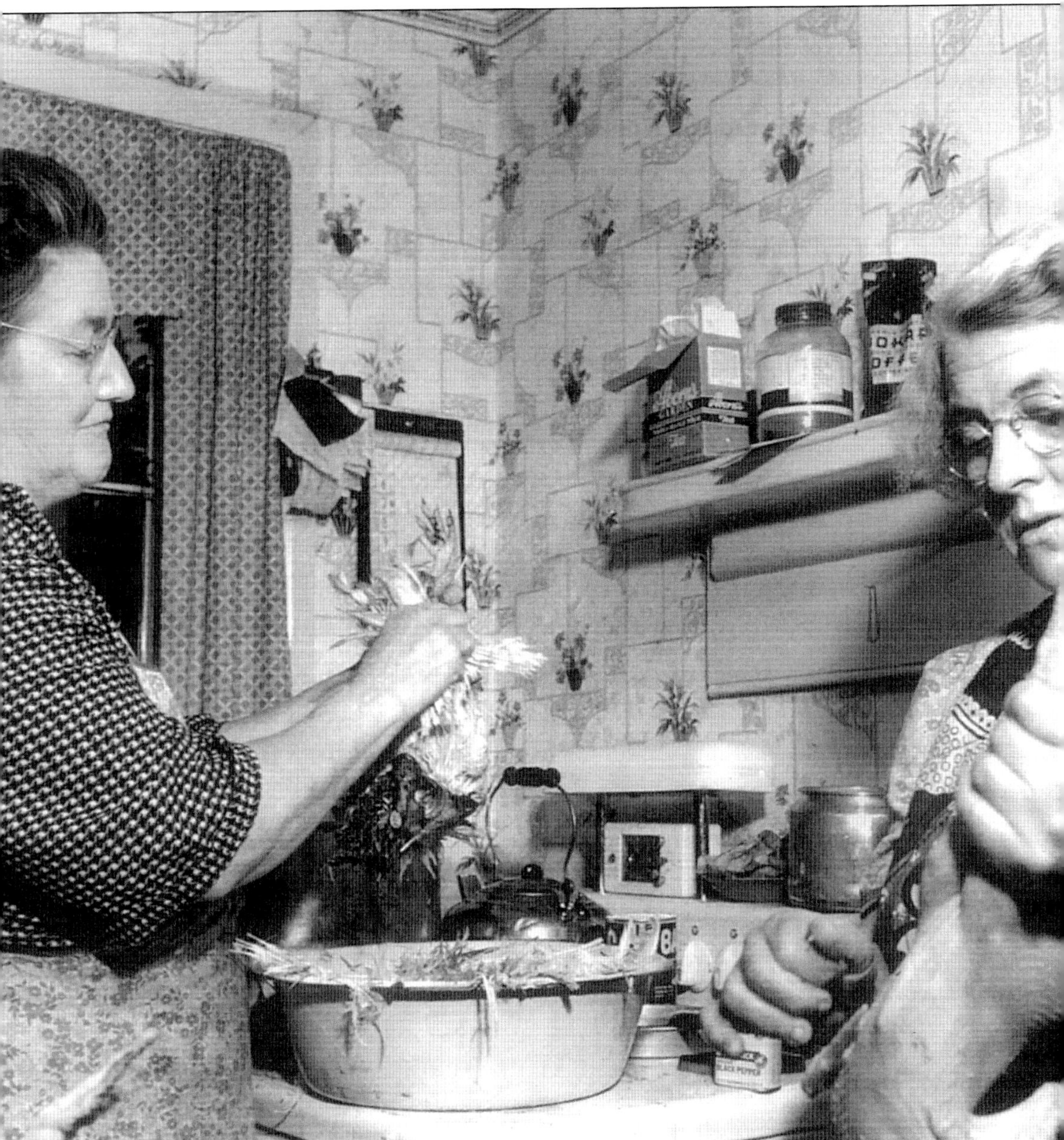

Farm Women Plucking Chickens, a Regular Job. Farm women and the children were often responsible for doing the chores. Doing the chores meant chopping kindling and kitchen stove wood, bringing in wood for heating stoves, pumping and carrying water, taking care of chicks and chickens, picking eggs, sometimes taking care of hogs, and the other routine farmstead little jobs. The extent to which the family women were routinely involved with the heavy work, raising crops and the large-animal husbandry, varied a good deal from family to family.

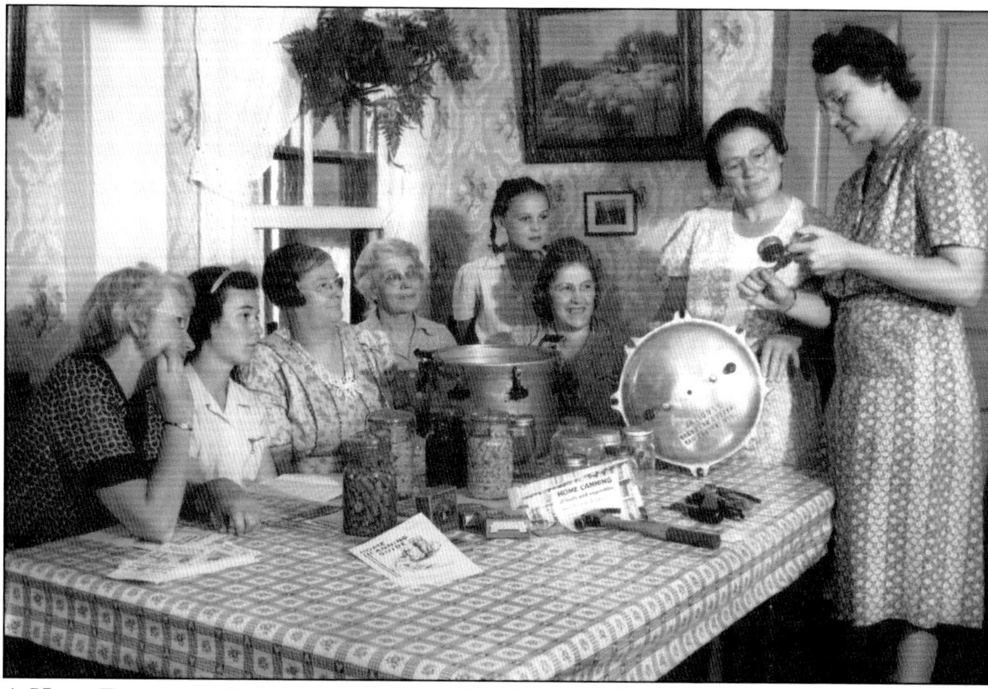

A Home Extension Agent Introducing The Pressure Cooker.

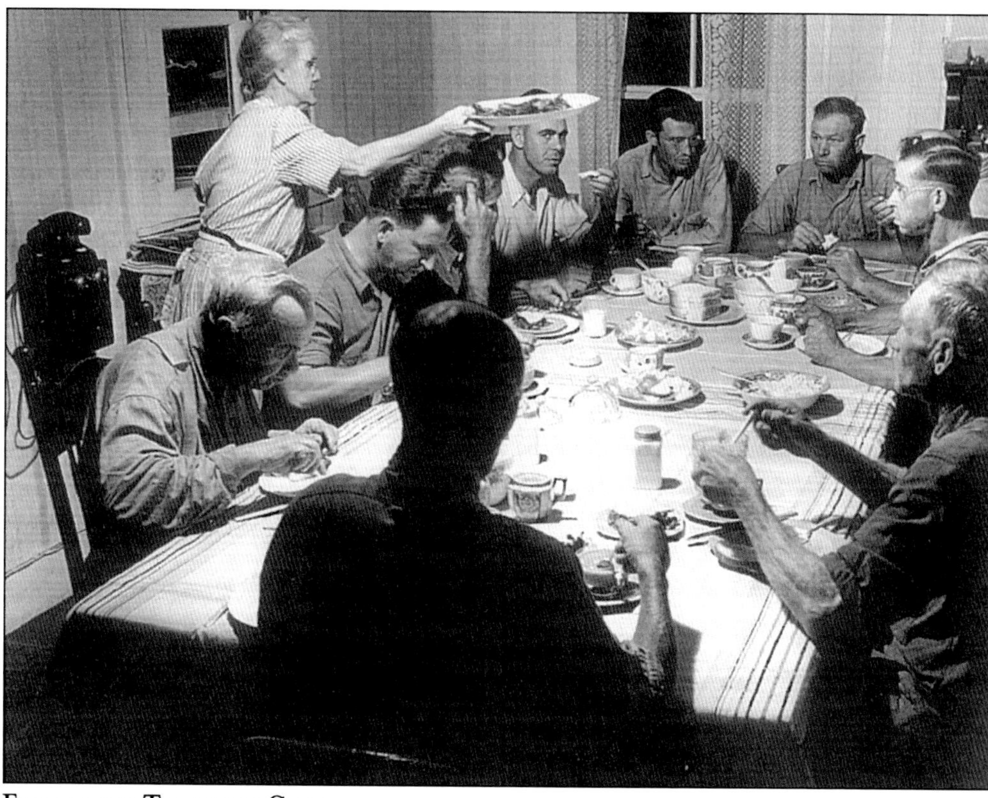

Feeding the Threshing Crew.

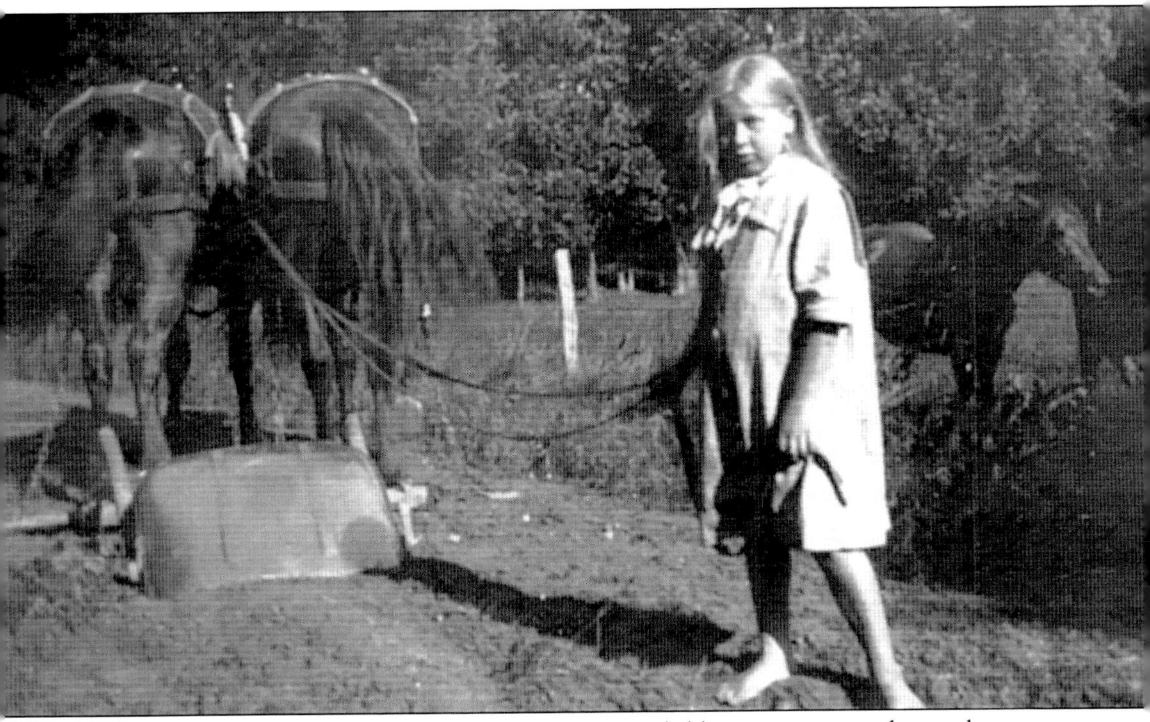

Evelyn Trogen Helping with the Fresno, c. 1912. Children were expected to work as soon as they were old enough. Amanda Abrahamson's diary records: "We *[the children]* had to learn to milk cows when we were six or seven years old. My folks had one cow by the name of Fanny who was very gentle and an easy milker. At first it was fun, but after learning how, we found that we couldn't quit, but had to help each night and morning. In the end, each of us *[children]* had four to six cows to milk. We also had to help feed the cows, go in for breakfast, clean up, and then go to school. We also had chores to do after school—carry in straw for bedding for the cows and horses, help feed them silage, and then it would be supper time. Milking time came later as did bedding the cows down with straw and feeding them hay from the mow. It was usually around eight or so before we were done with separating the milk and cleaning up the pails. I don't remember studying at night while in grade or high school. When we started to help in the fields, it was first to pick weeds in the potatoes and the corn. Ed and I had to cultivate, too, with a one-horse cultivator—one driving the horse and the other handling the cultivator. It took a long time to finish a field."

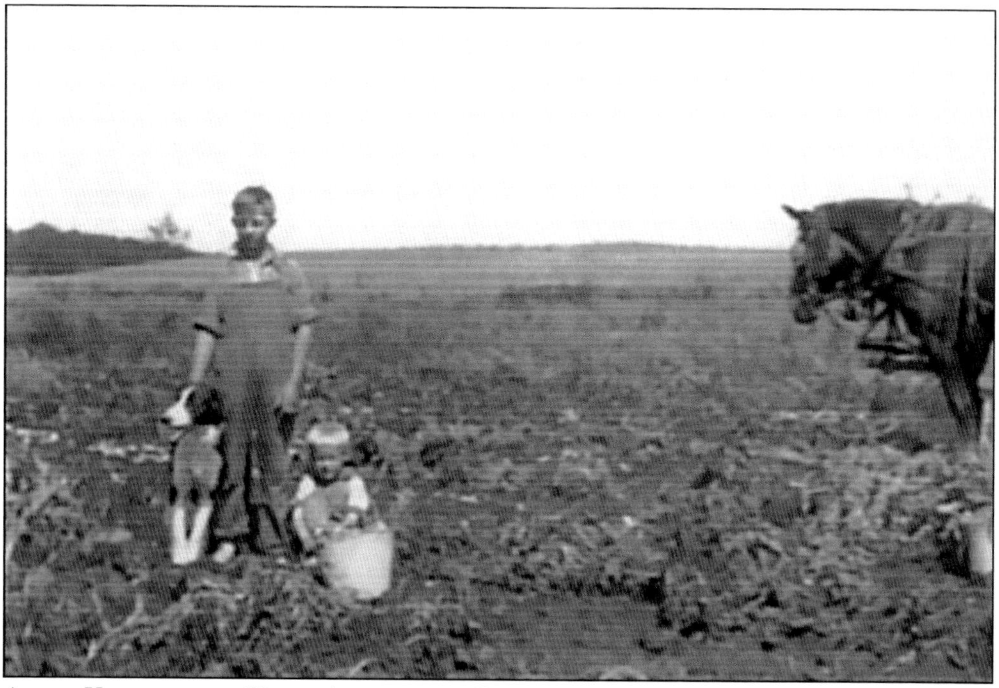

ALVIN, KENNETH, AND HELEN ABRAHAMSON PICKING POTATOES, 1927.

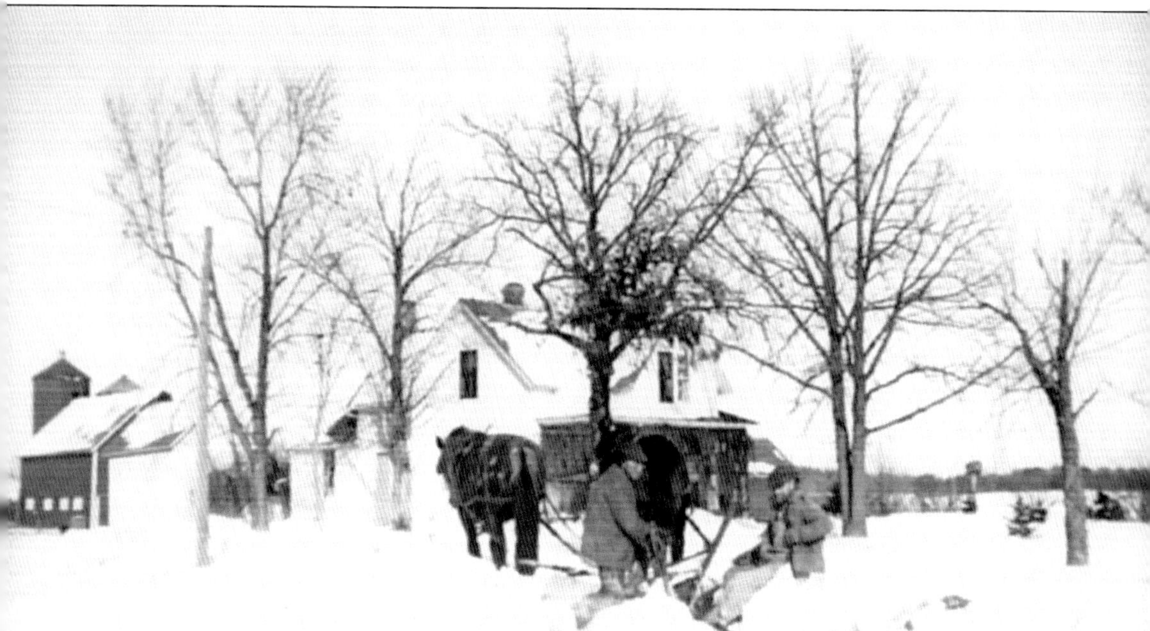

FRANK AND MARTY ABRAHAMSON CLEARING SNOW WITH A FRESNO, 1943.

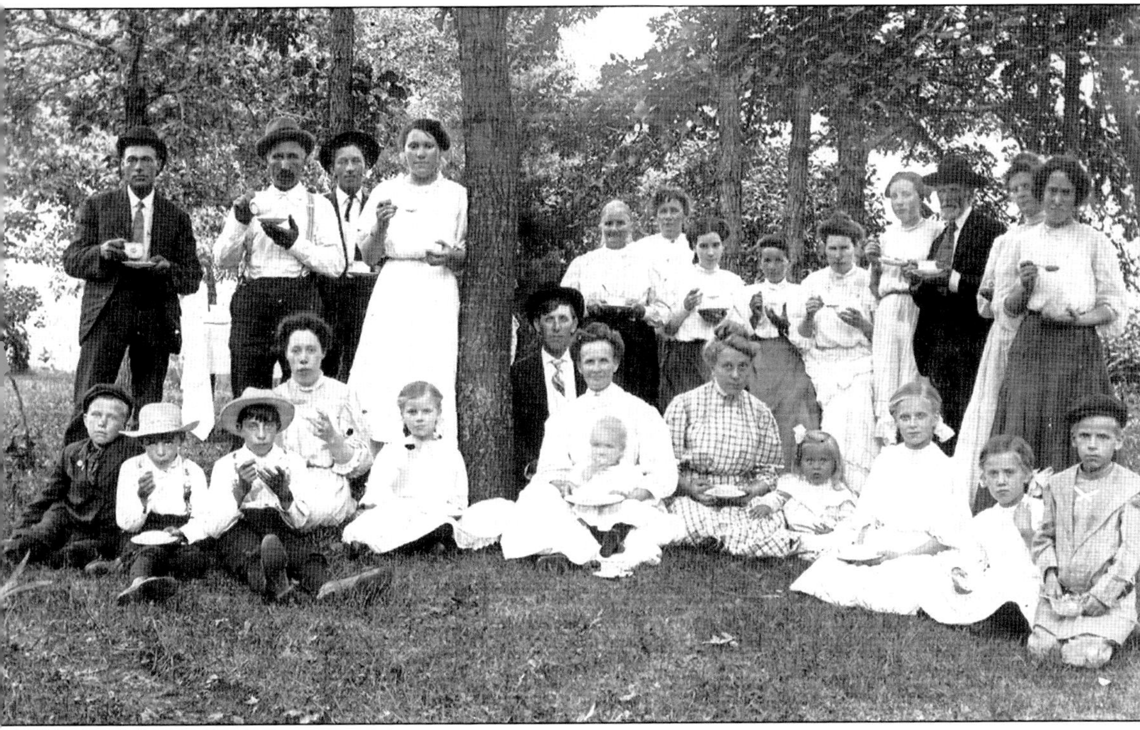

Chunking Stove Wood, a Regular Fall Job.

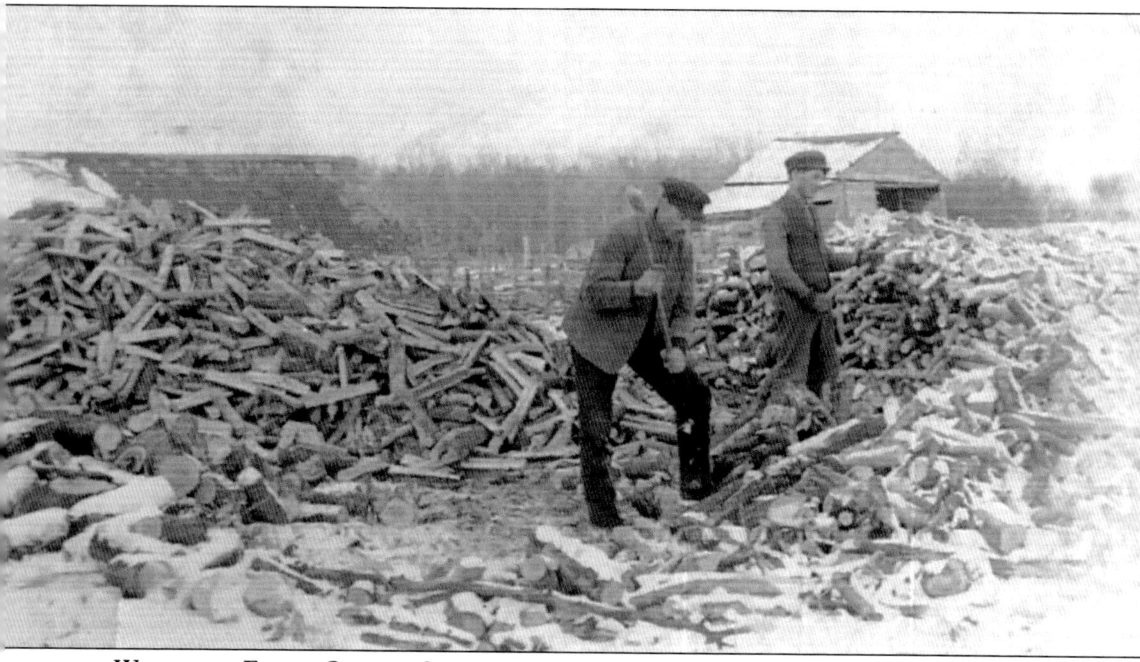

Willy and Frank Oswald Splitting Wood, 1908. Plowing was the first step in growing crops. Land was ploughed in either fall or spring. Plows evolved from single-bottom walking plows, pulled by one or two horses, to sulky and gang plows pulled by two or more horses. The fields were then disked and harrowed (a.k.a. dragged) before crops were planted. Except for the occasional planting of Rye or of Winter Wheat, all planting and sowing was done in the spring—small grains as soon as the fields were dry enough to work, usually by mid-April. Corn, and later Soybeans, were not planted until mid-May because of the likelihood of killing frost.

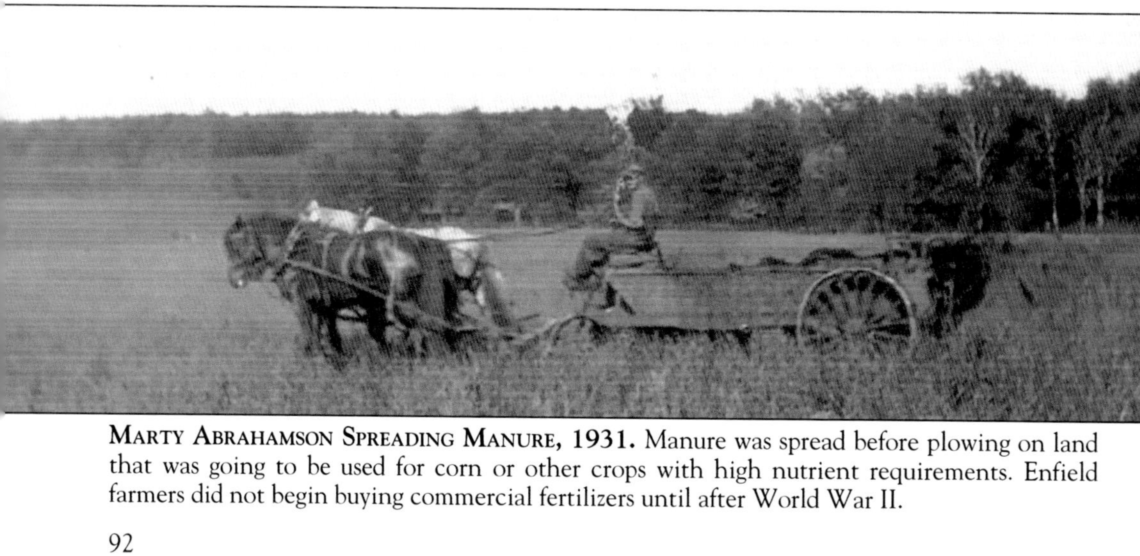

Marty Abrahamson Spreading Manure, 1931. Manure was spread before plowing on land that was going to be used for corn or other crops with high nutrient requirements. Enfield farmers did not begin buying commercial fertilizers until after World War II.

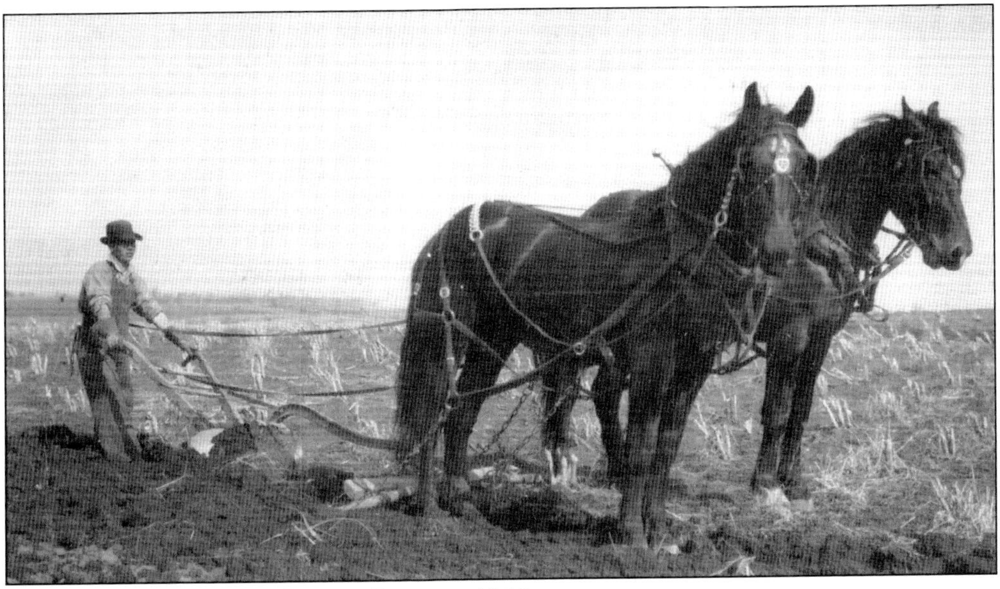

PETE WESTMAN WITH A WALKING PLOW, C. 1910.

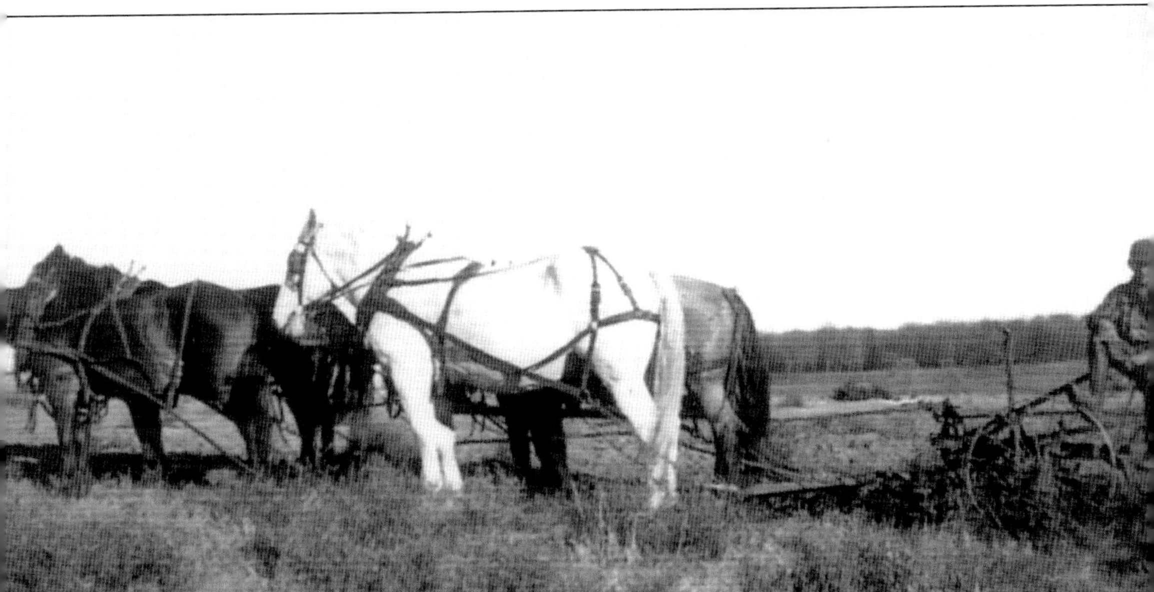

FRANK ABRAHAMSON WITH TWO-BOTTOM GANG PLOW, 1934.

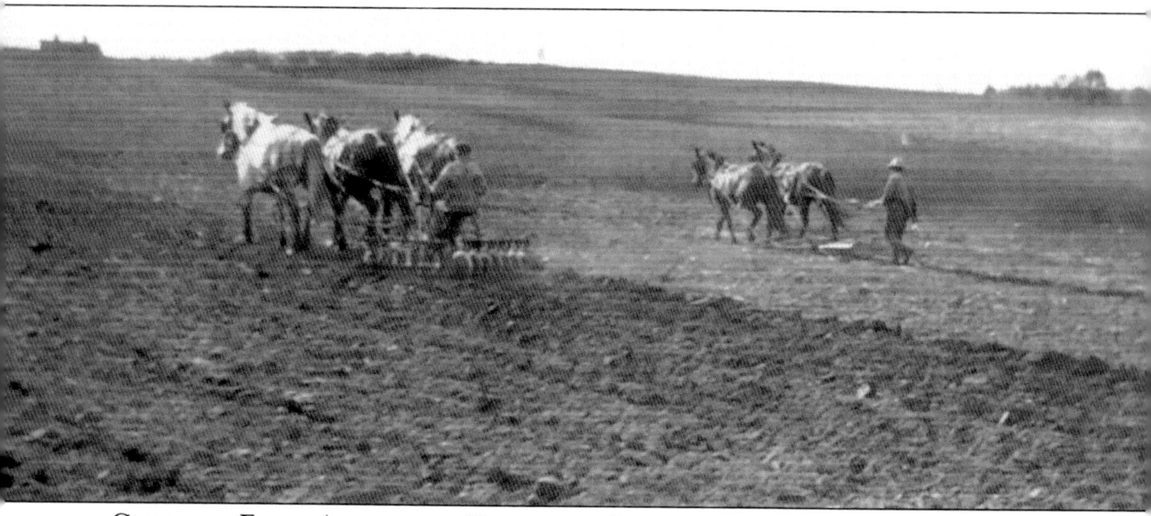

GLENN AND FRANK ABRAHAMSON DISKING AND PLOWING, 1931.

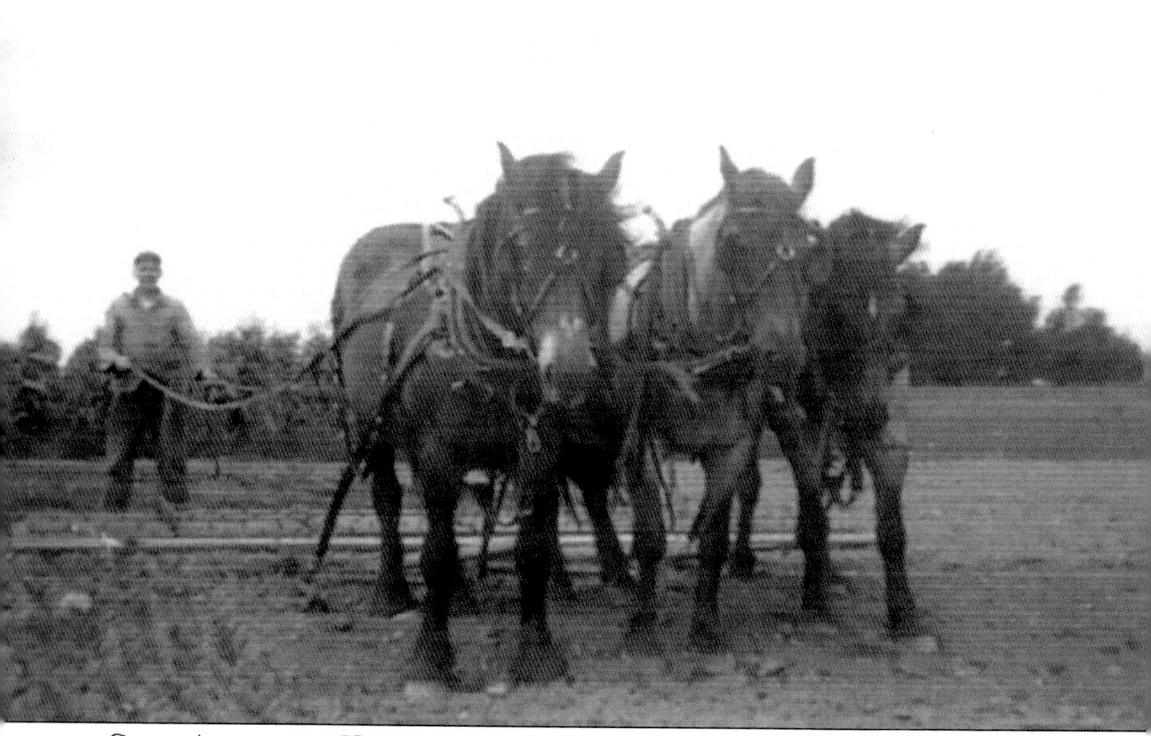

GLENN ABRAHAMSON HARROWING, THE LAST STEP BEFORE PLANTING. Horses were regarded as members of the family and many a horse led an active life of 20 or more years. Family photo albums and memoirs recorded the genealogy, births, and deaths of the family's horses. These notes often record individual horse's personalities: "Flora was a gentle horse, Mom's favorite; Fly was a good, gentle horse; Fox could not be trusted—he could open the barn doors and take off his halter . . . ."

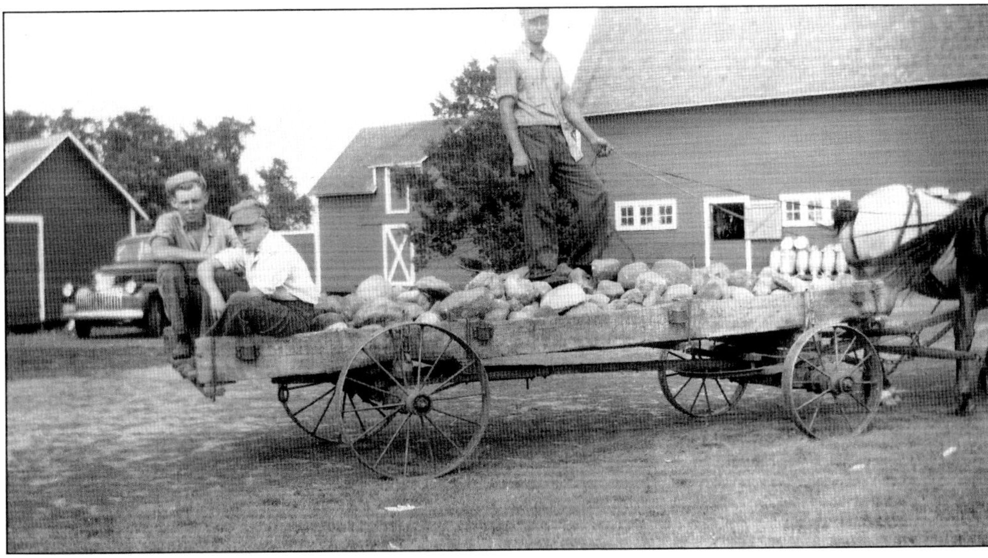

BILL AND WALLY BERG PICKING ROCKS, 1943.

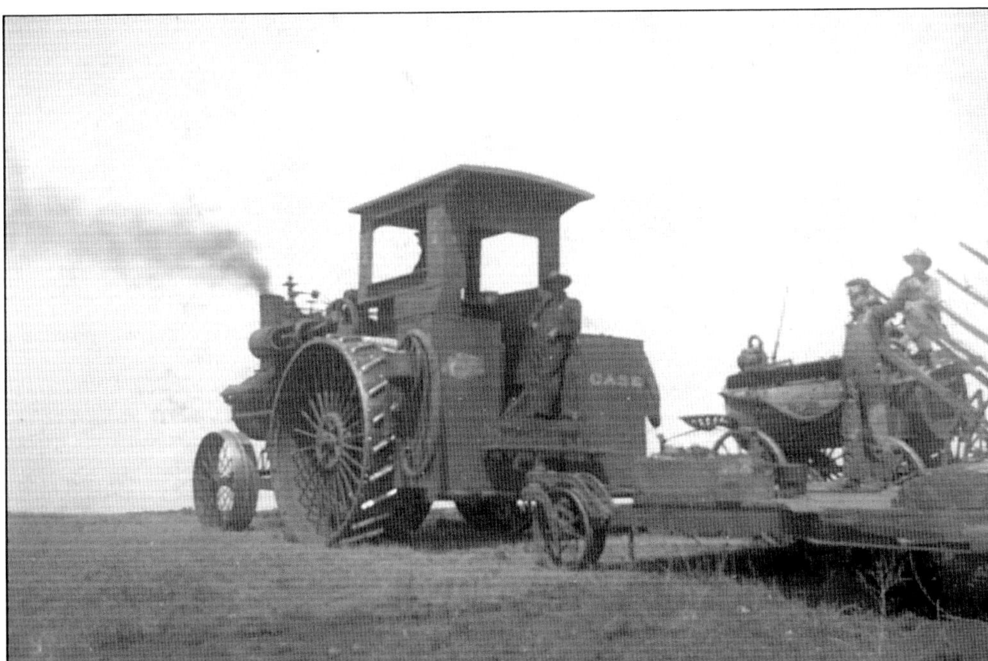

AN EARLY CASE STEAM TRACTOR, C. 1910. The transition from horses to tractors was gradual. The first tractors appeared on Enfield farms in the early 1900s. The earliest were large unwieldly devices that were not much used for pulling machines and were primarily used on the belt. Some early tractors made by Case, Rumley, and other makers had wood or coal-fired steam engines. Draft horses were in regular use in the community through the 1940s. Many farmers kept a team of horses well into the 1950s, in part for sentimental reasons, but also to use when there was too much snow for the motor vehicles or when it was so cold that engines could not be started.

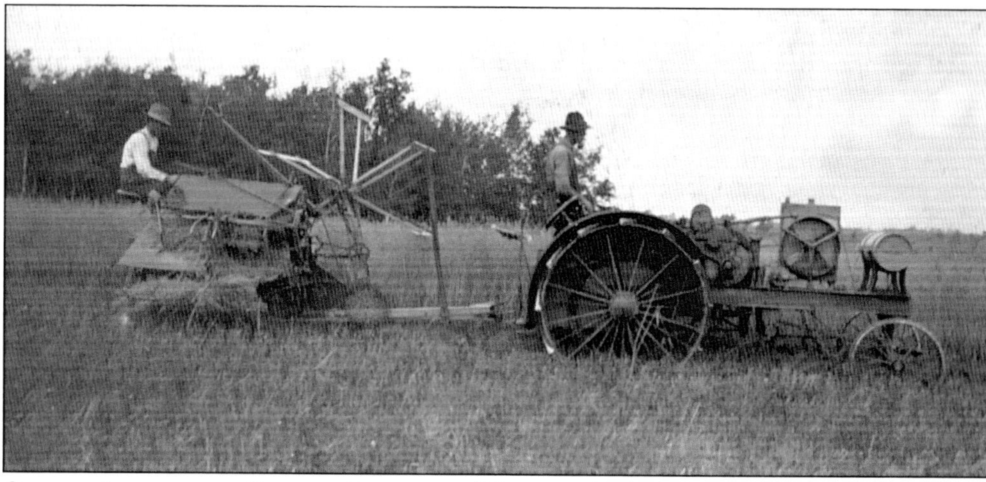

Charlie Abrahamson Cutting Grain with Waterloo Boy Tractor, 1916. Farm machinery changed little during the first few decades of the tractor era. The pole or tongue of the wagon, or the disk, or the grain binder was simply cut off and a tractor hitch added to replace the single or double-trees to which the harnesses were connected. Machinery specifically designed for tractors began to be introduced in the late 1930s, but was not in common use until well after World War II.

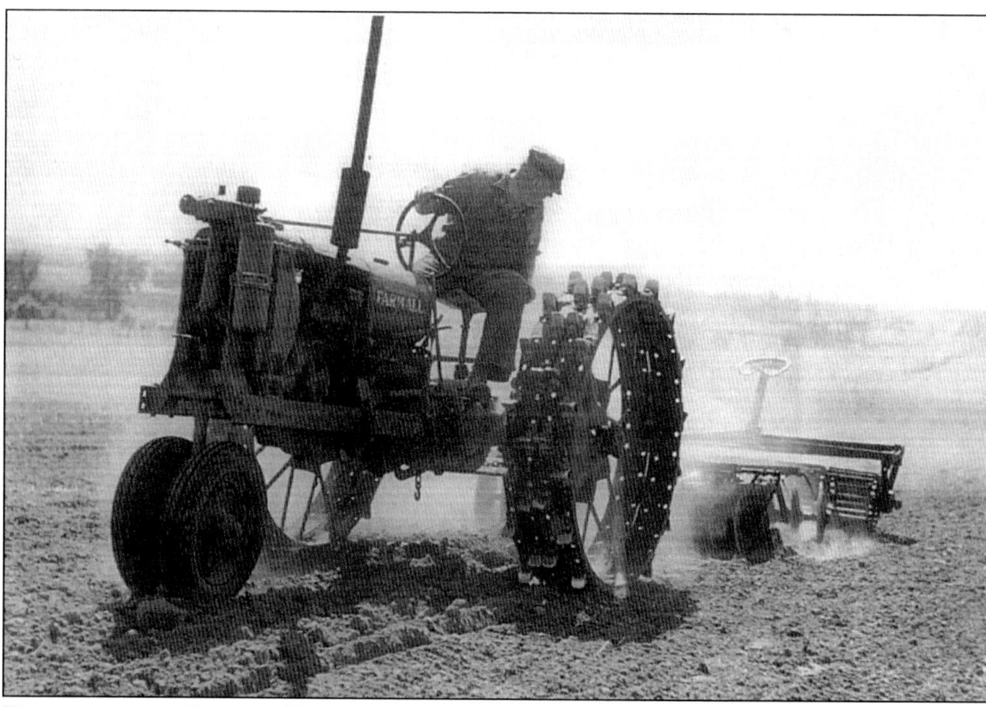

Disking with a Farmall F-14. Case, Ford, John Deere, International Harvester, and other manufacturers soon introduced relatively small and mobile tractors. Each farmer had his preference—some used only Case tractors, some only John Deere and so forth. The International Harvester Farmall-F series was particularly popular. The F-12 or F-14 pulled one-bottom plows (two-bottom plows in light soil). The F-20 pulled two 14 or 16-inch plows. Early models had steel wheels with lugs—later they were mounted on rubber.

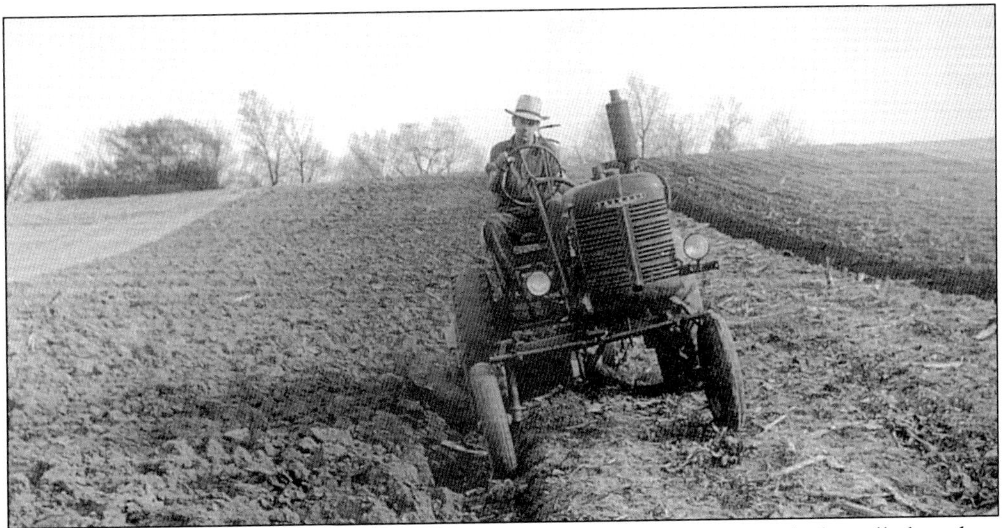

PLOWING WITH A FARMALL-A. The late 1930s brought the first of what might be called modern tractors from each of the major farm machinery companies. The International Harvester Farmall A, B, H, and M series was very successful. These tractors were easy to drive, very maneuverable, and had relatively comfortable seats. Like the comparable models made by Case, John Deere, and Ford, these tractors all had rubber tires and also had a relatively high-speed road gear. They all had power take-offs and soon the H and the M came equipped with hydraulic pumps—which enabled power-operated plows, cultivators, disks, and other machinery. The days of using brute force to handle farm machinery and of the bull wheel that supplied motive power to grain-binders and corn-binders was at an end.

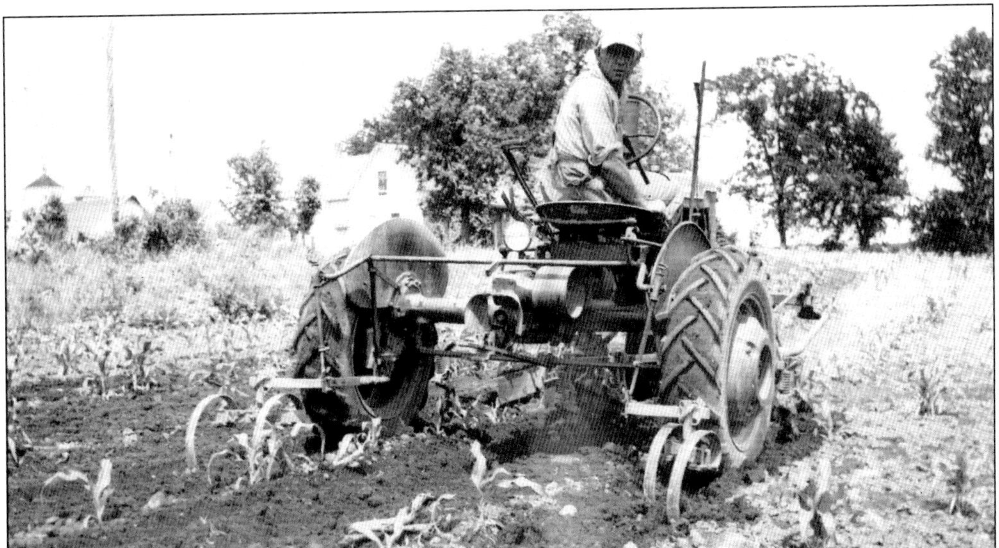

ED ABRAHAMSON CULTIVATING CORN WITH A FARMALL-B, 1948. The Farmall-B was a wonderful little tractor and many are yet in use in the 21st century. It was inexpensive, small, very easy to handle, reliable, and found much use in light jobs. The Farmall-A was essentially the same as the Farmall-B, but it had widely-spaced front wheels and was built on a narrower frame. The Farmall-B usually pulled a one-bottom 16-inch plow, the Farmall-H pulled two 14-inch plows, and the Farmall-M usually pulled three 14-inch bottom plows.

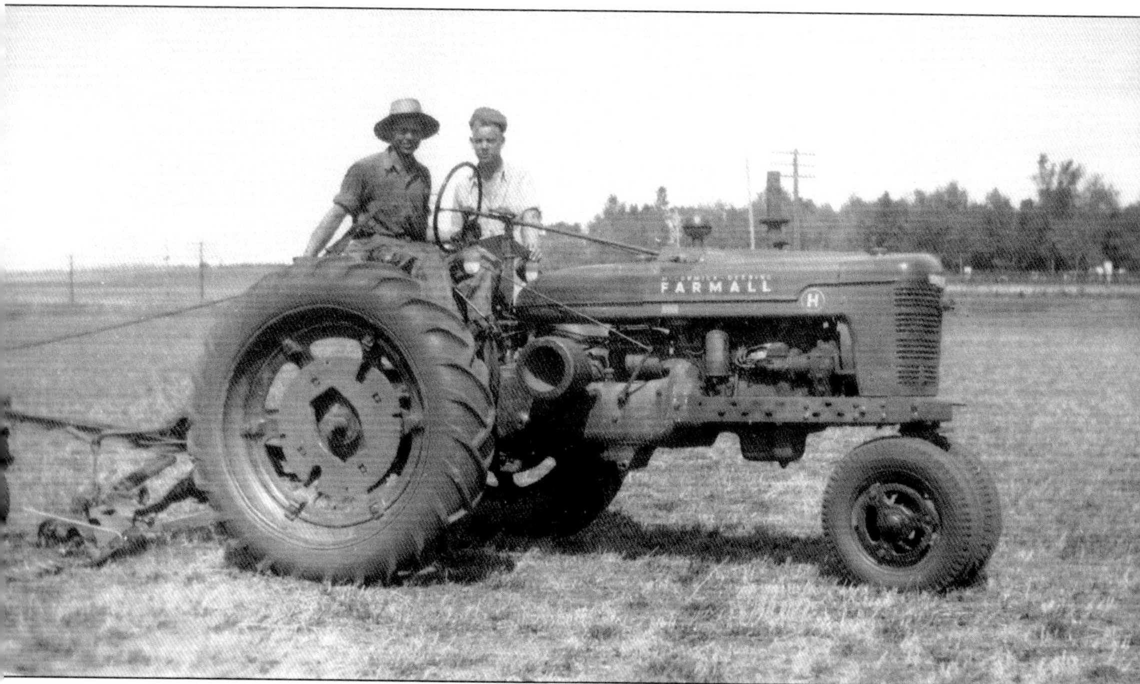

Bill Berg and his Farmall-H with Mounted Hay Mower, 1948. Hay was the staple everyday feed for both cattle and horses—much as bread was a staple food for the family. Canary grass, perhaps with a bit of timothy for garnish and sweet clover for flavor, was the usual winter horse hay. Cattle were fed with hay with the highest nutrient levels available; red clover or, more commonly, alfalfa often mixed with some timothy. Clover or alfalfa was planted at the same time as oats. The clover or alfalfa would grow after the oats were harvested and then either be plowed down in the fall as green manure or let stand as a hay field for a few years.

Opposite, Top: **Cutting Hay with a Scythe, c. 1890.** The technology for putting up hay changed enormously in the roughly 100 years from the homestead days to the 1950s. In the beginning hay, often native marsh grass, was cut with a scythe, collected with wooden rakes, and stacked either in the field or near the farm buildings.

Opposite, Bottom: **Collecting Hay with Wooden Rake, c. 1890.**

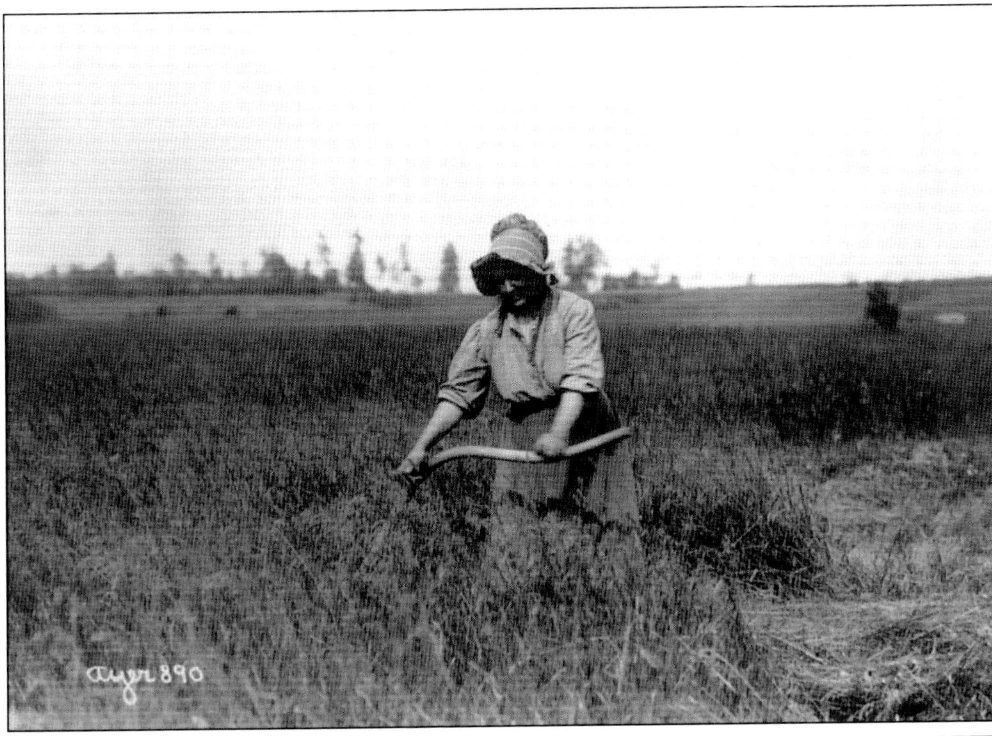
Ayer 890

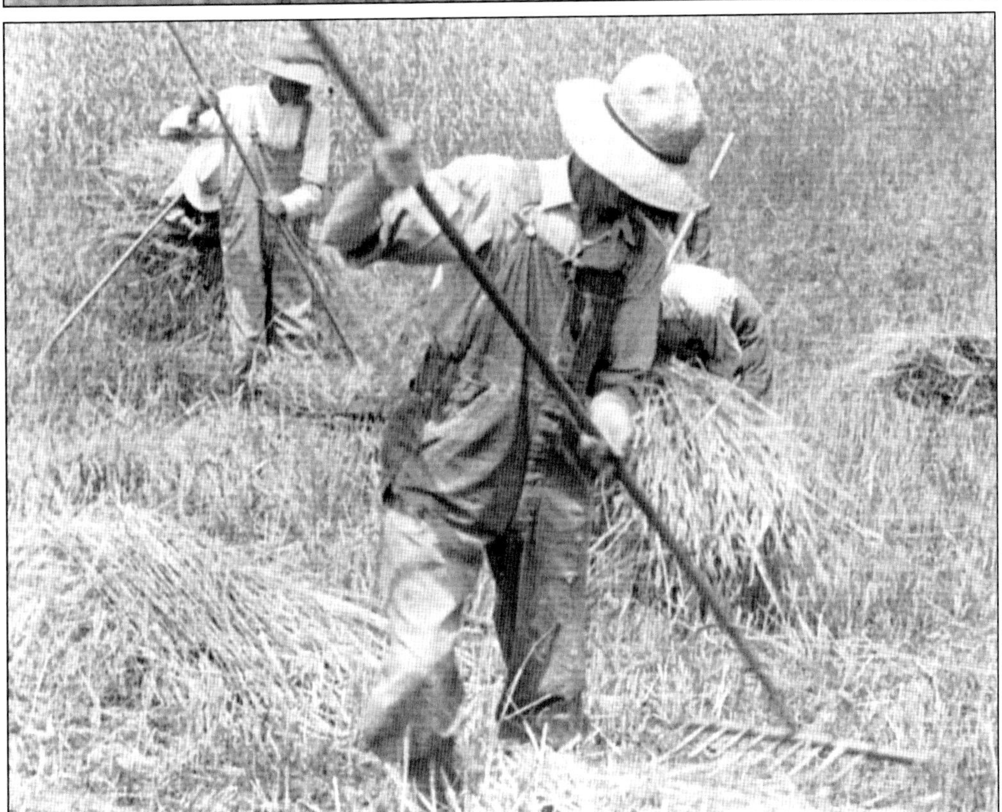

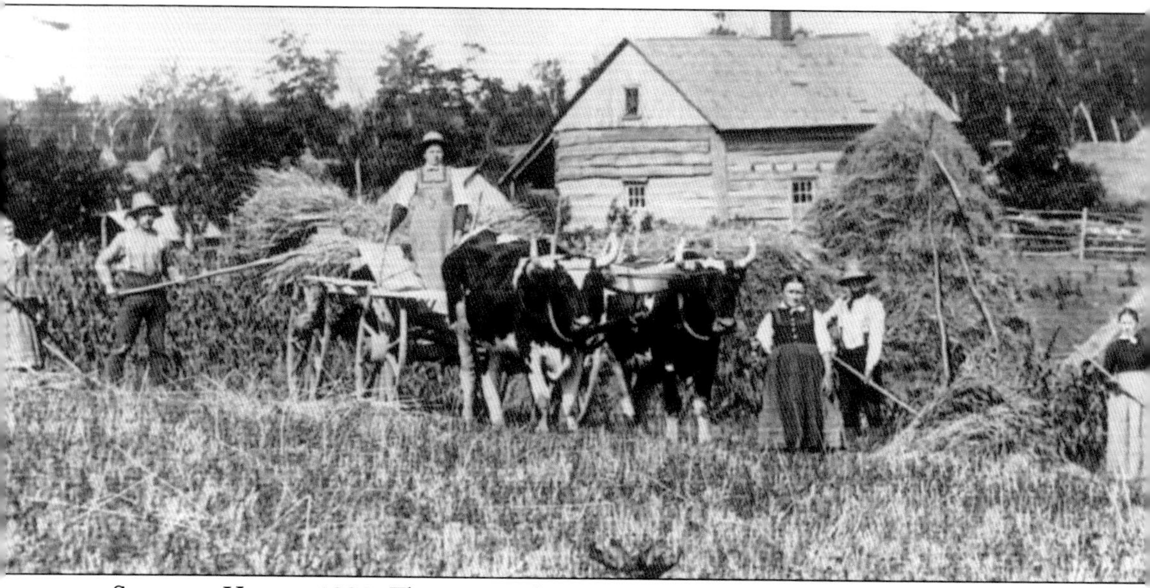

Stacking Hay, c. 1890. The next evolution was the introduction of hay mowers, with four or five-foot cutting bars. The hay was then collected with dump rakes. The hay was then left in the field to dry for a couple of days, depending on the availability of help and the weather, then collected into shocks in the field or gathered and stacked either at field's edge or near the barns.

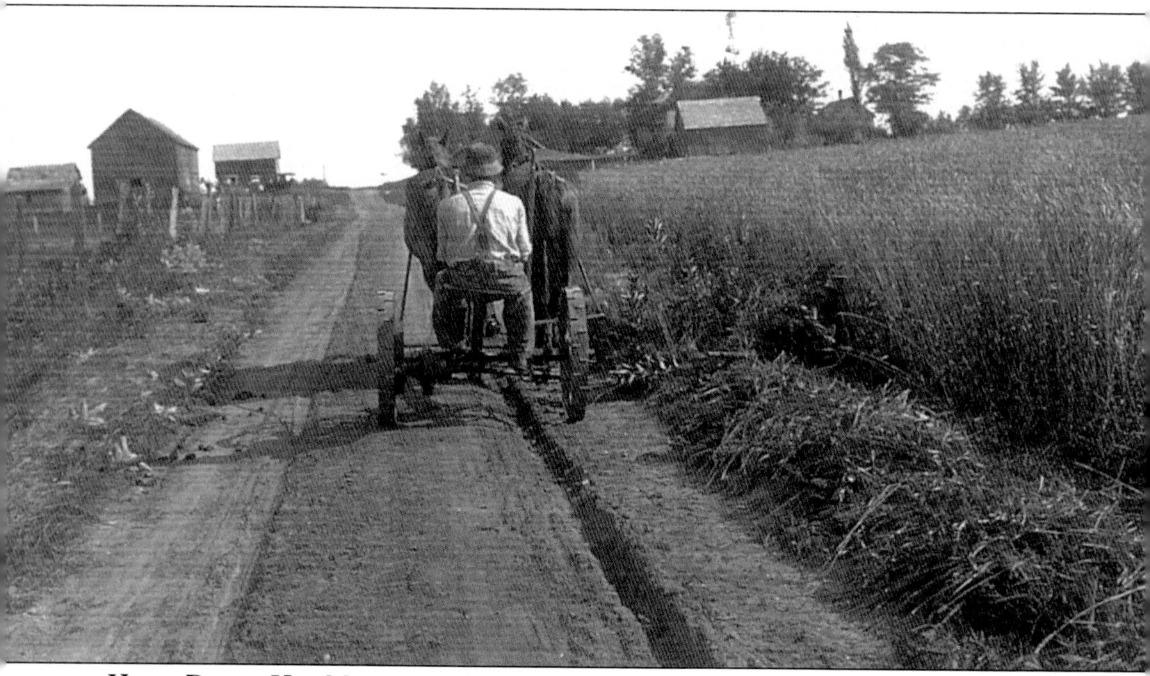

Horse-Drawn Hay Mower, c. 1910.

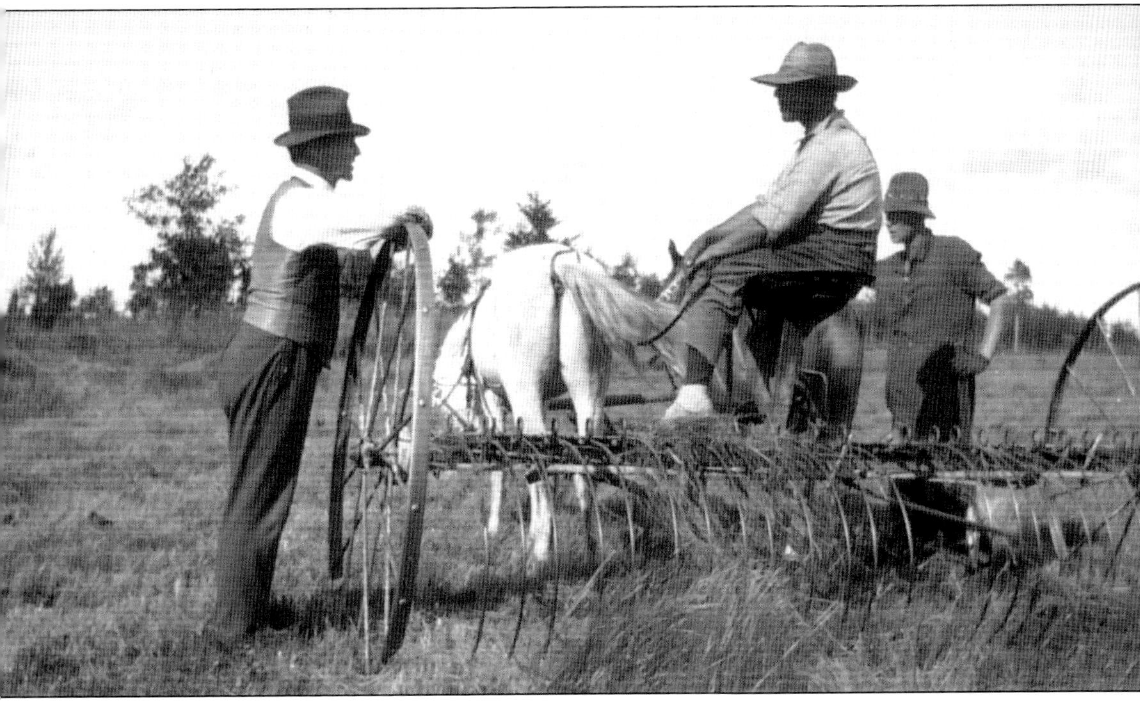

DUMP RAKE, C. 1910.

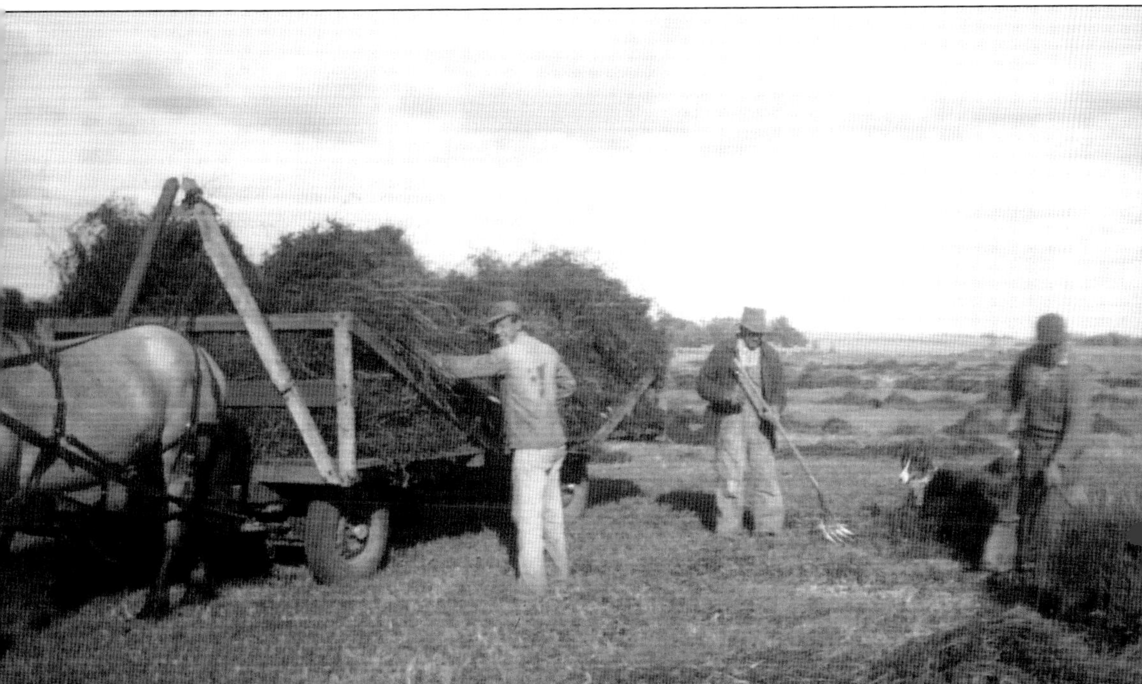

FRANK ABRAHAMSON FAMILY, HAULING HAY.

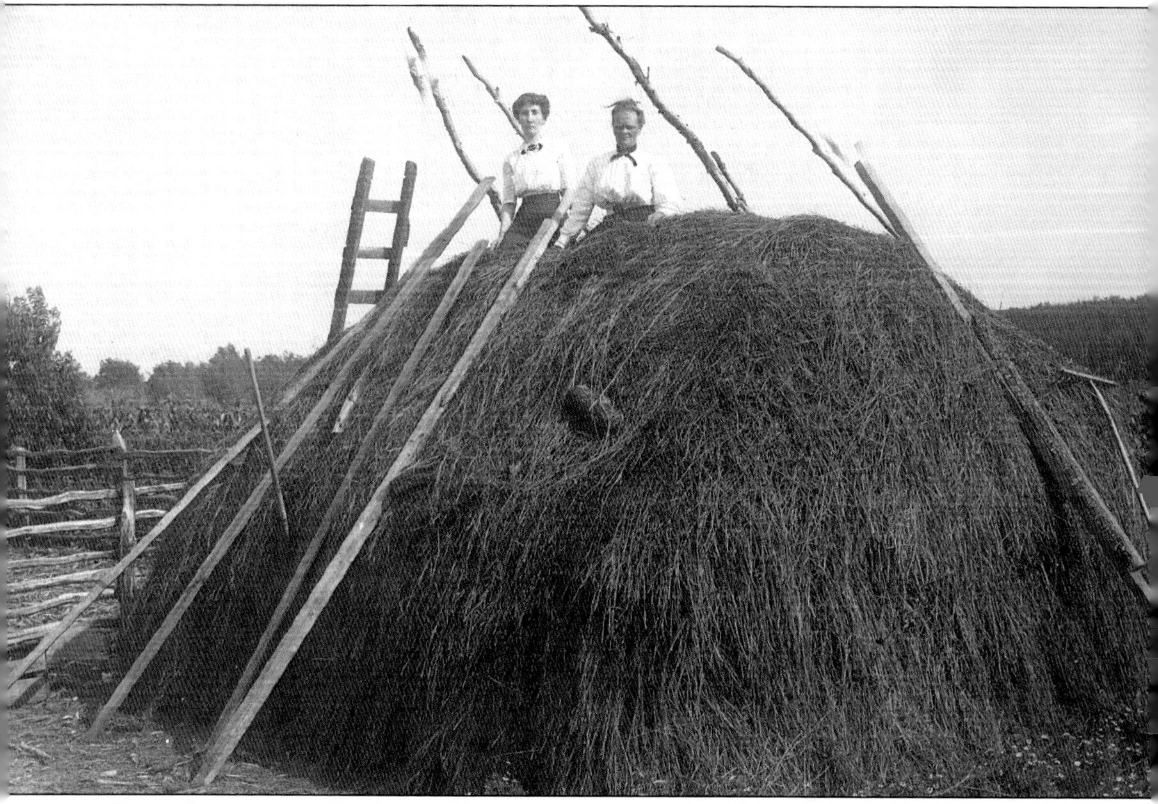

ELSIE OSWALD AND BERTHA WESTMAN ON HAYSTACK, 1913. The introduction of the side-delivery rake and mechanical hay loaders in about 1910 or 1920 was a major improvement in haying technology. The hay was cut with a horse or tractor-drawn mower, allowed to dry for a few hours or a day or so, and then raked. Side-delivery rakes rolled the hay into long, regularly-spaced windrows. It was then picked up by a mechanical hay loader hooked behind a wagon fitted with a hay rack. While it could have yet been stacked, it was usually moved directly into the hay mow of the cow or horse barns using a hay fork or slings.

The hay fork was a mechanical device that was pushed down into the load of hay, hooks to retain the hay were extended, and the hay was pulled into the hay mow. There was a long stout rope that extended from a rail mounted along the ridge of the barn roof, through a series of pulleys, out the side of the barn, and then hooked to a team of horses or a tractor. After being dumped into the hay mow, the hay was leveled by a couple of men or boys using pitch forks. Slings were rope contrivances that were laid across the hay rack, usually three per load of hay, and used to contain the hay when it was pulled into the hay mow.

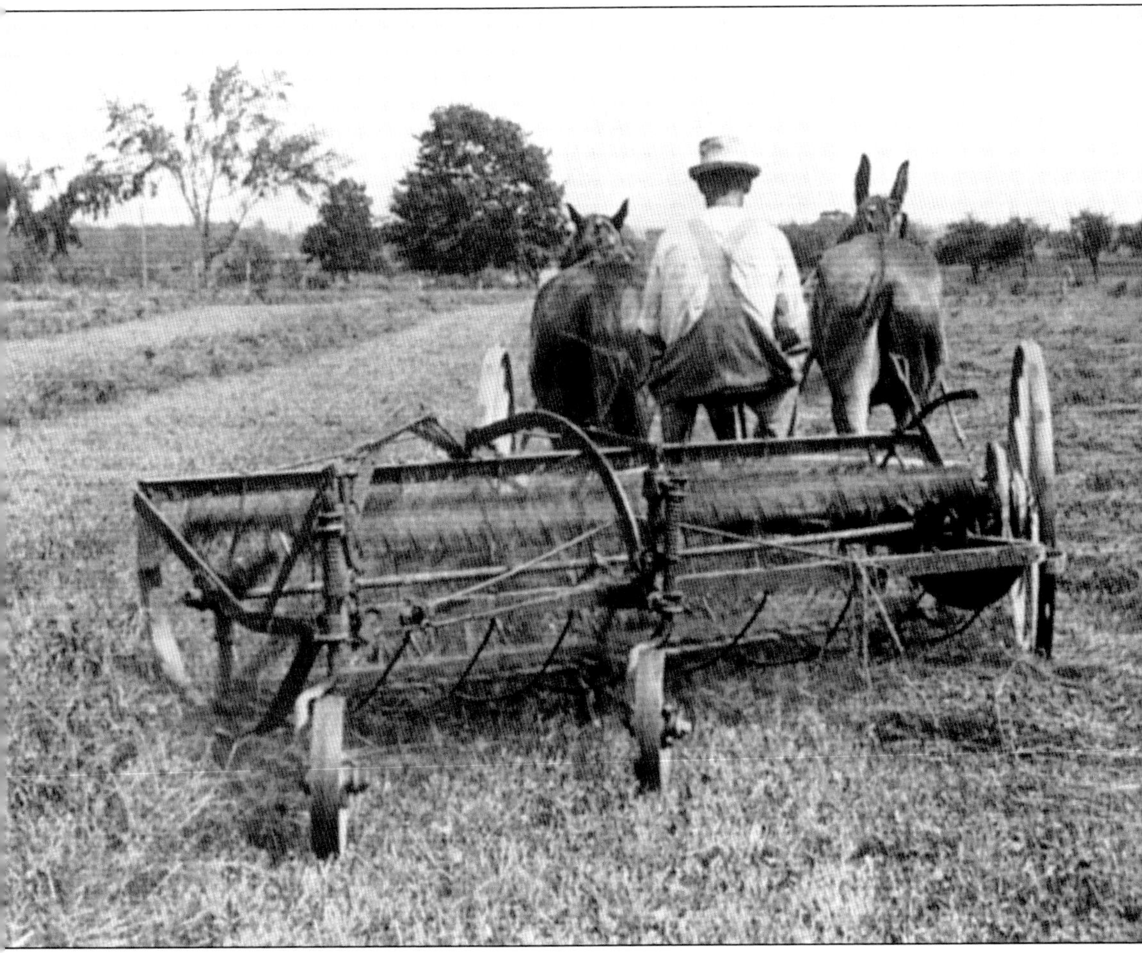

SIDE-DELIVERY RAKE, C. 1920.

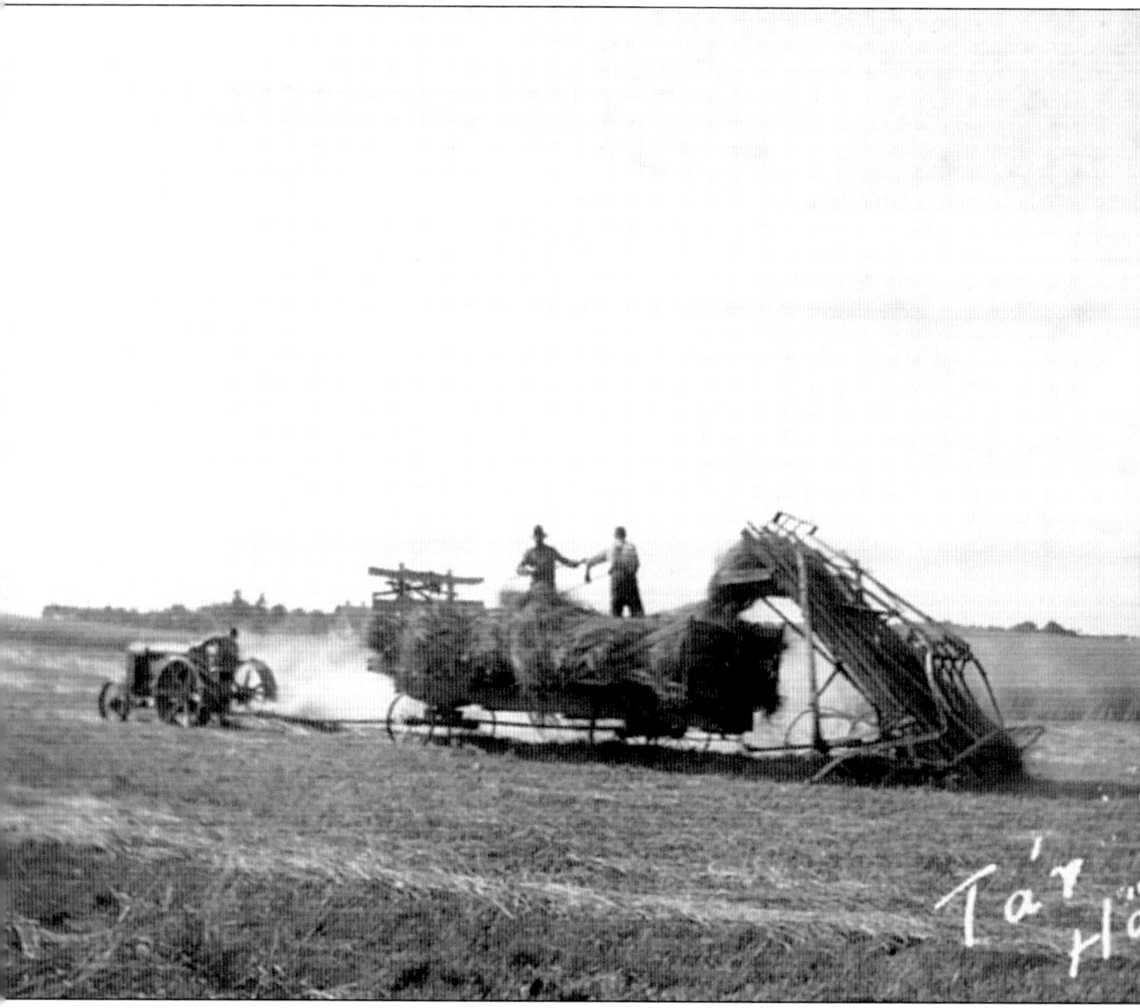

MECHANICAL HAY LOADER AND FORDSON TRACTOR ON FRANK ABRAHAMSON FARM, c. 1920.

Opposite: **PULLING HAY INTO THE HAY MOW, FRANK ABRAHAMSON FARM, 1927.** Hay balers first appeared in the late 1930s. The earliest baler in common use was the Case baler with wire ties. Hay was, as before, cut with a cutting-bar mower, raked with a side-delivery rake, allowed to dry for the appropriate time, and then baled. The Case baler was a large machine powered by its own motor. The business end was a chute through which the compressed hay was forced. The machine required three people: one to drive the tractor, and two to deal with the wires used to contain the bale. The needle man sat on an iron seat mounted on the left side of the rear end of the baler. His job was to insert steel needles into the stream of hay in intervals of about three feet. He then pushed wires through the needles. The tie man sat on another iron seat mounted just behind the apparatus that picked up the hay. His job was to pull the wires through the bales and to twist them together. The tie man was working in constant noise and a cloud of dust; it was a dirty job. The circumstances of the needle man was slightly better because he was on the outboard side of the baler and so was not exposed to the cloud of dust and dirt that enveloped the tie man.

Various self-tying balers soon appeared. Some used wires but balers using heavy hemp twine soon became the norm. Self-tying balers were a most welcome development.

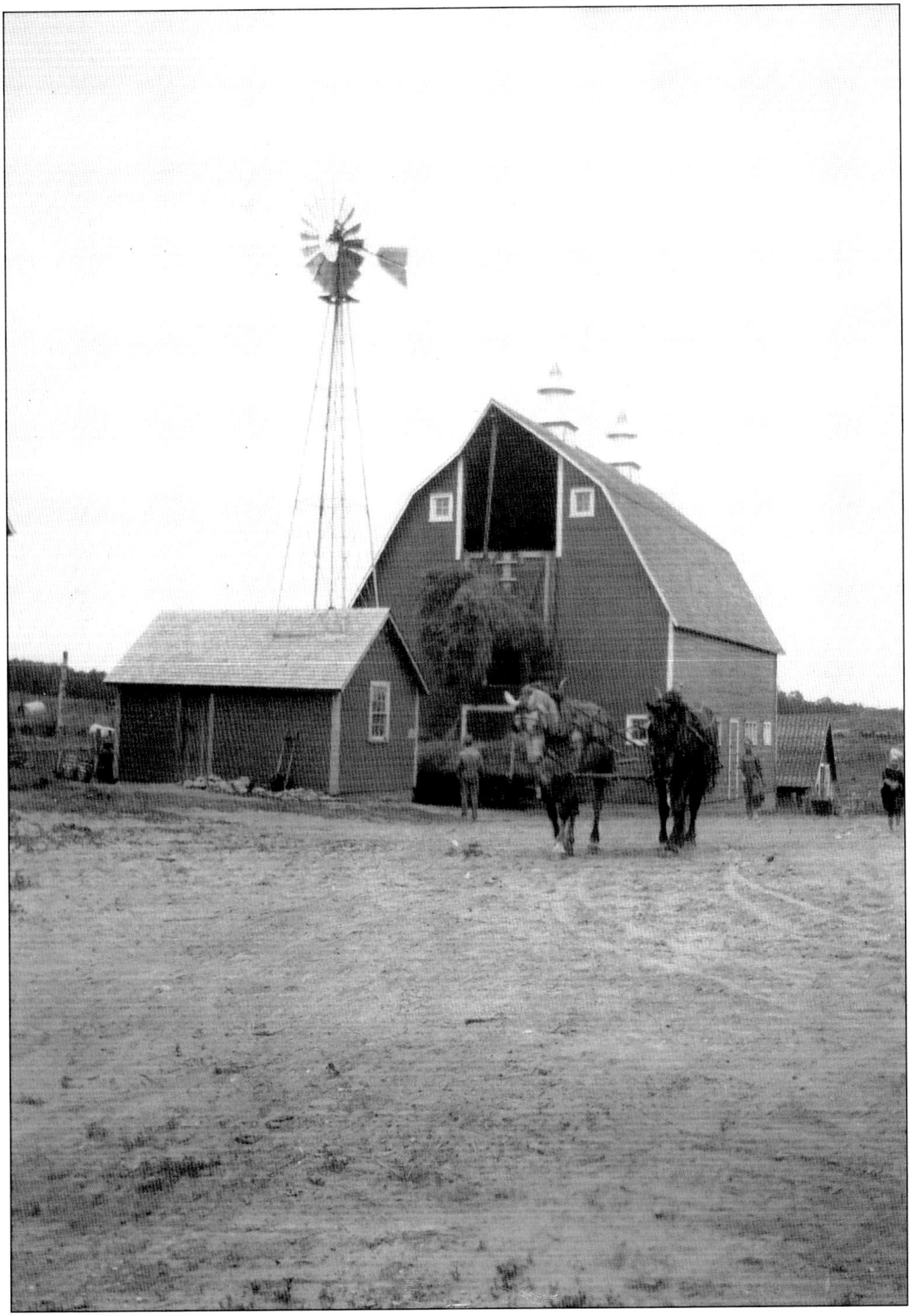

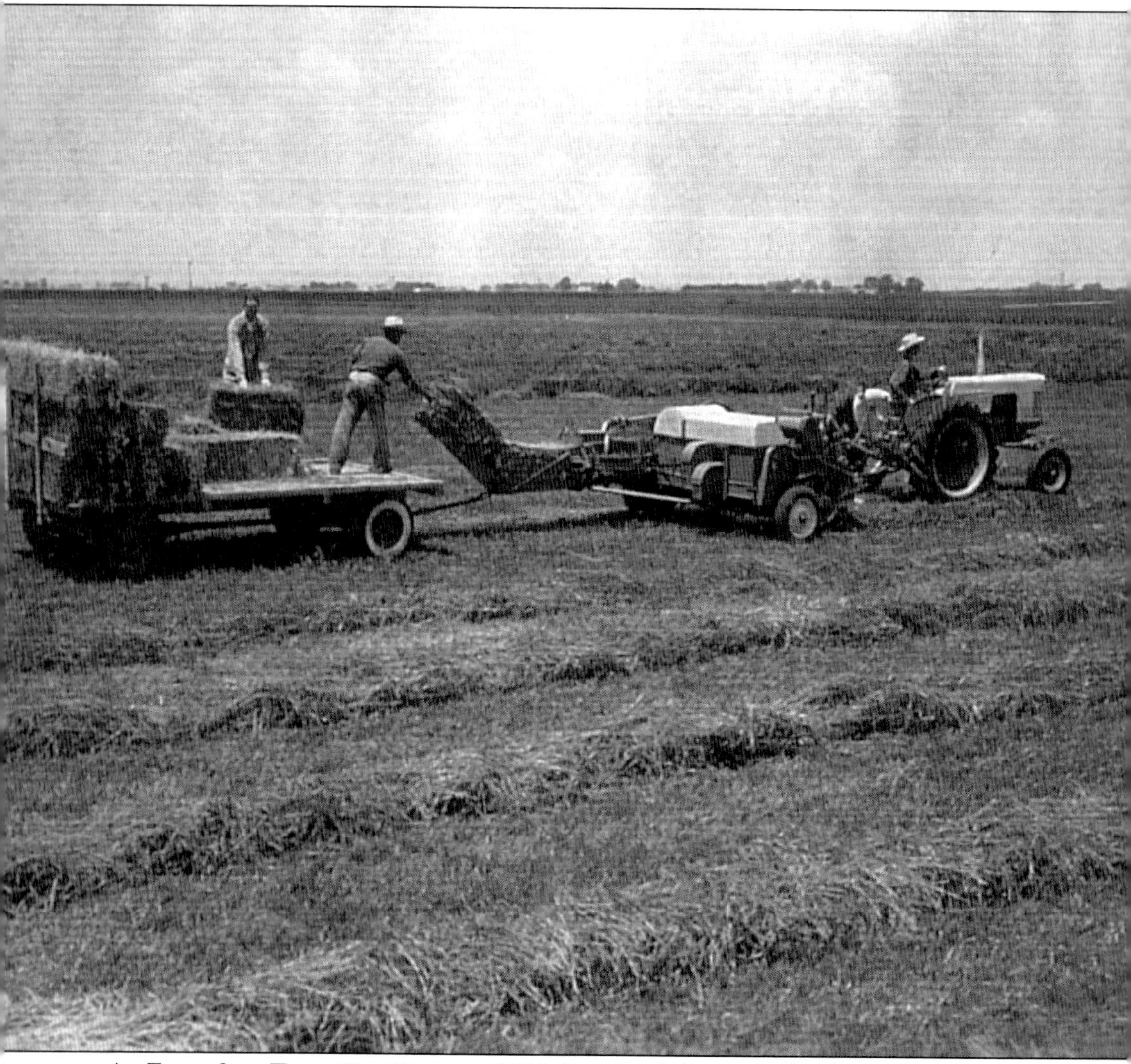

AN EARLY SELF-TYING HAY BALER, C. 1950. Case hay bales were either dumped on the ground or were pushed up a chute onto a trailing wagon. Either way they had to be manhandled and they were heavy—typically 70 to 90 pounds. The system was considerably more efficient than the hay-loader and sling system, but it was much harder work for those involved. The bales were then stacked, either in the field or near the barns, or they were moved into the hay mow with an elevator. The John Deere company began to market an elevator that could be used to move hay bales into hay mows or onto stacks, and could also be used to elevate grain into granaries. The elevator was a great labor saver. Hay was occasionally sold as a cash crop after the advent of hay bailers. It usually hauled by truck to beef cattle farms in the Dakotas or Nebraska.

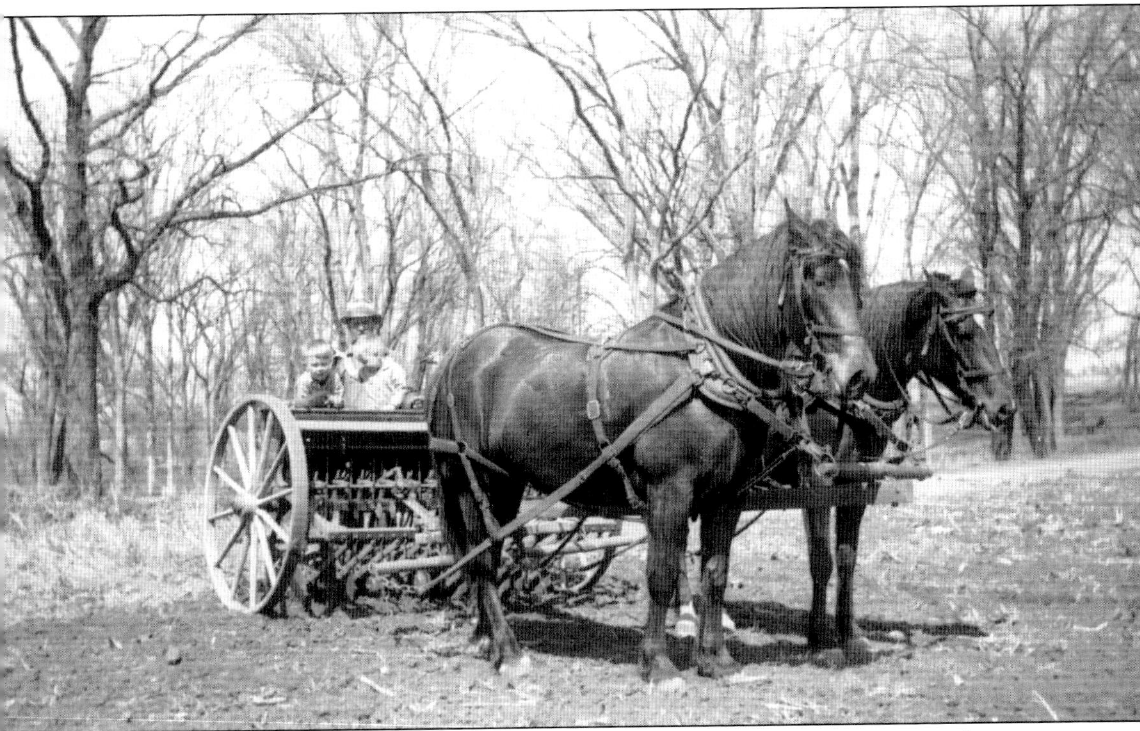

Ed Abrahamson with Dean and Bruce—Drilling Grain, c. 1939. Grain was primarily grown for feeding the farm animals, but some was sold as a cash crop through the grain elevators in Hasty and in Monticello. Much of the grain was ground. Gust Okerman installed a feed mill along with his blacksmith shop in Enfield in the early 1900s. There was a large feed mill at the grain elevator in Monticello that continued in use well into the 1960s. Many farmers had their own feed mills driven with belts run off their tractors. Rye and winter wheat were planted in the fall, other grains were planted in the spring as soon as the fields were dry enough to work—usually early or mid-April. The seed was planted, in the very early years, by broadcasting, either by hand or with little machines carried on a strap around the farmer's neck and powered with a hand crank. Grain drills soon replaced broadcasting. Grain drills, which had an attachment to seed grass seed at the same time, did not evolve as much as other farm machines—but they got larger.

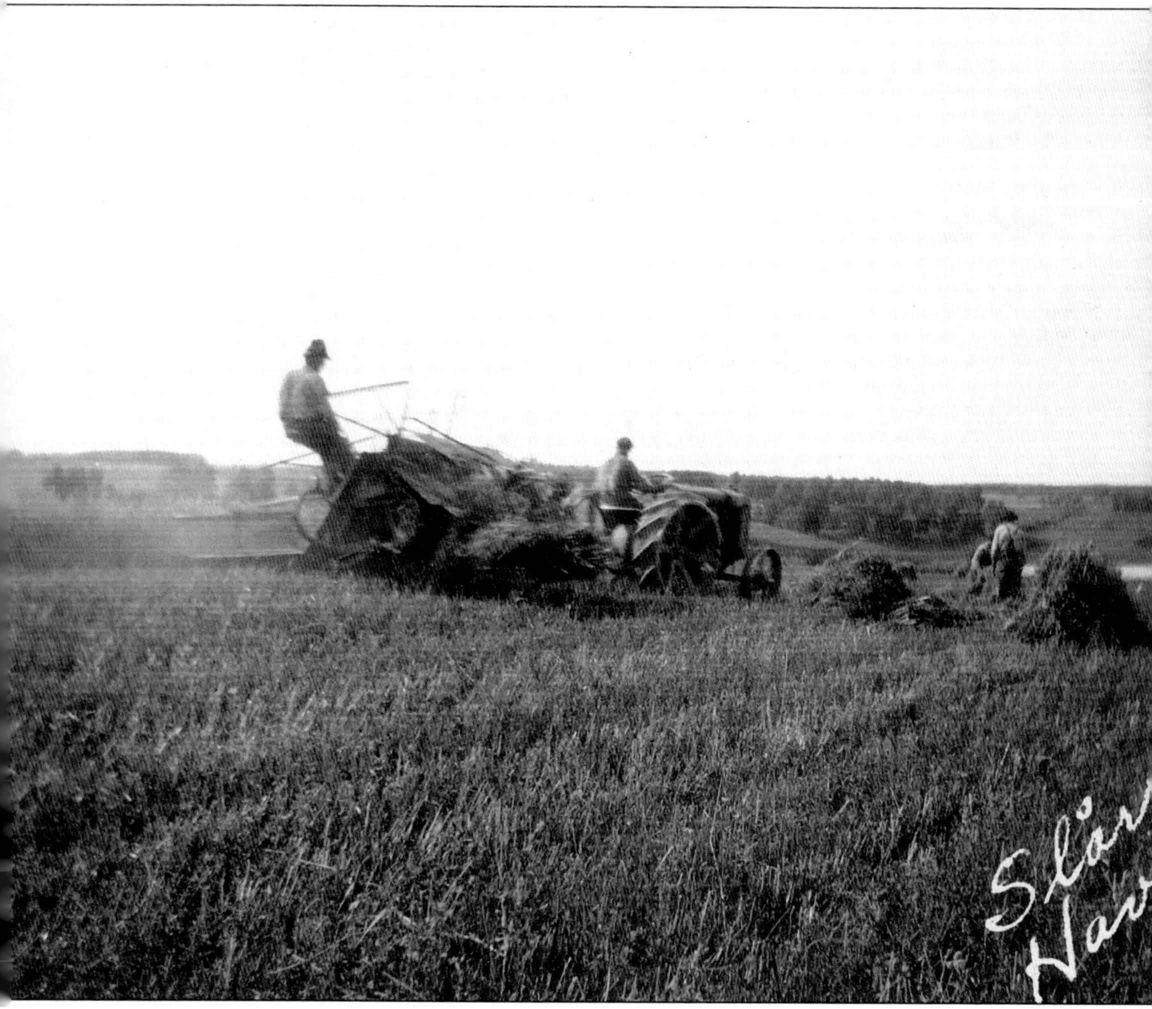

GRAIN BINDER PULLED BY A FORDSON TRACTOR, FRANK ABRAHAMSON FARM C. 1920. The earliest Enfield homesteaders probably cut their grain with a scythe and threshed it out with flails or small thresing machines powered by a horse walking on a treadmill. The mechanical reaper, invented by Cyrus McCormick in 1831, went into mass production in 1847 and was in common use by the late 1800s.

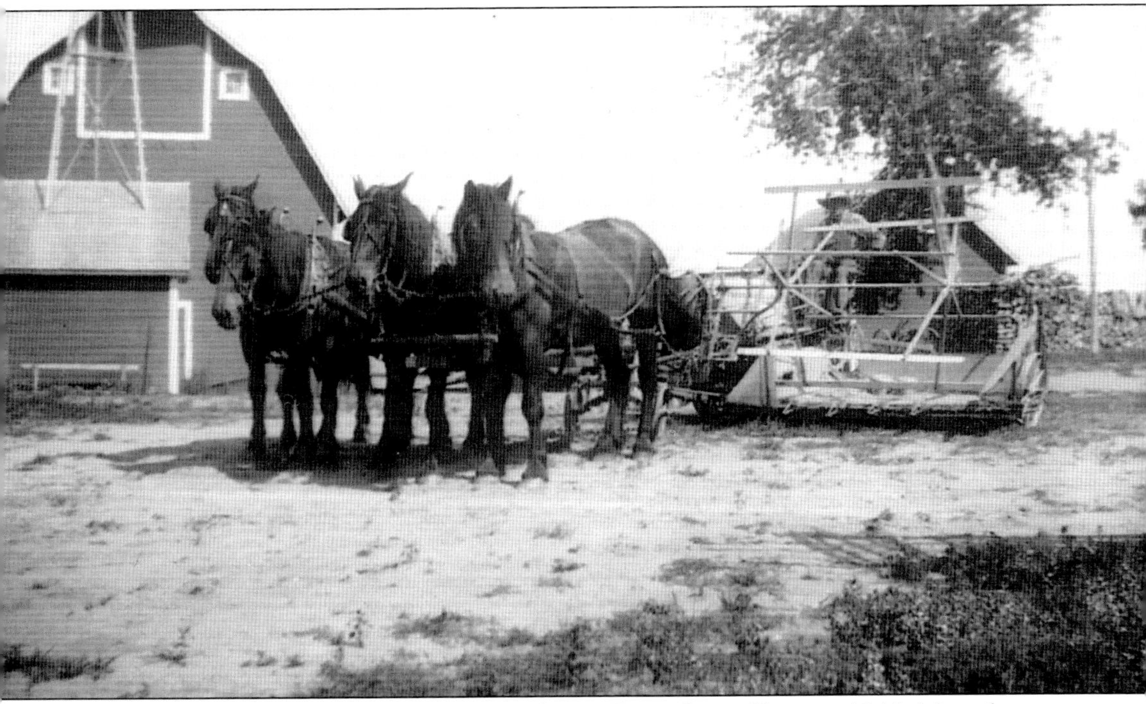

Frank Abrahamson and His McCormick Seven-Foot Grain Binder, 1944. Many farmers began to pull their grain binders with the early tractors, but some of them returned to horses for the job. There were probably two reasons: pulling the binder with a tractor required two men while a horse-drawn binder required only one, and the early tractors were extremely unwieldy and heavy which caused land compaction.

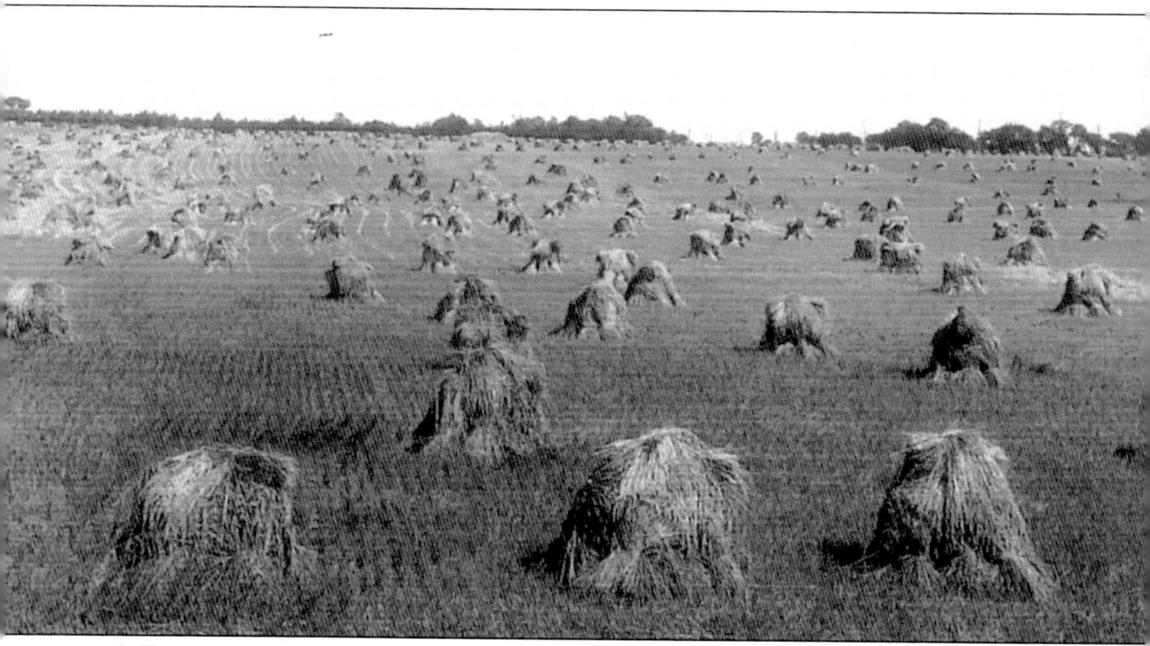

A FIELD OF WELL-SHOCKED GRAIN. The grain was then shocked and left in the field to dry. Shocking grain was not only hard work, it required considerable skill to make compact shocks that did not fall or blow down and were carefully capped with a single grain bundle in a way that shed rain. Men who were good grain shockers were in great demand.

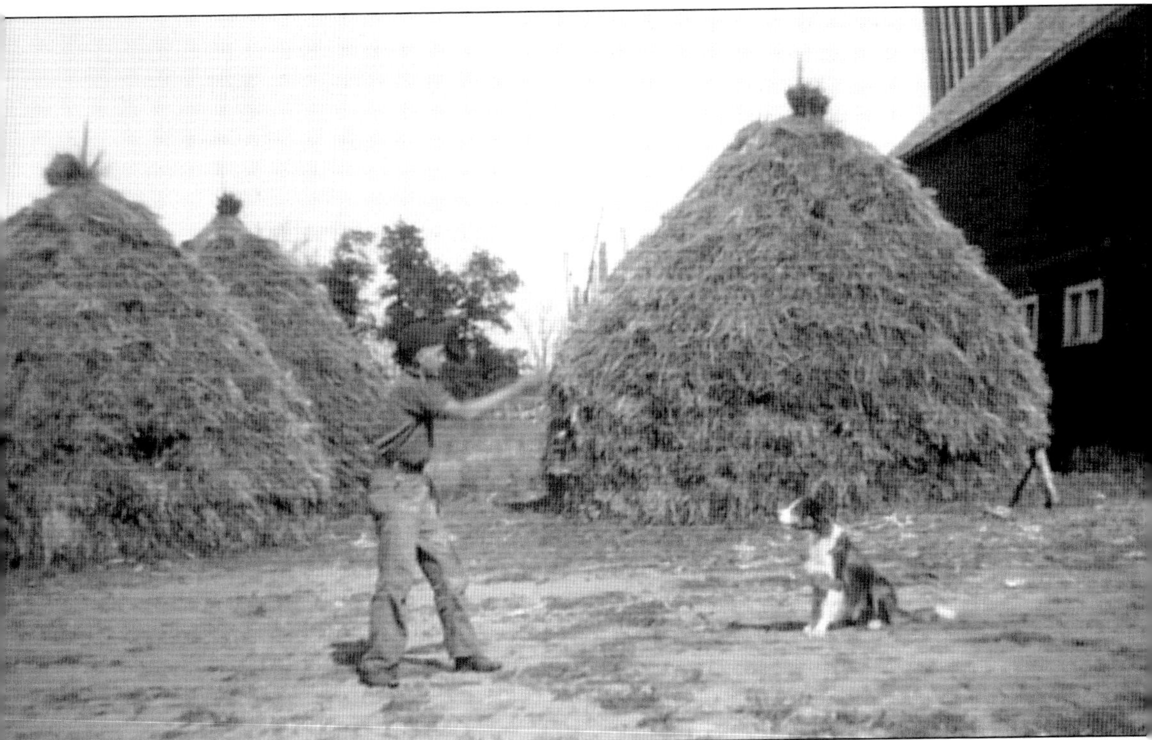

KENNETH ABRAHAMSON AND GRAIN STACKS READY FOR THRESHING, 1935. Small thresing machines that were inexpensive enough for a single farmer or for two or three neighbors appeared at about the time of World War II. Until that time, threshing was done by very large thresing machines, powered by steam tractors, and that required a large crew of men. These threshing crews would travel from farm to farm threshing them out as they went. Although neighbors formed part of the crews, part of the trading work that was the routine custom between family farms, a number of men were part of the crew that travelled with the thresing machine. Farm wives had to feed, and sometimes board, the threshing crew. It was a busy time and family photo collections are replete with pictures of threshing time.

The threshing had to be done as quickly as possible because the rig and crew had to serve many farms. It was usually not practical to have wagon crews hauling grain from the shocks on threshing day(s). So, after it had stood in the shocks for the necessary period of time, the grain was hauled to the farmstead and put into stacks spaced so that the bundles could quickly be thrown into the thresing machine. The straw would be blown into a straw pile from which bedding for the farm livestock would be taken during the winter.

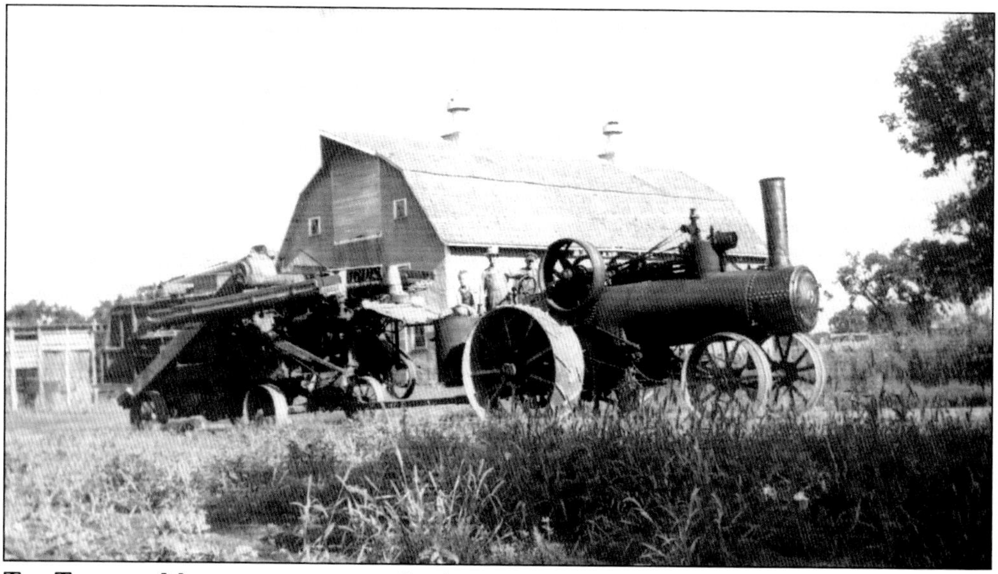

The Thresing Machine gets to the Ed Abrahamson Farm, 1938. The grain would either be run into tight, double wagon boxes and then shoveled into the granary, or it would be put into grain sacks. Each sack held a bushel or so of grain, would be hauled to the granary, carried into the bins, and dumped. (The author's first paying job was as sacker on his grandfather's threshing crew; he was 12 years old and the job paid 50¢ an hour—big money for a farm kid in 1947.) Sacks were no longer used after the advent of the versatile John Deere farm elevator.

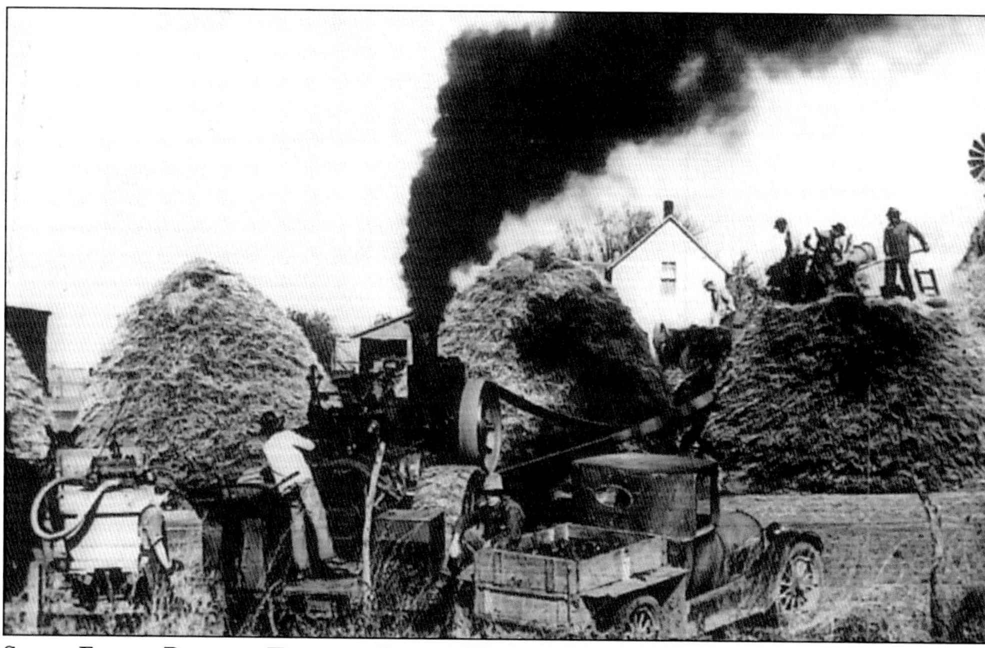

Steam-Engine-Powered Thresing System. The use of small, farmer-owned, thresing machines meant that the grain no longer had to be stacked, but could be conveyed directly from the shocks to the thresing machine. Many hands were still required, but the work could usually be done by individual farm families and their immediate neighbors. The threshing was still done on the farmstead so that the straw pile would be adjacent to the barns.

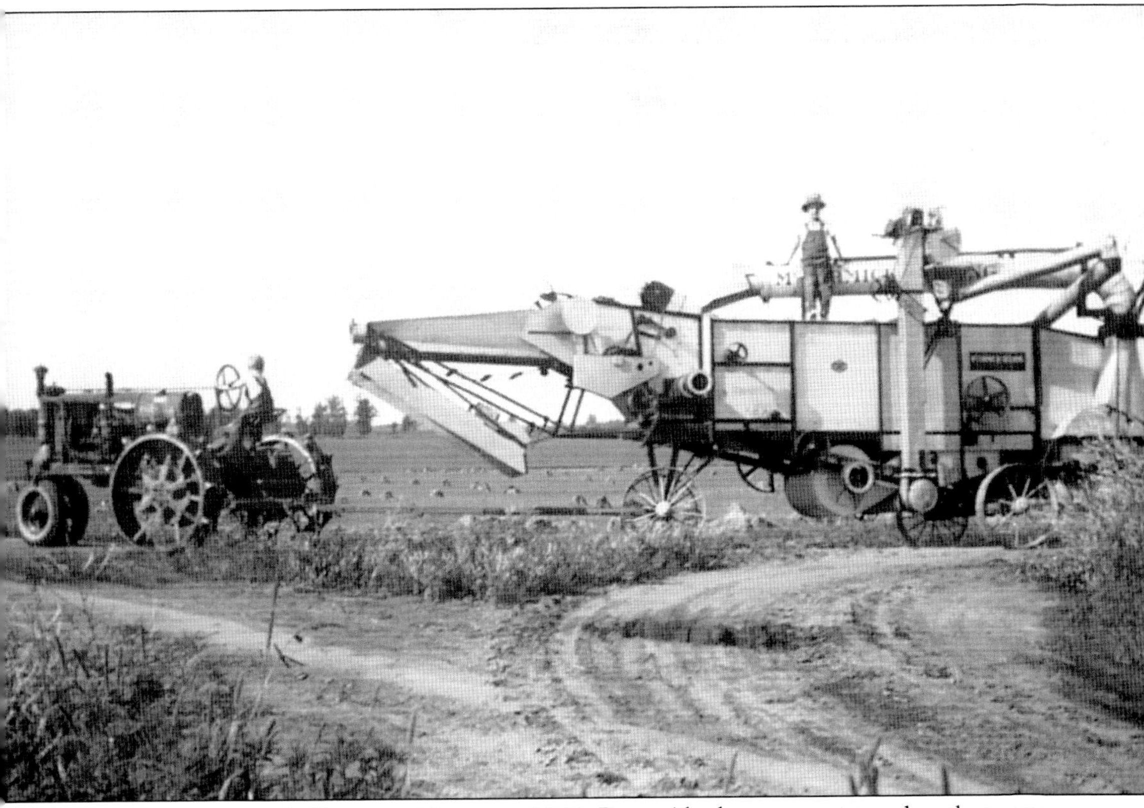

FRANK ABRAHAMSON'S THRESING MACHINE, 1943. Bruce Abrahamson is pictured on the tractor and Dean Abrahamson on the thresing machine. The 1950s brought the first practical small combines and the days of grain binders, shocking, stacking, and thresing machines were over. These combines were inexpensive enough for a single Enfield dairy farmer, perhaps bought with one or two of his neighbors. These small combines have long since been replaced by behemoth self-propelled machines with air-conditioned cabs and other bells and whistles.

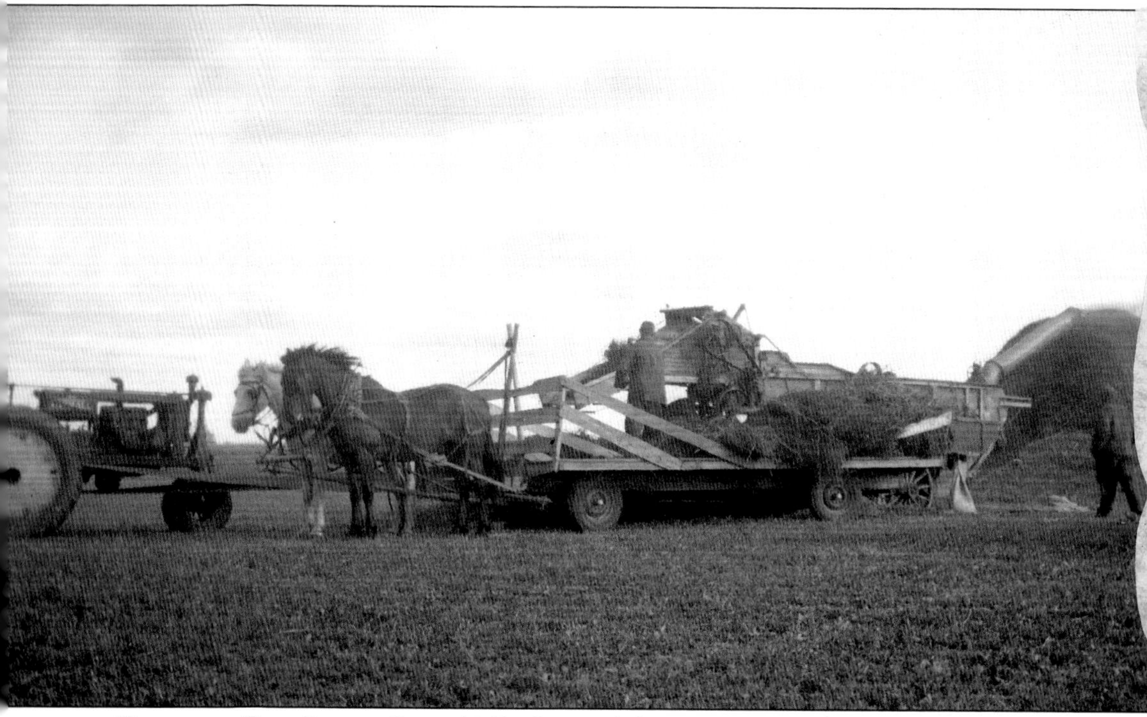

THRESHING OUT CLOVER SEED, 1943. One and then two-row mechanical corn planters were soon introduced. A wire was stretched across the length of field. Knots in the wire were spaced at intervals equal to the space between hills of corn. A fork-like apparatus on the corn planter ran along the wire and at each knot would release the seeds. A circular plate inserted in the planter had notches that determined how many seeds would be planted in each hill of corn. Considerable skill was required to place and stretch the wire so that the corn could be cultivated along both the length and breadth of the field. This was checking corn. Later the corn was drilled meaning that individual seeds were planted every few inches instead of the rectalinear hills of corn that could be cultivated both ways.

Opposite: **AN EARLY FAMILY-SIZED GRAIN COMBINE, C. 1960.** Corn harvesting techniques went through three stages. In early years the corn was cut, after the ears had ripened, with a hand-wielded corn knife or with a corn binder, often drawn by four horses. The corn bundles would be shocked in the field and then some time later, often not until after snowfall, the bundles would be brought to the farmstead and stacked near the barns. During the winter the ears would be husked out and the stalks and leaves used for fodder, bedding, or fed to horses.

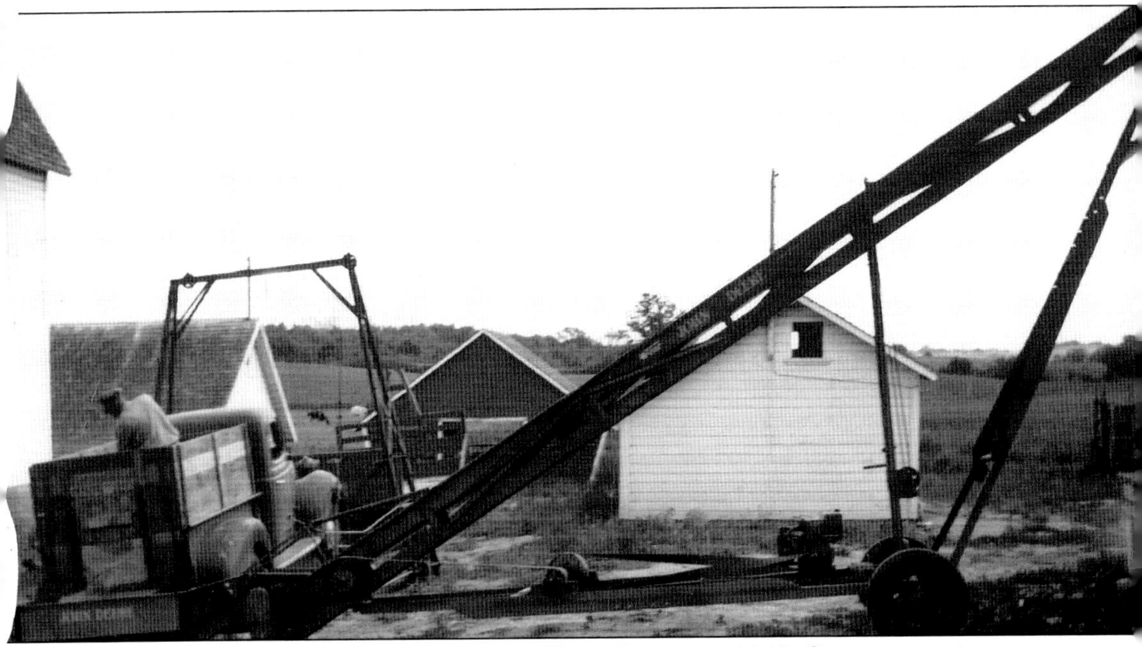

Elevating Grain into the Ed Abrahamson Farm Grainery, 1948. Corn was a major crop on Enfield dairy farms. During the first years a sled-like apparatus was twice dragged over the field making a checkerboard pattern. Corn was planted, with a hand planter, at the intersections of the lines so that the corn could be cultivated both ways. Usually three or four seeds were planted in each hill. It was then cultivated with a horse-drawn walking cultivator the width of which was a little less than the distance between rows. Children wielding hoes were also brought into play.

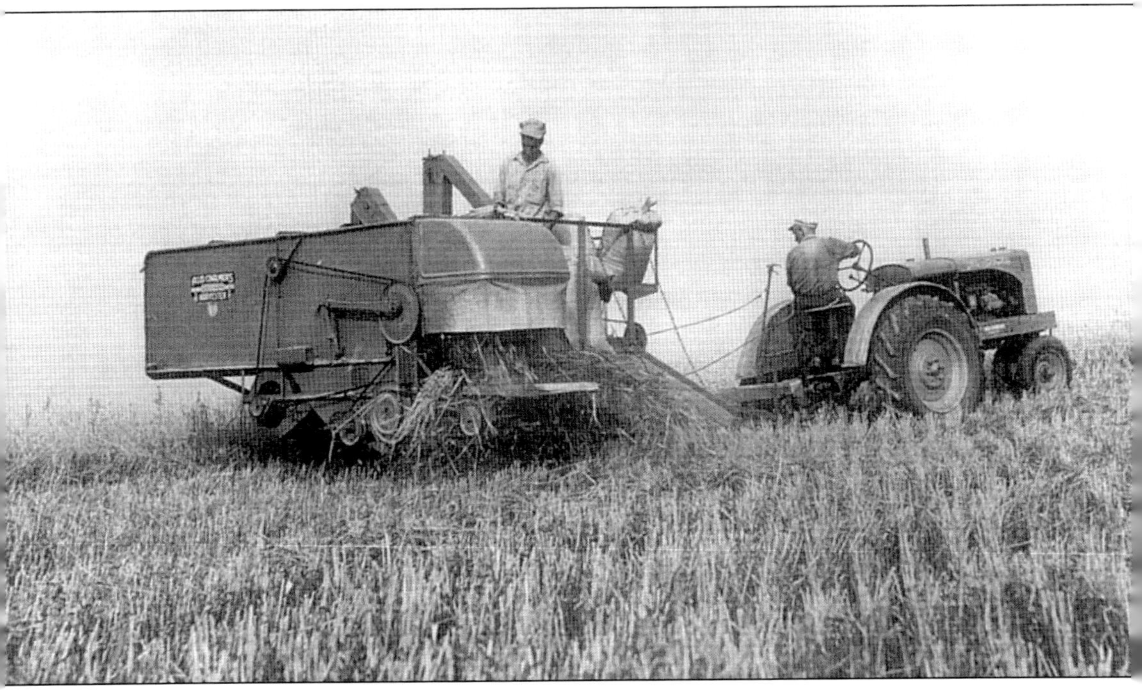

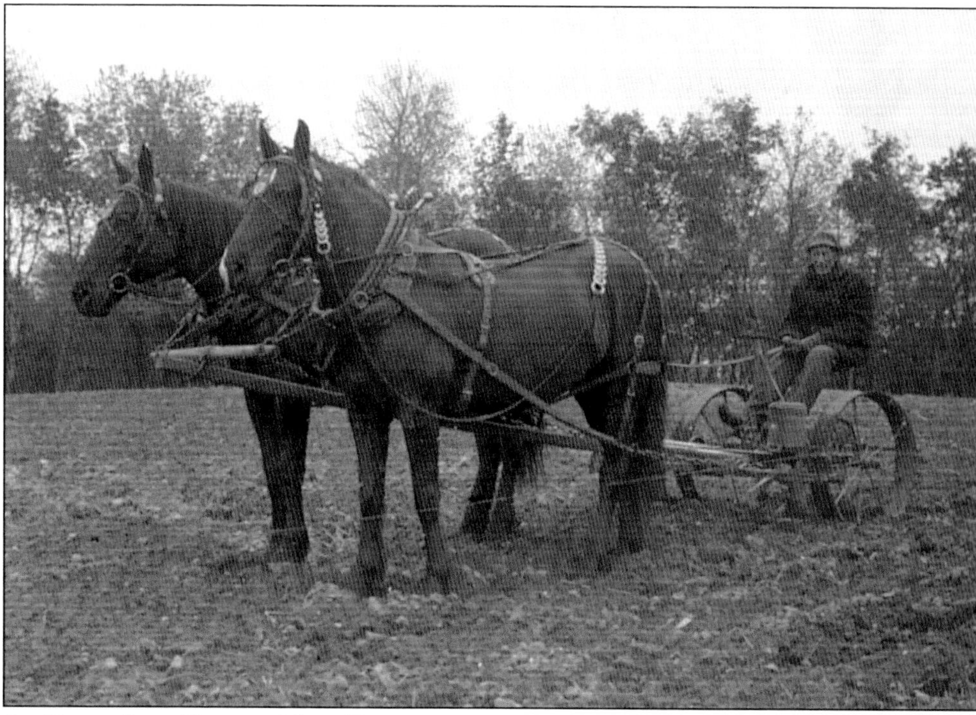

An Early Corn Planer, Matt Erickson, c. 1910.

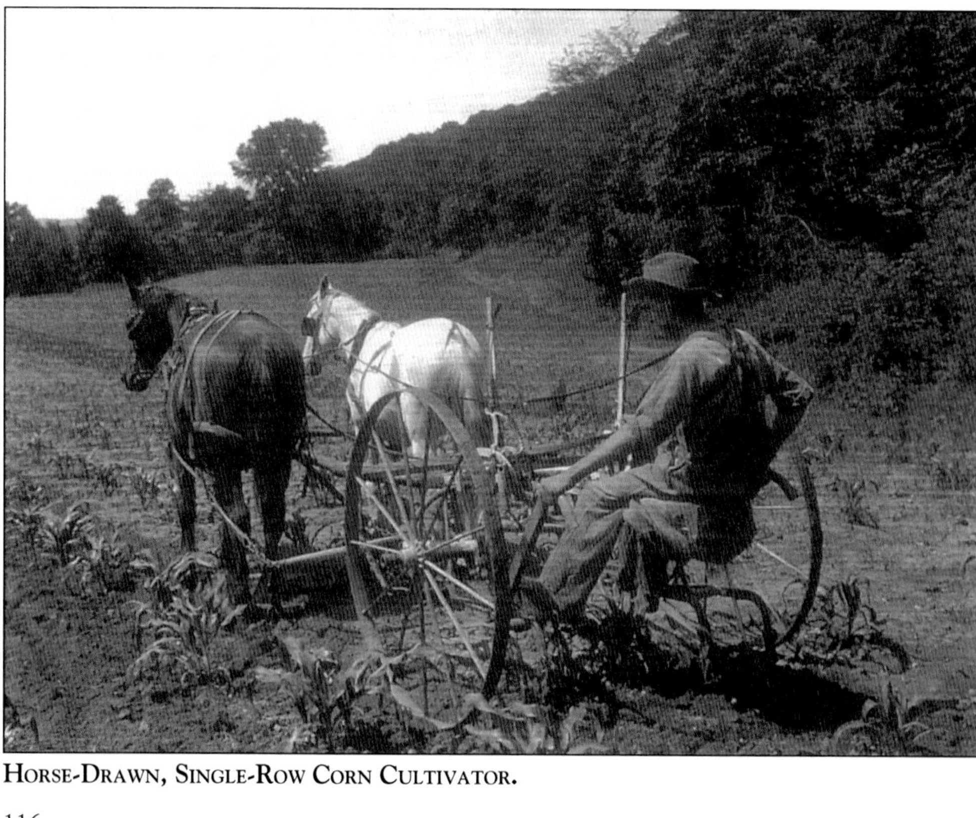

Horse-Drawn, Single-Row Corn Cultivator.

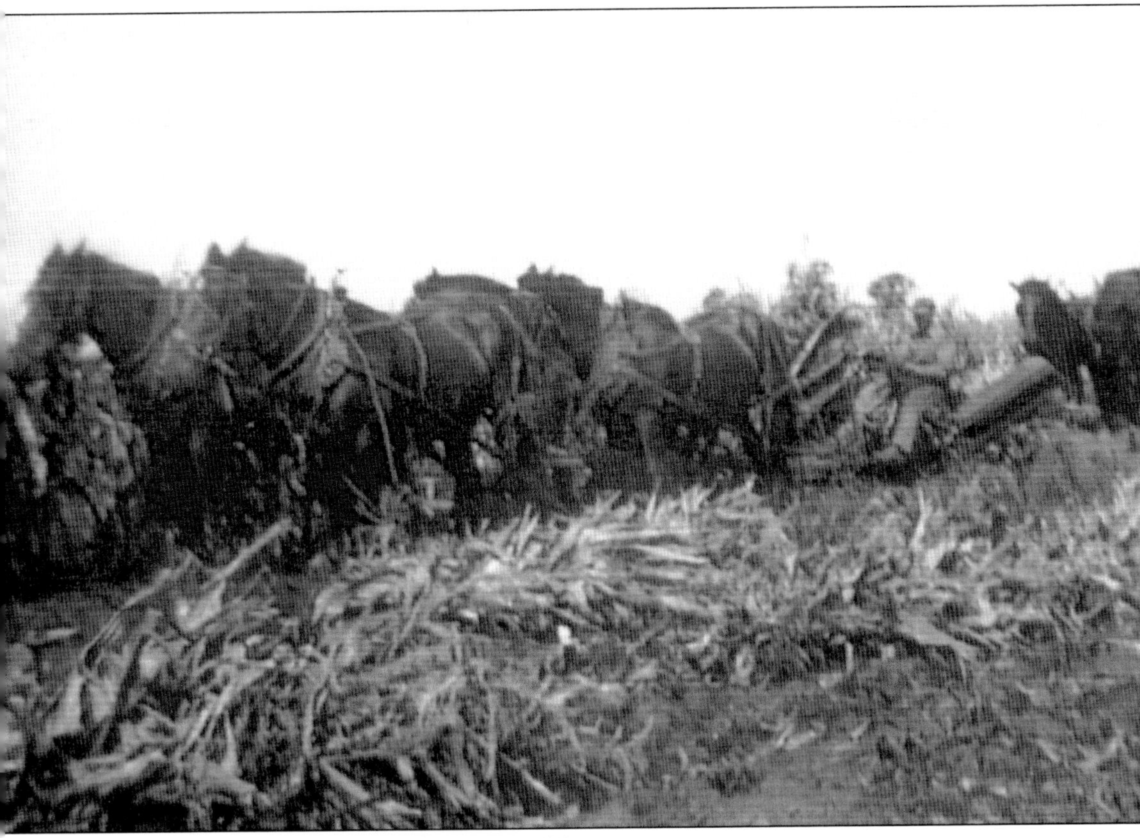

CHARLIE ABRAHAMSON CUTTING CORN, c. 1920.

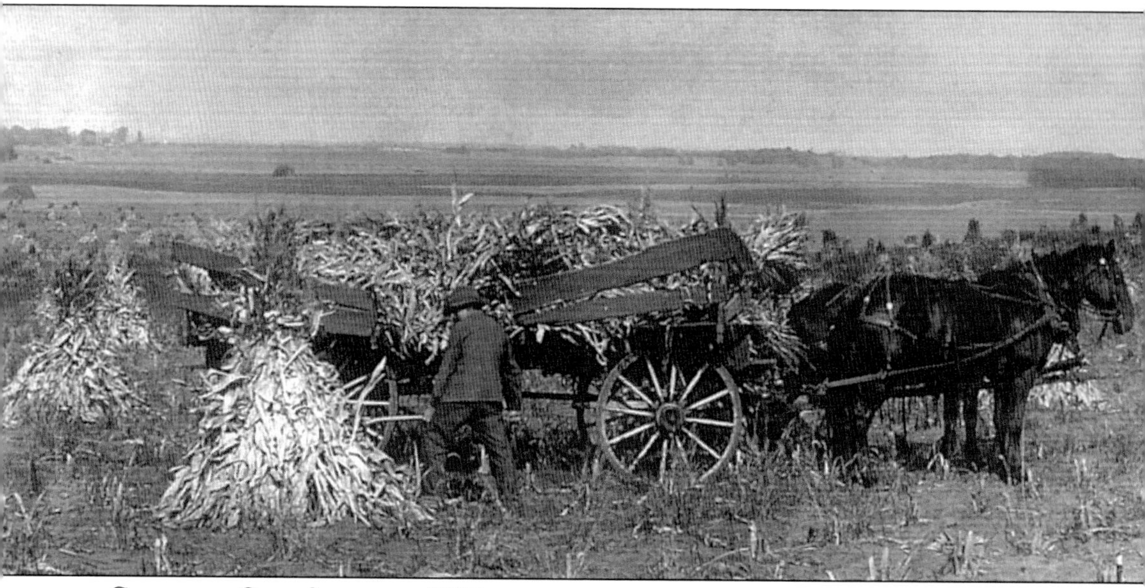

GATHERING CORN SHOCKS, C. 1920.

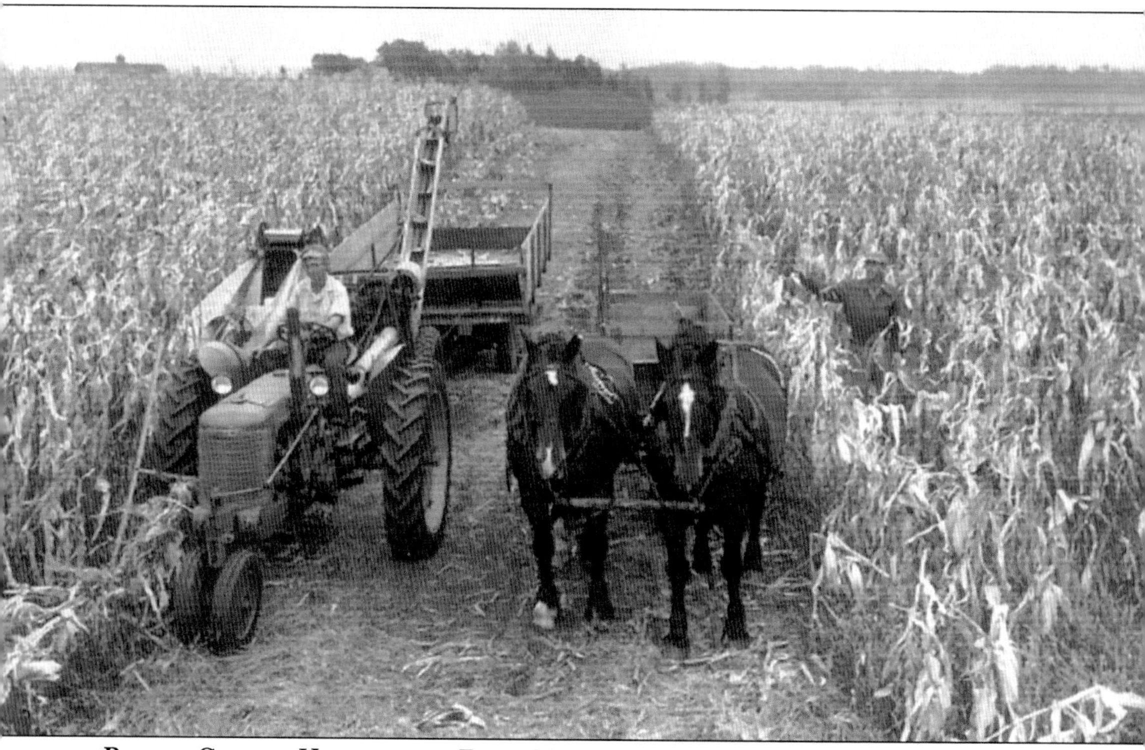

PICKING CORN BY HAND AND AN EARLY MECHANICAL CORN PICKER. Corn was also picked in the field—first by hand and then using mechanical corn pickers. Corn was picked and husked by hand and thrown, ear by ear, into a horse-drawn wagon equipped with a double box with a bang-board along the far side. It was slow work and required good leather gloves and a hook-like device that was strapped on the picker's hand. The unshelled corn was stored in cribs, often made of snow fencing.

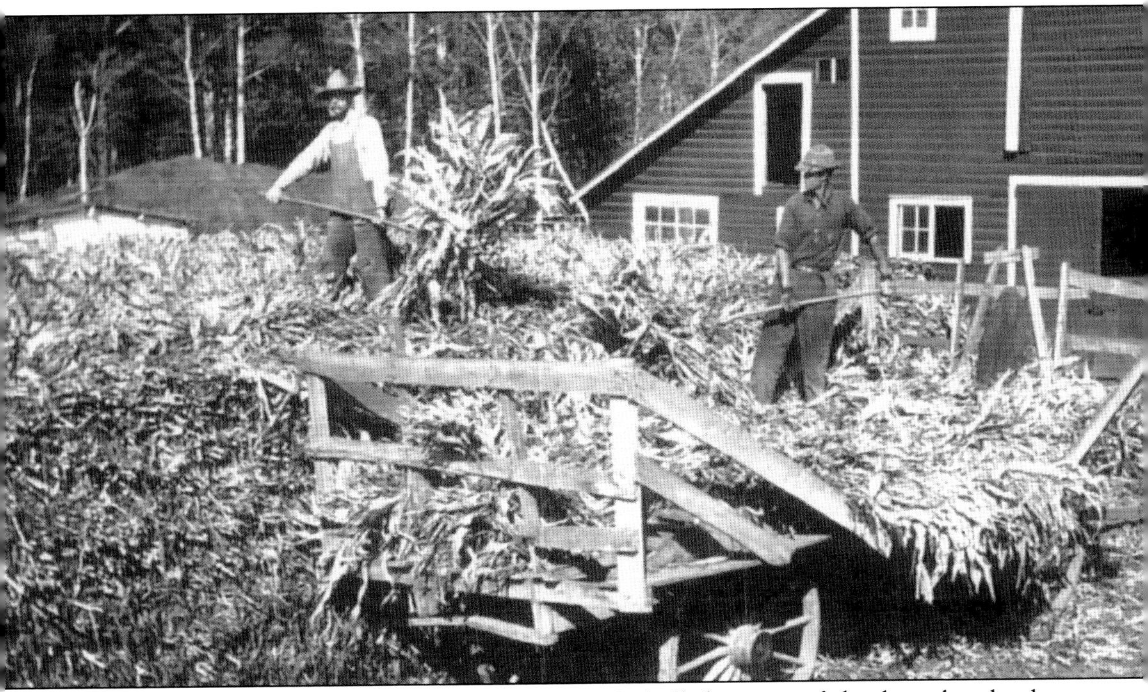

STACKING CORN BUNDLES BY THE BARN, C. 1920. Unshelled corn was fed to hogs, but the the corn had to be shelled, and often ground, for cattle and chickens. Shelling was done with small corn shellers, usually powered by two boys; one who fed ears into the machine and the other who turned a crank. The corncobs were saved and put to good use. Dry corncobs were burned in the kitchen range or brought into use in the privy. Field corncobs were rough, popcorn cobs were a bit softer, but while old Sears Roebuck or Montgomery-Ward catalogs were most often used, the soft paper used to wrap peaches in crates was best of all.

Corn silage became a staple winter feed for milk cows beginning in the early 1900s. The corn was cut with a corn binder, hauled to the silo, and fed into the silo filler—which chopped it and blew it into the silo. It was dangerous work. More than one farmer lost a hand or an arm trying to unplug the silo filler.

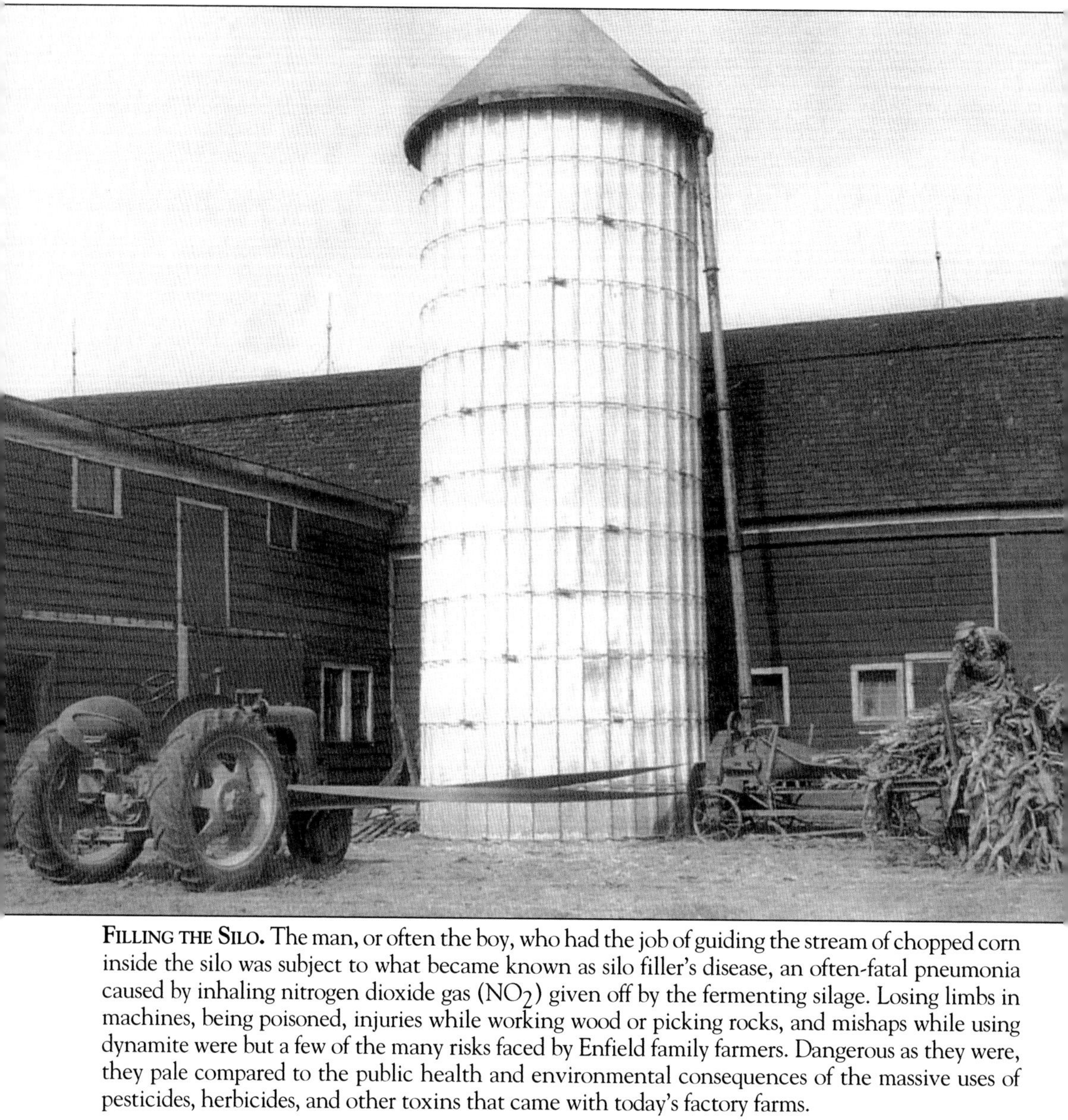

Filling the Silo. The man, or often the boy, who had the job of guiding the stream of chopped corn inside the silo was subject to what became known as silo filler's disease, an often-fatal pneumonia caused by inhaling nitrogen dioxide gas (NO_2) given off by the fermenting silage. Losing limbs in machines, being poisoned, injuries while working wood or picking rocks, and mishaps while using dynamite were but a few of the many risks faced by Enfield family farmers. Dangerous as they were, they pale compared to the public health and environmental consequences of the massive uses of pesticides, herbicides, and other toxins that came with today's factory farms.

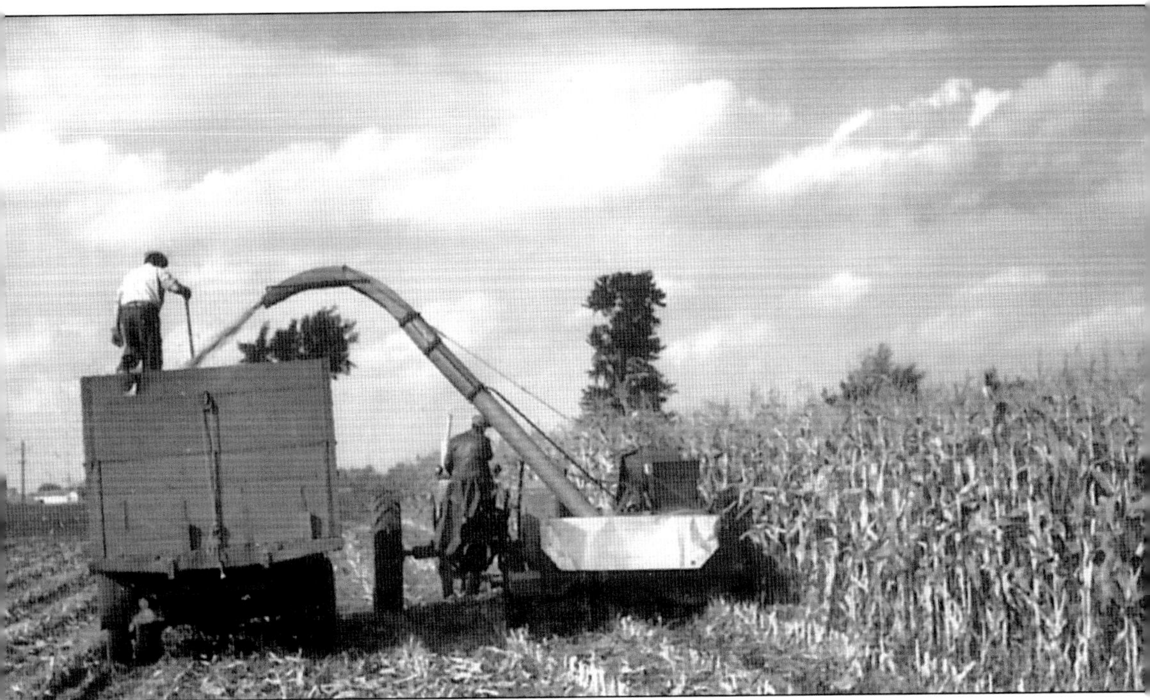

AN EARLY CORN FIELD CHOPPER, C. 1960. The silo filler, in turn, was replaced with another machine, the field chopper, which cut and chopped the green corn in the field. It was then blown into the silo or, in later years, stored in plastic-lined trenches.

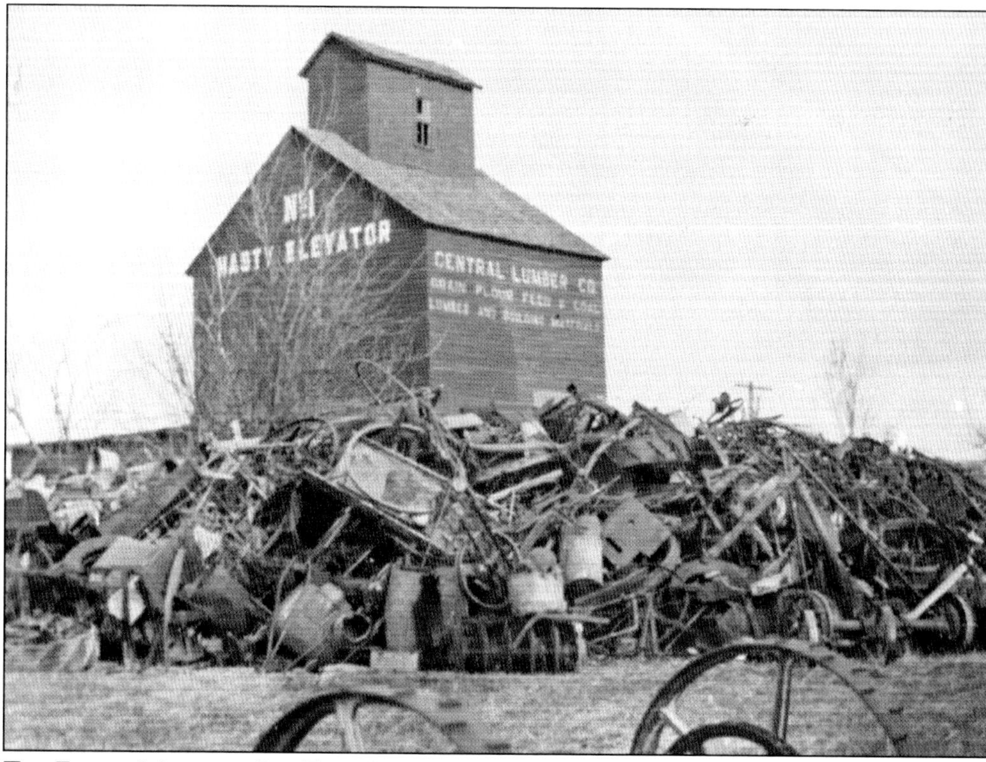

THE END OF MANY AN OLD FARM MACHINE; THE WORLD WAR II SCRAP DRIVE, 1942. This little summary touches on only a few of the many tasks completed regularly by the Enfield farm families. Hopefully, what has been included here gives some flavor of farm life from the homestead days until the days of the mega-machines and factory farms.

Ten

THE END

The Enfield Scandinavian-American family farm community had a life of nearly 150 years—beginning with the homesteaders who came to Minnesota's Big Woods in the late 1850s and 1860s with their scythes, rakes, and axes—and ending with the evolution to commercial farming and the conversion of the land into what is now largely a residential community. A hundred and fifty years—only a blink in the eye of history—but those years spanned a major evolution in Minnesota.

The young people who came alone or with their young families to Silver Creek Township in the mid-1800s came from families that had not travelled more than a few miles from their home villages or farms for centuries. Their decisions to abandon their ancestral homes and come to the New World required enormous courage and they faced great challenges during their first years in Minnesota. Most survived and prospered; some did not. Other members of their families often followed, as with today's immigrants to the United States. After they had become established here, few returned to Sweden except for visits.

All of the homesteaders and their children are now gone, but their legacies live on. Some of their descendants still live and work in the community. The old farm equipment has been relegated to scrap drives or to the dump except for examples preserved in museums. There are no longer any draft horses and only one family in the Enfield community now husbands a herd of dairy cows. The land that is yet farmed is tilled by a decreasing number of farmers using large machines—each of which costs far beyond what would have been the wildest imagination of the family farmers of bygone years.

It is easy for those of us who are no longer directly dependent on the land to be sentimental about the good old days. But those days are gone. We now drive the old roads remembering how it used to be and wondering what the next 150 years will bring.

Sources

Much of this history comes from my own files and the memoirs written in the late 1980s by my Father, Edwin T. Abrahamson, and his brothers, Verner F. Abrahamson, and Glenn E. Abrahamson. I also greatly benefited from discussions with a number of current or former residents of the community, including Rebecca Barnett, Wesley "Bill" Berg, Lenore and Bill Johnson, Richard Anderson, Russell Nelson, my brother, Bruce Abrahamson, and my sister, Mavis Abrahamson Ward. Considerable use was made of Franklyn Curtis-Wedge, *History of Wright County Minnesota*, H.C. Cooper, Jr. & Co, Chicago (1915). Much of the early Minnesota information is from William Watts Folwell, *A History of Minnesota*, Minnesota Historical Society, St. Paul (1956, two-volume edition), and Theodore C. Blegen, *Minnesota: A History of the State*, University of Minnesota Press, Minneapolis (1975 edition).

The context of the Swedish emigration to Minnesota is wonderfully detailed in the four-volume historical novels by Vilhelm Moberg: *The Emigrants [Utvandrarna], The Immigrants [Invandrarna], Into a New Land [Nybyggarna]*, and *The Last Letter Home [Sista Brevet Till Sverige]*. The best English edition is that of the Minnesota Historical Society Press.

Most of the photographs are from collections of my family: Edwin and Evelyn Abrahamson, Frank and Amanda Abrahamson, Edward and Anna Trogen, Bruce E. Abrahamson, Rebecca Abrahamson Barnett, Frieda Westling Cullen and her daughter Marlys Cullen Lilja, Amelia Erickson Westman and her niece Joyce Erickson DeVries, Ruth Westling Berg and her son Wesley "Bill" Berg. Several photographs are from the collections of the Wright County Historical Society and the Minnesota State Historical Society. Don Smith, editor and publisher of the *Monticello Times* gave me complete access to the photographs published from August 1968 and August 1975 in its *Monticello Remembers* series. I have used a few photographs, that I could not find in Enfield collections, from *Clearwater Remembers* (an extensive collection of early photos from Clearwater, Minnesota but the editor, publisher, and publication date are not identified). Several of the farming photographs are from the archives of the University of Minnesota Agricultural Extension Service.

Jerry Stockham and Peter Kissinger gave me access to the records of the Lake Side Cemetery and the Faith Lutheran Church respectively. Richard Anderson helped me understand the fate of the Enfield Baptist Church and the Enfield I.O.G.T. hall. Diana Magnuson, Bethel College Archivist, helped me locate what appear to be the only existent written records from the Enfield Baptist Church in the annual: *Årsbok för Svenska Baptists-Församlingara inom Nord Amerika (Annual Report of the Swedish Baptist Congregations in North America)*, M.A. Rosenlund Publishers, Chicago. The history of Enfield School District #121, compiled by Gladyce Anderson in 1991 on the occasion of the 100th anniversary of the school, provided many details of the school.

Photograph Attributions

From Family Collections Unless Otherwise Noted

Abbreviations
DFR = Delores Frehner Ramerth; LPJ = Lenore Platten Johnson; CR = *Clearwater Remembers;* MNHS = Minnesota Historical Society; MT = Monticello Times Archives; UMN = University of Minnesota Extension Service; WCHS = Wright County Historical Society

Cavalry Troop Passing Through Monticello (MT); Ox Cart (MNHS); An Early Enfield Family (WCHS); Carter School and Students: 1910 (MT); Sorensen School: 1925 (MNHS); Enfield School Students: 1905 (MHHS); Enfield School and Students: 1910 (MT); Enfield School with Students Identified: 1910 (MT and DEA); Baptist Church: *c.* 1878 (WCHS); Baptist Church Building Being Moved to Enfield Village: 1905 (WCHS); Baptist Church in Enfield Village: 1910 (WCHS); Lutheran Church: 1947 (WBB); Enfield Cream Station and Railroad Siding: 1910 (MT); Locomotive "The William Crooks": First through Enfield in 1882 (CR); Enfield Depot, Cream Station, and Train: *c.* 1911 (WBB); Great Northern Train Crossing Silver Creek Bridge: ca. 1910 (MT); Rural Minnesota Stagecoach: 1876 (MNHS); Clearwater-Clear Lake Ferry: ca. 1910 (CR); Mail Carrier on Enfield Route (Monticello Rural Route #1); ca. 1909 (MT); Pre-Electricity Farm House Work (RAB); "Greetings from Enfield" Postcard Montage: ca. 1910 (MT); Chunking Wood by Berglund Store: ca. 1910 (MNHS); Enfield Cheese Makers, Carl and John Frehner and August Witz: 1934 (DFR); Enfield Cheese Factory: *c.* 1934 (DFR); Healy Company Potato Warehouse: ca. 1910 (MT); Cattle Enclosure and Loading Chute: ca. 1940 (CR); Gust Okerman's Blacksmith Shop: *c.* 1910 (MT); Enfield Town Hall and I.O.G.T. Hall: 1910 (WCHS); Carpenters Finishing I.O.G.T. Hall: 1910 (MCL); I.O.G.T. Dedication and Convention: 4 September 1910 (MCL); I.O.G.T. Halloween Party at I.O.G.T. Hall: 31 October 1910 (WBB); Silver Creek Siding Grays Baseball Team: *c.* 1909 (WCHS); Enfield Baseball Team: June 1912 (WBB); Baseball Team Cheering Section: June 1912 (WBB); Enfield-Hasty Baseball Team, Members Identified: 1933 (LPJ); Olof Anderson House, Built 1897: photo *c.* 1940 (MNHS); L.P. Enfield-Becker Ferry: 1900 (WBB); Picnic on Locke Lake: *c.* 1910 (MT); Pond Overlooked by Andrew Ezra Trogen Farmstead: 2001 (DEA); Log Drive Near Mouth of Silver Creek: *c.* 1910 (MT); Logs Collected at Boom Island: *c.* 1915 (MT); Log-Driving Crew Cook- and Bunk-Barges at Berg Farm: *c.* 1910 (MT); Local Ladies on "Left-Behind" Logs at Berg Farm: *c.* 1910 (MT); The *J.B. Bassett* Stern-Wheeler: 1909 (CR); The *Sampson* Stern-Wheeler Below Enfield: *c.* 1915 (MT); Sawmill in Monticello: 1890s (MT); Blasting Stumps with Dynamite (MNHS); Silver Creek Logging Crew: *c.* 1890 (MNHS); Silver Creek Sawmill: *c.* 1890 (MNHS); A Mature Enfield Community Farmstead (WBB); A Family's Canned and Cellar Goods (UMN); Plucking Chickens (UNL) Introducing the Pressure Cooker (UMN); Feeding the Threshing Crew (UNL); Farm Woman Cutting Haw With Scythe (MNHS);

Collecting Hay With Wooden Rake (MNHS); Stacking Hay: *c.* 1890 (MNHS); Horse-Drawn Hay Mower (UMN); Dump Rake (MNHS); Side-Delivery Rake (MNHS); An Early Self-Tying Hay Baler (UMN); Elevating Hay Bales into Barn (UMN); Field of Well-Made Grain Shocks (UMN); Steam Engine Threshing Crew (UMN); An Early Grain Combine (UNL); Horse-Drawn, One-Row Corn Cultivator (UMN); Horse-Drawn Corn Binder (RAB); Corn Shocks (UMN); Stacking Corn (UMN); Picking Corn: By Hand and With Early Corn Picker (UMN); Corn Crib Made From Snow Fencing (UMN); Silo Filler (UNL); An Early Corn Field Chopper (UMN); World War II Scrap Drive: The End of Many a Farm Machine (MT)

Maps

Map of Territory of Minnesota: 1849 (University of Minnesota Borchert Map Library); Indians of Minnesota at Time of Settlement (Modified from Theodore C. Blegen, *Minnesota: A History of the State*, University of Minnesota Press, Minneapolis [1975 Edition]; Pre-Settlement Military Roads (Modified from Blegen, *ibid.*); Silver Creek Township: 1874 Andreas Atlas (Jerry Stockham); Land Sessions by Indians in Minnesota (Modified from Blegen, *op cit.*); Major Pre-Settlement Minnesota Land Areas (Modified from Blegen, *op cit.*); Key to Silver Creek Township Survey Map (DEA); Aerial Photographs: 1940 (Borchert Map Library, University of Minnesota).

About the Author

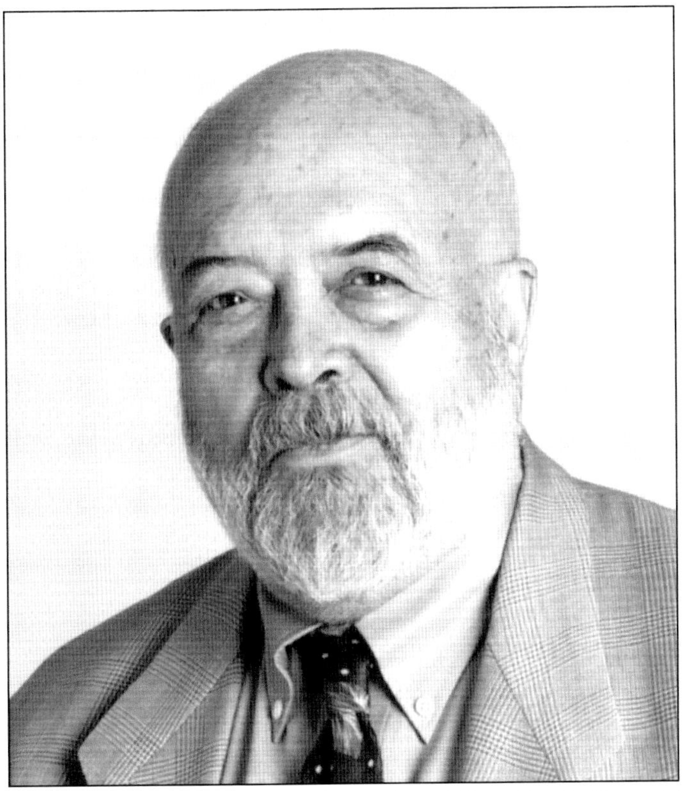

Dean E. Abrahamson. Dean was born and raised in Silver Creek Township. His parents, Edwin T. and Evelyn Trogen Abrahamson, lived out their span of years in the Enfield Community. His paternal grandparents, Frank and Amanda Felien Abrahamson, and his maternal grandparents, Edward and Anna Westling Trogen, lived in the Enfield community after they emigrated from Sweden in the 1890s. His great-grandparents, Erick Johnson Trogen and Kestin Andersdotter Trogen, were among the Enfield pioneers, having homesteaded in Section 26 in 1871. Dean spent 32 years as a professor at the University of Minnesota with guest professorships at the University of Iceland, and in Sweden at Lund University and Chalmers Institute of Technology. He lives in Minneapolis and has a son, a daughter, four grandsons, two stepsons, one step-grandson, and two step-granddaughters.

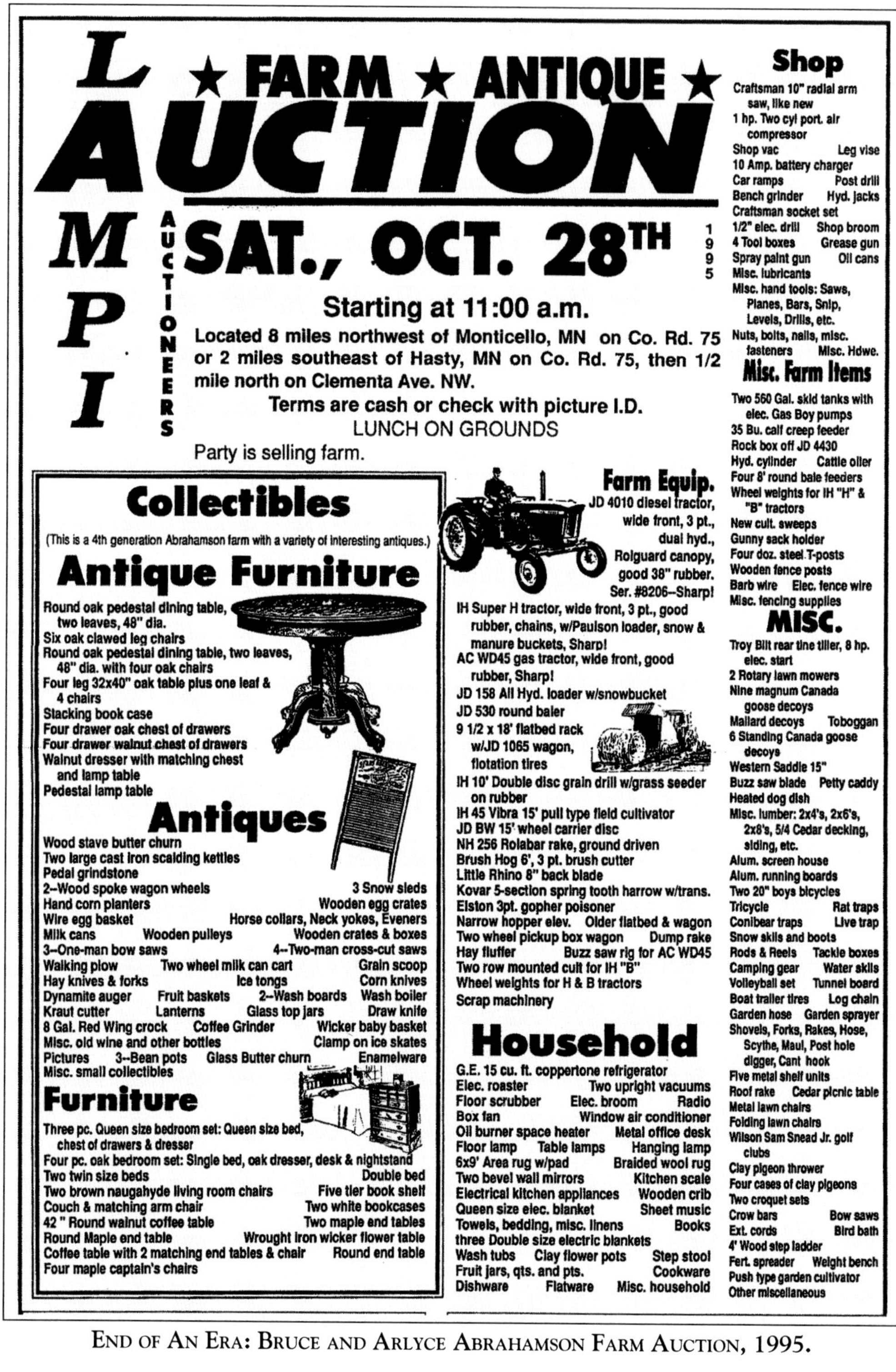

L M P I

AUCTIONEERS

★ FARM ★ ANTIQUE ★

AUCTION

SAT., OCT. 28TH 1995

Starting at 11:00 a.m.

Located 8 miles northwest of Monticello, MN on Co. Rd. 75 or 2 miles southeast of Hasty, MN on Co. Rd. 75, then 1/2 mile north on Clementa Ave. NW.

Terms are cash or check with picture I.D.

LUNCH ON GROUNDS

Party is selling farm.

Collectibles

(This is a 4th generation Abrahamson farm with a variety of interesting antiques.)

Antique Furniture

Round oak pedestal dining table, two leaves, 48" dia.
Six oak clawed leg chairs
Round oak pedestal dining table, two leaves, 48" dia. with four oak chairs
Four leg 32x40" oak table plus one leaf & 4 chairs
Stacking book case
Four drawer oak chest of drawers
Four drawer walnut chest of drawers
Walnut dresser with matching chest and lamp table
Pedestal lamp table

Antiques

Wood stave butter churn
Two large cast iron scalding kettles
Pedal grindstone
2–Wood spoke wagon wheels — 3 Snow sleds
Hand corn planters — Wooden egg crates
Wire egg basket — Horse collars, Neck yokes, Eveners
Milk cans — Wooden pulleys — Wooden crates & boxes
3–One-man bow saws — 4–Two-man cross-cut saws
Walking plow — Two wheel milk can cart — Grain scoop
Hay knives & forks — Ice tongs — Corn knives
Dynamite auger — Fruit baskets — 2–Wash boards — Wash boiler
Kraut cutter — Lanterns — Glass top jars — Draw knife
8 Gal. Red Wing crock — Coffee Grinder — Wicker baby basket
Misc. old wine and other bottles — Clamp on ice skates
Pictures — 3–Bean pots — Glass Butter churn — Enamelware
Misc. small collectibles

Furniture

Three pc. Queen size bedroom set: Queen size bed, chest of drawers & dresser
Four pc. oak bedroom set: Single bed, oak dresser, desk & nightstand
Two twin size beds — Double bed
Two brown naugahyde living room chairs — Five tier book shelf
Couch & matching arm chair — Two white bookcases
42" Round walnut coffee table — Two maple end tables
Round Maple end table — Wrought iron wicker flower table
Coffee table with 2 matching end tables & chair — Round end table
Four maple captain's chairs

Farm Equip.

JD 4010 diesel tractor, wide front, 3 pt., dual hyd., Rolguard canopy, good 38" rubber. Ser. #8206–Sharp!
IH Super H tractor, wide front, 3 pt., good rubber, chains, w/Paulson loader, snow & manure buckets, Sharp!
AC WD45 gas tractor, wide front, good rubber, Sharp!
JD 158 All Hyd. loader w/snowbucket
JD 530 round baler
9 1/2 x 18' flatbed rack w/JD 1065 wagon, flotation tires
IH 10' Double disc grain drill w/grass seeder on rubber
IH 45 Vibra 15' pull type field cultivator
JD BW 15' wheel carrier disc
NH 256 Rolabar rake, ground driven
Brush Hog 6', 3 pt. brush cutter
Little Rhino 8" back blade
Kovar 5-section spring tooth harrow w/trans.
Elston 3pt. gopher poisoner
Narrow hopper elev. — Older flatbed & wagon
Two wheel pickup box wagon — Dump rake
Hay fluffer — Buzz saw rig for AC WD45
Two row mounted cult for IH "B"
Wheel weights for H & B tractors
Scrap machinery

Household

G.E. 15 cu. ft. coppertone refrigerator
Elec. roaster — Two upright vacuums
Floor scrubber — Elec. broom — Radio
Box fan — Window air conditioner
Oil burner space heater — Metal office desk
Floor lamp — Table lamps — Hanging lamp
6x9' Area rug w/pad — Braided wool rug
Two bevel wall mirrors — Kitchen scale
Electrical kitchen appliances — Wooden crib
Queen size elec. blanket — Sheet music
Towels, bedding, misc. linens — Books
three Double size electric blankets
Wash tubs — Clay flower pots — Step stool
Fruit jars, qts. and pts. — Cookware
Dishware — Flatware — Misc. household

Shop

Craftsman 10" radial arm saw, like new
1 hp. Two cyl port. air compressor
Shop vac — Leg vise
10 Amp. battery charger
Car ramps — Post drill
Bench grinder — Hyd. jacks
Craftsman socket set
1/2" elec. drill — Shop broom
4 Tool boxes — Grease gun
Spray paint gun — Oil cans
Misc. lubricants
Misc. hand tools: Saws, Planes, Bars, Snip, Levels, Drills, etc.
Nuts, bolts, nails, misc. fasteners — Misc. Hdwe.

Misc. Farm Items

Two 560 Gal. skid tanks with elec. Gas Boy pumps
35 Bu. calf creep feeder
Rock box off JD 4430
Hyd. cylinder — Cattle oiler
Four 8' round bale feeders
Wheel weights for IH "H" & "B" tractors
New cult. sweeps
Gunny sack holder
Four doz. steel T-posts
Wooden fence posts
Barb wire — Elec. fence wire
Misc. fencing supplies

MISC.

Troy Bilt rear tine tiller, 8 hp. elec. start
2 Rotary lawn mowers
Nine magnum Canada goose decoys
Mallard decoys — Toboggan
6 Standing Canada goose decoys
Western Saddle 15"
Buzz saw blade — Petty caddy
Heated dog dish
Misc. lumber: 2x4's, 2x6's, 2x8's, 5/4 Cedar decking, siding, etc.
Alum. screen house
Alum. running boards
Two 20" boys bicycles
Tricycle — Rat traps
Conibear traps — Live trap
Snow skiis and boots
Rods & Reels — Tackle boxes
Camping gear — Water skiis
Volleyball set — Tunnel board
Boat trailer tires — Log chain
Garden hose — Garden sprayer
Shovels, Forks, Rakes, Hose, Scythe, Maul, Post hole digger, Cant hook
Five metal shelf units
Roof rake — Cedar picnic table
Metal lawn chairs
Folding lawn chairs
Wilson Sam Snead Jr. golf clubs
Clay pigeon thrower
Four cases of clay pigeons
Two croquet sets
Crow bars — Bow saws
Ext. cords — Bird bath
4' Wood step ladder
Fert. spreader — Weight bench
Push type garden cultivator
Other miscellaneous

END OF AN ERA: BRUCE AND ARLYCE ABRAHAMSON FARM AUCTION, 1995.